Electronic Currency Trading
for Maximum Profit

Electronic Currency Trading for Maximum Profit

Manage Risk and Reward in the Forex and Currency Futures Market

KEITH LONG AND KURT WALTER

PRIMA MONEY
An Imprint of Prima Publishing
3000 Lava Ridge Court • Roseville, California 95661
(800) 632-8676 • www.primalifestyles.com

PRIMA MONEY and colophon are registered trademarks of Prima Communications, Inc. PRIMA PUBLISHING and colophon are trademarks of Prima Communications Inc., registered with the United States Patent and Trademark Office.

Library of Congress Cataloging-in-Publication Data
Long, Keith.
    Electronic currency trading for maximum profit : manage risk and reward in the forex and currency futures markets / Keith Long, Kurt Walter.
        p. cm.
    ISBN 0-7615-2520-3
    1. Foreign exchange futures. 2. Foreign exchange market.
I Walter, Kurt. II. Title.
    HG3853 .L656 2001
    332.45—dc21

                                                                00-069303

01 02 03 04 05 HH 10 9 8 7 6 5 4 3 2 1
Printed in the United States of America

How to Order
Single copies may be ordered from Prima Publishing, 3000 Lava Ridge Court, Roseville, CA 95661; telephone (800) 632-8676, ext. 4444. Quantity discounts are also available. On your letterhead, include information concerning the intended use of the books and the number of books you wish to purchase.

Visit us online at www.primalifestyles.com

Contents

Acknowledgments   vii

Section One
An Introduction to the Electronic Currency Markets

1   How the Currency Markets
Got to Where They Are Today   3

2   A Close Look at the Forex
(Foreign Exchange) Market   19

3   Conceptual Blueprint for Maximizing
Profits in Forex   41

4   A Close Look at the Exchange Futures Market   55

5   Conceptual Blueprint for Maximizing Profits in
Exchange Futures Trading   71

Section Two
A Strategic Framework for Maximizing Profits

6   Making Profits "Happen" in Currency Trading   89

7   Forex Trading Strategies   103

8   Trading Strategies in Exchange Futures Markets   119

9   Option Trading Strategies   135

10   Closing the Deal: Profit Is the Name of the Game   155

Section Three
Using Technical Analysis

11   Advanced Use of Charts for Currency Trading   171

12   A Close Look at Technical
     Analysis for Forex Markets   187

13   A Close Look at Technical Analysis
     for Futures Markets   203

14   A Close Look at Technical Analysis
     for Currency Options   221

15   Integrating Fundamental Analysis
     with Technical Analysis   239

Section Four
Navigating a Course to Maximize Profits

16   Some Rules of Trading and Order Entry   255
17   Watchword—Be Careful!   271
18   Case Histories of 10 Forex Trades   283
19   Case Histories of 10 Exchange
     Futures/Options Trades   301
20   Fateful Decisions   323

Resources   335
Glossary   339
Index   345

Acknowledgments

Keith Long: When one writes a book, especially a book that incorporates detailed and technical elements on complex subjects, such as the global financial markets in general and currency markets in particular, the author soon comes to the conclusion that his text is being constructed on the shoulders of a great many authors who have come before him. Also, all scribes, some more than others perhaps, will find themselves compelled by the honesty of their own journalistic principles to conclude that opinions they have held prior to the work being published will in some way or another be subject to a new interpretation or perhaps even a complete revision. I have had the benefit of that process, and I trust the readers will discover that reinterpretation of a few of their previously held perspectives will be an enlightening and salutary experience for them as well.

On a practical level, I want to acknowledge the contributions of the folks at Prima Publishing, who initiated a relationship with me, supported my outline for the book, and then stuck with me as I developed a theme that will lead the reader to a cutting edge understanding of our new fast-paced, contemporary financial markets. The title of this project references "maximizing profits," and that ultimate objective was never far from the standards by which David Richardson, acquisitions editor at Prima, guided the completion of our project for the benefit of the reader. Also, Andrew Vallas, as project editor, coordinated the many contributors who polished and occasionally honed the raw text into a final, readable manuscript. Readers will be able to confirm the high standards underlying all these efforts. Kurt Walter, is an artist of Web-based financial markets whose efforts made a substantial contribution to the finished product.

On another level, I want to acknowledge Suzanne Claessens, of Clearwater, Florida, a wife and mother of two children who carries on a personal agenda with a subtle ambition that is only limited by the mortal restrictions of those she shares it with.

Kurt Walter: First, I would like to thank my loving wife and family for supporting me and accepting my demanding work schedule in a guilt-free fashion. I will make it up to you! Thanks also to Prima Publishing for providing an opportunity to deliver this useful tool to currency traders at a time when the currency market is red hot. Finally, Keith deserves the vast majority of the credit for writing the book. Thanks, Keith, for collaborating with theFinancials.com to create such an excellent resource.

SECTION

I

An Introduction to the Electronic Currency Markets

1

How the Currency Markets Got to Where They Are Today

One half of all American households now own stock, and international market participation is expected to catch up with that of the United States sooner rather than later. It is thus inevitable that this global wave of "human investment" in financial markets will spread beyond the equity (stock) markets into other attractive investment vehicles such as currencies, bonds, and commodities, to name just a few. There is no more natural attraction for this new international engagement in investments than the world's largest and most efficient market—global foreign exchange. Combine that market with the opportunity expansion that the online format offers and that increasingly underlies the global business environment, and one can easily predict that participation in electronic currency trading will continue marching apace with the information technology revolution for decades to come. That is the premise of this book. And its purpose? Well, simply put, to mine these opportunities and extract for readers the riches held by this new high-tech environment.

Given that investors in all global financial markets base their livelihood and professional success on the medium of exchange between peoples around the globe, called currencies, it is certainly appropriate to begin our journey together through this new world of electronic currency trading by reviewing not only the nature of currencies but by briefly describing how they evolved into their present contemporary relationships. First, the reader must bear in mind that foreign currency "trading" implies—nay, requires—a relationship.

Globalization, along with IT—information technology—has prompted international trade, M & A, and cross-border stock and bond investments to grow at an ever-increasing pace. The framework for this newly developing international business model is based on currency relationships, which is to say, foreign exchange (forex). So as public familiarity with currency exchange relationships increases, so, too, will forex participation around the globe, not only at the institutional and commercial bank level, but at the corporate, fund, and retail (individual investor) levels as well.

For international electronic currency trading, IT is, of course, the vehicle that makes it all happen. Readers of this book will gain insights and knowledge that will provide them with a valuable edge in the highly competitive world of online currency trading.

Because globalization is the handmaiden of information technology, readers need to acquire a facility with international aspects of electronic currency trading that will establish the comfort level they need to profit in modern currency markets. Inevitably, internationalism will impact every currency trader, no matter which country he or she resides in.

The term *forex* is a contraction of FOReign EXchange, which can exist only as a relationship between two different national currencies. Indeed, it is the change in a market value relationship between two given currencies (at a particular point in time) that produces profits, or losses, for all foreign currency traders. From that vantage point, then, we will proceed apace and travel together seamlessly into the contemporary world of electronic currency trading in a global market.

Let's start right off with a framework that takes note of the international character of forex trading. Question: What led to the creation of the world's first currency zone invention—the euro—and what have been the implications of this new single currency for the time-worn national currencies like the deutschemark, lira, and French franc? Well, the euro was officially introduced on January 1, 1999. On that date, 11 national currency exchange values became frozen, linked to the euro and in effect to each other, for the duration of their (national currency) lives. Table 1.1 shows the 11 currencies and their official fixed exchange rate created for the duration of their existence.

Those lives have a time limit. The European Council's membership required that by January 1, 2002, at the latest, each member country would then have only six months in which to redeem every last lira

Table 1.1 *Final Euro Currency Valuations*

Official Exchange Rate 1/1/99	Official Euro Abbreviations	
1 euro = 40.3399	Belgian franc	BEF
1.95583	German mark	DEM
166.386	Spanish peseta	ESP
6.55957	French franc	FRF
0.787564	Irish punt	IEP
1936.27	Italian lira	ITL
40.3399	Luxembourg franc	LUF
2.20371	Dutch guilder	NLG
13.7603	Austrian schilling	ATS
200.402	Portuguese escudo	PTE
5.94573	Finnish markka	FIM

(Italy), franc (France, Belgium, and Luxembourg), deutschemark (Germany), schilling (Austria), escudo (Portugal), punt (Ireland), guilder (Holland), markka (Finland), or peseta (Spain) for euros. So 11 national currencies were slated for extinction in this transition to the new zonal currency called the euro.

Currency traders need to know that the answers to "big picture" questions are driving world currency values even as we speak. As an example, in 1999, its inaugural year, and upon consolidation of these 11 national currencies into a single currency, the new euro promptly suffered a 25 percent decline up until June 2000 (see figure 1.1). Understanding how currency traders profited from this macro currency move is a key to opening *your* doors to profits.

By the same token, on the other side of the world, the Asian currency crisis had a major impact not only on the (former) Asian Tigers' national currencies but on the strength of the dollar as well. These events, the introduction of the euro and the Asian currency crisis, presented enormous profit opportunities for global currency traders who possessed the perspective and knowledge that prepared them to take advantage of these tsunami-like transformations in global currency relationships.

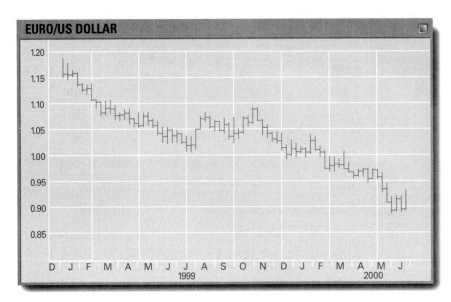

Figure 1.1   *The euro fell from $1.17 to below $0.90 in the first 16 months after its introduction onto the currency markets.*

So our journey begins with a brief but necessary grounding in some important big-picture background into currency relationships, which, I predict will translate into trading profits for readers of this book, and sooner rather than later. Currency markets begin from a macro or fundamental framework, and from there day-to-day technical- and software-based analysis can flourish. So let's get started.

The Dollar

Why is the U.S. dollar the world's reserve currency, and what are the implications for currency traders of that status? Well, the U.S. currency is the base currency for most forex trading, being involved in over 80 percent of all forex transactions. Understanding that "King Dollar" has a leadership role in global currency relationships is fundamental for profitable day-to-day trading in currency markets.

In 1944, during the last days of the destruction from the Second World War, the soon-to-be-victorious free world nations came together in Bretton Woods, New Hampshire, for a conference that created the famous IMF, International Monetary Fund and World Bank. This conference laid the groundwork, successfully, for the currency relationships of the postwar era, which, as it turned out, lasted nearly 30 years.

The hallmark of Bretton Woods was, of course, the fixed exchange rate regime that, briefly put, made exchange rates theoretically immovable in terms of their relationship to each other (subject to a 1 percent incremental range). Many currencies were actually devalued in the Bretton Woods era, but its framework was, on balance, successful in providing overall stability and discipline for the postwar reconstruction era.

The design of the Bretton Woods framework was to have the United States become an anchor for all free world currencies. What enabled the dollar to in fact assume a new role of "reserve currency" for the world was a guarantee by the U.S. Treasury to redeem those national currencies for dollars at their agreed-upon rates.

The IMF did its part, from time to time, by loaning governments (central banks) money to maintain this agreed-upon exchange structure (value), and so long as the U.S. currency was strong enough to exchange a dollar for gold at the fixed rate of $35 per ounce, everything worked well. The postwar gold standard ultimately relied on the ability of the United States to redeem dollars for gold. No other country guaranteed to exchange its currency for gold, although England, as a gesture to reinforce the Bretton Woods regime, promised to exchange U.S. dollars for sterling.

In the late 1960s and early 1970s, as the United States tried unsuccessfully to meet the gold standard test of leadership that the Bretton Woods framework imposed, it became apparent that nothing would be able to staunch the global economic crisis brought on by the worldwide inflationary environment. Many nations found themselves unable to maintain the value of their currencies under the Bretton Woods regime. Inflation, we now know, is the mortal enemy of both stable prices and stable exchange rates. As inflation became rampant, more dollars became worth less, and dollar holders around the globe sought the safety of gold in the vaults at Fort Knox. As a result, the U.S. supply of gold went down. Inflation had infested the U.S. economy. In fact, in 1970, the U.S. gold reserves fell below $12 billion, an amount that world government claims for gold could exceed. By the 1970s, the inflationary environment and perception that the United States was exporting its inflation to other economies led to tensions. Economically, the United States was in trouble, and so was the rest of the world. France threatened to demand redemption in gold for its sizable dollar reserves—a threat that, if carried out, would have destroyed the gold standard overnight. The real significance of the threat was that it laid bare the European desire for currency independence from the United States, something that would ultimately evolve into the creation of the euro. Bretton Woods and the gold standard were on their way to becoming discarded, but in 1971 the world was not quite ready for market-driven exchange rates.

With global currency relationships under stress, brought on by the worldwide inflation crisis that would not be resolved for a decade, the U.S. commitment to preserve the gold standard was tested. Ultimately, the United States was unable to preserve its promise of $35 for every ounce of gold at its gold window. With that, the Bretton Woods era was finally over and the modern floating exchange rate system was born in 1973.

Markets were quick to react. The Chicago Mercantile Exchange created the IMM, International Monetary Market, where currencies were quickly accommodated (and defined) as "commodities," along with pork bellies and wheat and so forth. Seven international currency contracts were developed, and so modern currency trading was born. An interbank market was also developing, and that market is what became known as forex.

The Euro

The genesis for a European economic community can be traced back to before the breakup of the Bretton Woods regime in 1971–1973, going all the way back to 1957 and the Treaty of Rome. Then Europe's economies, led by Germany's concern for its deutschemark, wanted to protect eurozone economic growth and the European business culture from a growing U.S. global influence. Europe's road to the single currency has been fitful and, like the Bretton Woods experience, has had some missteps. But from the Treaty of Rome, a European monetary system, EMS, eventually emerged in 1979, six years after the collapse of the gold standard.

By 1992, 15 European countries would sign the Maastrict Treaty, amending the Treaty of Rome, to create the European Union. They were: Austria, Belgium, Denmark, Finland, France, Germany, Great Britain, Greece, Ireland, Italy, Luxembourg, the Netherlands, Portugal, Spain, and Sweden.

Soon thereafter, all but four of these original 15 nations in the EU (Greece, Sweden, Denmark, and Great Britain) took another step down the economic convergence path by forming an economic union, the EMU. (Greece could not meet the convergence or economic criteria and was delayed entry into the EMU. England, Sweden, and Denmark opted out for essentially nationalistic reasons.)

Once established, the single currency zone in Europe, known as the European Monetary Union, quickly became a major force for change on the global currency landscape and promises, in my opinion, to presage currency zone developments all over the globe. We want to look at the European Monetary Union's early attempt to reconstruct the fixed exchange rate regime of Bretton Woods into its new EMS model.

The EMS came up with something called the ERM, or Exchange Rate Mechanism, in 1979. This unique pan-European currency relationship attempted to provide a format similar to the Bretton Woods fixed-rate discipline for Europe but with a larger valuation range.

That discipline would eventually crumble 13 years later, however, in the fall of 1992, as England, which had only joined the ERM in September 1990, had in the event insisted on establishing an overvalued exchange rate of DM 2.95 per GBP. The overvaluation of this rate of exchange was confirmed on the first day of trading, when no one would buy the pound at that rate.

Slowly, England came under more and more pressure for trying to prop up the pound at such a high rate, first spending $40 billion per month to purchase its own currency through its central bank, the BoE, then lobbying other governments to do likewise—predictably, however, to no avail. Markets, as usual, trumped central bank intervention. Finally, the BoE raised its interest rates to as high as 75 percent, and still the pound found more sellers than buyers. Mercifully, England withdrew from the ERM, as its currency fell 27 percent in three months, while an international currency investor named George Soros, by anticipating this major reversal in the British pound, profited to the tune of $1 billion.

The ERM was abandoned, and the world financial hierarchy, it seemed, had finally broken its attachment to fixed exchange rates for currencies. Market-oriented, or floating, valuations are now the institution-supported environment that permits currency traders to participate in establishing international currency rates.

There are good economic reasons underpinning the drive for a single European currency. The United States, for example, as a federal republic of 50 states uses its dollar as a common currency, and there are thoughts that, eventually, Europe may evolve into a union not too dissimilar from this U.S. federal model.

Let's look at the euro as it affects real businesses that trade in forex. DaimlerChrysler Corporation in Germany, of course, sells automobiles across international borders and must trade in forex. It offers an excellent illustration of how the euro is being integrated into euroland economies. The euro, which began to trade as a book currency on January 1, 1999, and in forex and exchange futures markets, was not scheduled to be introduced into circulation until 2002, meaning that all old script would vanish by July 1, 2002, at the latest. However, Manfred Gentz (Board of Management, DaimlerChrysler) led his corporation in converting to the new euro currency for all corporate accounting statements on the date it was launched. In the event, DaimlerChrysler immediately eliminated all currency exchange costs, which over recent years had totaled DM 100 billion. For this German-based business, converting currencies across euroland's 15 borders immediately became a thing of the past.

Another reason business is eager to embrace the euro is to avoid the costs that simply do not show up as explicit balance sheet expenses on a corporate spreadsheet. There are intangible costs associated with planning and executing contracts involving so many different currency rates. So those intangible costs were also eliminated at DaimlerChrysler. Mr. Gentz, it is likely, will also want to rethink the need for having satellite offices throughout euroland, with their hundreds of employees who in the past had to help facilitate the price differentials for customers in their own countries because of currency exchange requirements. With a single currency, comparative prices to the retail consumer became transparent for the first time.

Net-net, these kinds of cost savings derived from a currency union are considerable and are responsible in no small measure for the economic recovery euroland has made from its long economic funk in the 1990s.

The management of such an innovative restructuring, and on such a large scale, is daunting, but bear in mind that markets ultimately pass judgment on the work. Currency traders are always looking for opportunities anyway in every currency environment, especially one such as the euro. When establishing an inaugural benchmark exchange rate for the euro with existing international currencies, especially the dollar, currency traders evaluate whether the new ECB benchmark is too high, too low, or, like Goldilocks's appraisal, something that is "just right." Recalling the experience in 1992 of the pound sterling and how its exchange rate value was set too high, the market concluded that the euro, in its first year, 1999, was overvalued almost 20 percent, and traders who accurately shorted the euro in its first 17 months made 25 percent gains.

Keep in mind, euro currency contracts in the forex market are typically $1,000,000 or more. A 25 percent total gain on a contract amounts to $250,000. With margin leverage, which can amount to 50 to 1 in forex trading, one can see that enormous profits available to forex traders are not only short term—those traders, like George Soros, who pay attention to these big-picture dynamics in the global currency markets can participate in major gains.

Strong growth ultimately is reflected in currency valuations. Besides in Greece, plans were already in place coincident with the introduction of the euro for the "first wave of enlargement," which includes the Eastern European countries of Czech Republic, Estonia, Hungary, Poland, and Slovenia.

The Russian Bear

The Russian default episode in August 1998 merits a brief nod here as an example of another macro trading event that can define our trading environment. Russia declared a 34 percent devaluation of the ruble, a default on external debt, and controls on capital trying to move out of the country.

As we all know, the Russian economy is making a monumental transition from its former Soviet "command" framework to a transitional form of free markets and interaction with the West. That such a transition will be fraught with difficulties is rather easy to predict. The Russian ruble was valued for international exchange at about eight to the dollar in 1997. Sophisticated traders knew that could change dramatically at any moment.

As Russia was looking for foreign capital to modernize its infrastructure and economic base, many investors speculated with loans throughout the Russian economy, often with an unfunded Kremlin guarantee of repayment. As the economy faltered in the summer of 1998, those guarantees came due, and neither the government nor anyone else had the cash to pay back their foreign creditors. The price of oil, which is an important source of cash flow for Russia, was dropping. On July 21, 1998, the IMF handed Russia a check for $4.2 billion. In less than a month, it had disappeared. The markets paid close attention as problems continued accumulating for Russia. As the impending default became apparent, there was a widespread flight of capital out of the country, which precipitated a scenario that, for currency traders, was absolutely predictable. History now notes the August '98 default period and the dramatic implications that ensued worldwide. The ruble devalued to nearly 30 to a dollar. Here is what happened. Look how bad it got.

There was a run on banks in the country as confidence in the currency tanked. Because everyone wanted to trade rubles for dollars, virtually every bank in Russia became insolvent overnight. Interest rates skyrocketed to 200 percent. Then, finally, what was predictable actually occurred.

On August 20, 1998, the government, as a policy, declared a default on foreign debt, a 34 percent devaluation in the ruble, and controls on foreign assets already in the country. For currency markets, there were more sellers than buyers of the ruble, and, not surprisingly, the ruble plummeted.

Foreign investors who only a few months earlier had been welcomed into the economy, were now persona non grata, and, as is well known, you do not have to hit global investors over the head. They left "town" post haste, along with as much of their money as they could get out in a hurry, and Russia was left to go it alone. Their stock market plummeted and the government resorted to selling some of its gold reserves for cash.

This environment led to worries in the investment world that this Russian formula of devaluation, default, and capital controls would spread to other emerging countries, particularly western hemispheric Latin America, which then could turn world currency markets into a sort of moral hazard gone amuck. These fears led creditors into becoming highly risk-averse as far away as the United States, where spreads between high-risk corporate bonds and U.S. Treasuries expanded, threatening a major credit contraction.

When Alan Greenspan saw the possibility of credit markets seizing up, he moved quickly, lowering U.S. Federal Funds rates 75 bps in a few weeks by October 1998. In January 1999, as Alan Greenspan celebrated his 11th year as chairman of the Federal Reserve Board, he noted that "the outlook for 1999 for the U.S. economy has weakened measurably in the aftermath of the Russian devaluation and debt moratorium. The building *sense of stability* in international markets has been undermined as the belief that the Asian contagion had moved into remission has been proved quite wrong.

"Clearly the size of the Russian economy, either in real terms or in financial terms, can scarcely be an element that would engender the types of consequences that have occurred subsequent to the (debt) moratorium. [In other words, the undermining of that "sense of stability" was an intangible that created turmoil in currency markets. Readers take note.] The Russian experience has created a major shift towards risk aversion pretty much throughout the world, as exhibited mainly in the financial markets"[1]

The Russian default accelerated the Japanese retreat from Asia. In the years 1997–1998, Japanese investors sold 687 billion yen in securities in East Asia, and 144 billion yen in bonds. Direct investment from Japan in the Asian Tigers fell 42 percent, or 57 billion yen in two years. In total, Japan withdrew financial resources from East Asia equal to 2.5 percent of Southeast Asia's GDP. Capital flows affect exchange rates. Money flowing back into Japan was going to increase the value of the yen.

Of course, currency exchange rates reacted. Beginning in August 30, 1998, 10 days after Russia announced the devaluation of its ruble, the yen rose 20 percent in 30 days, from 140 to 110 per dollar.

So, this Russian default experience illustrates that opportunities for currency traders exist literally in every environment, and as currency traders, we need to pay attention to "macro" forces like the Russian default and Asian currency crisis.

A lesson to carry away from knowledge of these macro economic crises is that currency movements can very often reflect intangibles that currency traders need to be alert for. As U.S. Fed Chairman Greenspan said, the actual or real impact on the financial markets from Russia's debt moratorium was marginal, while the indirect and intangible impact was tsunami-like.

The Yen

Our review of how currencies evolved to where they are today now turns to Asia, where the yen is the 900-pound Godzilla. Japan's currency has an interesting modern origin. In the immediate aftermath of

World War II, the institutions that were helping Japan reorganize its economy had to establish an exchange rate value for the yen. The story has come down that they saw the Rising Sun on the Japanese flag one day and ordered that the yen's value should be 360 yen to the dollar. Their rationale? *The sun's circumference was 360 degrees, of course!*

Since then, in spite of the appreciation of the yen over the years to a high of 80 yen to the dollar in 1995, Nippon Telegraph & Telephone, one of Japan's premier stocks, still sells for millions of yen per share and daily share prices move in the tens of thousands of yen as a routine. During the millennium year of 2000, Japan established a commission to consider "re-denomination" that would convert the yen from a 100-yen-per-dollar range to a parity relationship of 1 yen per dollar. Part of the rationale for re-denomination is to create a tripolar parity among the world's major currencies: the euro, yen, and dollar.

This tripolar parity relationship among the world's preeminent currencies will be a confirmation of not only the globalization within modern financial relationships but of the zonal character of that relationship. In this future model, Europe, Asia, and the northern hemisphere (United States) will each hold its own dominant currency, the euro, yen, and dollar. Of course, the dollar will continue to hold special reserve currency status, owing to its economic supremacy as the 21st century dawns.

This review of how currency markets got to where they are today should lead readers to pay attention to this looming zonal character of currency relationships and the emergence of three primary currencies in global currency markets. Alertness to this emerging relationship will translate into profits, as will become apparent as we move along together through *Electronic Currency Trading for Maximum Profit.*

A Look at Asia

For many years, as Japan's economy grew to the world's second largest, Japan's concomitant self-realization of its equal player status in world economic affairs has generated an interest within this island people's government for establishing an Asia Fund. The purpose of this, as explained on April 20, 2000, by Eisuke Sakikibara, the former vice finance minister in Japan (and one who proudly accepted the moniker "Mr. Yen"), was "for Asia to develop both an integrated debt market and its own regional currency system as a safeguard against future economic crisis."[2] A concern throughout the Asian region, though barely below the surface and for the most part unspoken, is the feeling that the United States–led IMF has had too much influence in Asian economies during recent periods of turmoil, especially during the 1997 Asian currency crisis.

Prior to 1997, there were 117 currency crises in 105 developing nations,[3] all of which got the IMF's attention to a greater or lesser degree. But the Asian currency crisis of late summer 1997 got the IMF involved big time, and not without criticism. South Korea, Indonesia, and Thailand, three Asian Tigers, received IMF loans totaling $17.7 billion, plus an additional $35 billion of non-IMF money. Let's look briefly at that episode and emerge with a better understanding of Asian currency relationships (valuations) in the process.

The Asian currency crisis reinforces the experience of the Russian default episode and the conclusion that in the world of foreign exchange, every problem represents an opportunity. The charts of the Thai baht, Malaysian ringgit, Philippine peso, and Korean won showed the currency devaluations underlying the economic and financial costs that the former Asian Tigers experienced in the late summer of 1997, as their economies collapsed.

Very briefly, here is the backdrop for this problem/opportunity in foreign exchange. The Asian currency crisis was, bottom line, a crisis in liquidity. For currency traders, liquidity means capital flows and foreign exchange. Because this flow of capital, as we have seen, affects exchange rates directly, it provides an insight into the big-picture forces behind exchange rate valuations. Many banks among the Asian Tiger nations, for instance, had gotten into the habit of borrowing funds abroad at low interest (such as in Japan) and then loaning them out at higher rates domestically.

Structurally, however, these economies were infested with government-supported investments in businesses that relatives and business alliances had cultivated for private gain at the expense of economic efficiency. In plain English, they were not profitable or resilient. Foreign investors who were operating in this environment began demanding greater returns for their investments there in Asian Tiger–land as the risks began escalating in 1997. When the domestic markets in Asia would not support higher returns, capital began flowing out of these economies and, predictably, their currencies tanked.

Indonesia, Thailand, the Philippines, and Malaysia had a predisposition for short-term debt (because of lower interest costs) and a lack of adequate reserves. What these economies needed to have happen was a preemptive fiscal policy to increase interest rates early, thus attracting foreign investments back into the country in order to then support domestic demand. Unfortunately, the governments were resistant to raising rates initially and the structure of their economies would not encourage higher rates anyway. Then, too, because so much of their debt was denominated in foreign currencies, their eventual policy decision to devalue only increased their foreign-denominated debt burdens.

What began as a currency liquidity problem soon evolved into a business solvency problem throughout the area. The IMF stepped in with huge loans to grease the skids for a return of foreign capital, which by now had gotten the blame for the currency crisis to begin with. *Devilish speculators* was a term heard quite often in the region.

Many smart currency traders were prepared and took advantage of this devaluation of national currencies during the crisis. Experienced traders know that foreign exchange is very much a two-way street. Traders can participate in a depreciating currency environment and profit as equally as they can in an appreciating currency valuation environment.

IT

Finally, no review of how currency markets got to where they are today would be complete without a reference to IT—information technology. Figure 1.2 shows an online trading platform offered to currency traders by a forex dealer. With a PC, a laptop, or even hand-held wireless devices, forex transactions can not only be visual and instantaneous, they can be done from anywhere at any time that markets are open. The same can be said for exchange futures and options online trading.

Q & A

Question: What are some of the benefits of IT for online currency traders?

Answer: With the online trading platform vehicle, bidders and sellers are filling orders, making markets, and changing currency values liter-

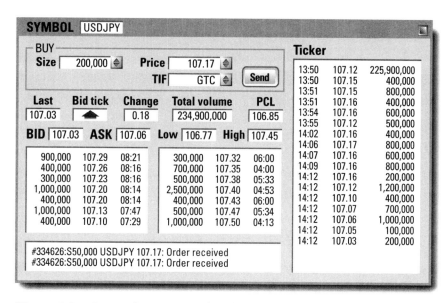

Figure 1.2 *One of a genre of online trading platforms with low spreads (in this case a three-pip spread) with trader information never before available to the small, retail trader.*

ally thousands of times per hour all over the globe. Software can be purchased that customizes your own trading system in a specific currency market. It identifies entry points, exit points, trading profit and loss in the position, and alternative positions—an entire menu of trading options in real time for the currency trader. This evolving vehicle for trade execution, the online trading platform, promises even more improvements in trade execution in the near term.

These software trading systems, the online brokers' trading platforms, and the technical analysis framework, however, must be integrated with the macro dynamics of the real world and will be explained in a thorough, step-by-step manner in the pages ahead. We begin with a look at the forex markets.

Notes

1. *Business Economics,* vol. 34, no. 1 (January 1999): 20 (5).

2. *Wall Street Journal,* April 21, 2000.

3. *Brookings Review,* vol. 16 (Summer 1998): 6 (4).

CHAPTER

2

A Close Look at the Forex (Foreign Exchange) Market

The abandonment of Bretton Woods' fixed exchange rates in 1973 did not mark the end of an era so much as it marked the beginning of what we today know as market-oriented currency valuations. After the turmoil of World War II, there was an understandable predisposition to provide a stable framework for economic relationships in order to facilitate rebuilding the devastated economies in Europe and Asia. The Bretton Woods gold standard fulfilled that purpose, and, indeed, its role fit a period that accomplished successful postwar reconstruction.

The subsequent three post–Bretton Woods decades of market-driven currency exchange rates, however, have made an even more important, lasting contribution to economic growth, and in the event, this new model has supplanted the gold-standard (fixed exchange rate) thinking throughout the world's institutional-financial framework. This new model has educated the institutions of world finance to the benefits— nay, the requirements—that the markets' price rule is the most efficacious and, in the long run, more stable framework for economic growth. That knowledge, coupled with the globalization that will define the world's economic relationships from here on out, makes market-determined currency valuations an inexorable reality for the foreseeable and, if one may say so, even unforeseeable future.

NAFTA, the European Union, and China's emergence as an equal player in the fastest developing area of the world, all are coming together to form new globally interdependent relationships that ensure currency exchange markets will be around for generations to come.

Table 2.1 shows the global character of foreign exchange trading in volume in dollars.

This is an important perspective that currency traders need to pay attention to: This new framework upon which future global economic development depends is in fact a new dynamic, generating ever greater trade and capital flows. Why is that important to a currency trader? Very simply, look at Asia and Japan, as these export-oriented economies perform "about-faces" and open up their domestic markets to global (foreign) participation. Capital flow into these new markets affects currency rates daily. The extent to which nations embrace this dynamic of globalization will be an important tip-off as to whether and to what extent capital flow enters a given economy at any given time. Already, total forex trading volume is a high multiple of total world trade volume. Table 2.2 shows the growth of forex trading,

Table 2.1 *Daily Average Net Foreign Exchange Market Turnover in Forex Trading Centers Around the World*

United Kingdom	$ 464 bn	Japan	$ 161 bn
Hong Kong	$ 90 bn	Germany	$ 76 bn
Australia	$ 39.5 bn	Canada	$ 29.8 bn
United States	$ 244 bn	Singapore	$ 105 bn
Switzerland	$ 86 bn	France	$ 58 bn
Denmark	$ 30.5 bn	Sweden	$ 28.1 bn
		TOTAL	$ 1.412 trillion

Source: National surveys 1995

Table 2.2 *The Growth of Forex Trading*

1977	1982	1987	1992	1998
$5 bn	$40 bn	$600 bn	$1 tr	$1.5 tr

Source: BIS, Bank for International Settlements

beginning with $5 billion in 1977 and growing 280-fold to $1.5 trillion in 1998.

So our expanding global market environment, along with the more open and transparent financial relationships that are being demanded of emerging growth economies, are a consequence of this new dynamic, much of which is ignited by floating exchange rates. In that understanding lies the perspective that will enable traders to anticipate trends in global currency rates. In this new world of currency trading, technical analysis will increasingly have for its foundation big-picture dynamics. That will become apparent and explained as we move through sections two and three, describing modern technical analysis.

Figure 2.1 shows the yen appreciation from market-driven capital inflows during the summer of 1999, even as Japan's government, whose policy wanted the offshore investment but not the currency appreciation (that necessarily accompanies capital investments), unsuccessfully intervened to weaken the yen. No clearer demonstration exists that market forces trump unilateral (and sterilized) central bank intervention in currency markets.

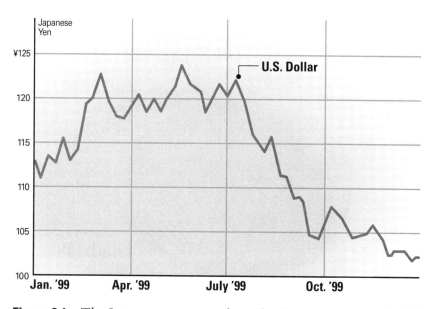

Figure 2.1 *The Japanese yen gained nearly 15 percent versus the U.S. dollar during the months of July through September in 1999.*

How the Forex Market Is Structured

The forex market is an amalgam of banks, other financial institutions, hedge and pension funds, international corporations, dealers, brokers, and individuals who all trade currencies. From time to time, the U.S. Federal Reserve Bank, BoE, BoJ, ECB, and other central banks use forex to buy and sell currencies or initiate other activities that adjust their national accounts. Forex is the marketplace where the exchange of currencies occurs in the most efficient, liquid, and accessible market in the world.

Figure 2.2 shows that in the London market only 7 percent of transactions are placed by private traders; the balance are institutional. Studies show the international character of the institutional forex market. Only 20 percent of London's forex trading is UK-centered. Table 2.3 shows how the approximately 5,000 banks that participate in the interbank forex market help to make it a 24-hour, 5-day-per-week market.

At 7 P.M. Sunday, New York, time trading begins, as markets open in Tokyo, Japan. Next, Singapore and Hong Kong open, followed by the European markets in Frankfurt and then London. The American markets open first in New York, then in San Francisco, and finally, before

Private Versus Institutional

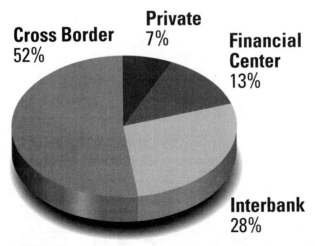

Figure 2.2 *Most forex trading is done by institutions. In the London market, for instance, only 7 percent of forex trades are for private accounts.*

Table 2.3 *The Seamless, Worldwide Character of Forex Markets*

Forex Week Starts

Sunday 7 P.M.	opens in Tokyo
Sunday 9 P.M.	opens in Hong Kong, Singapore
Monday 2 A.M.	opens in Frankfurt, Germany
Monday 3 A.M.	closes in Tokyo
Monday 3 A.M.	opens in London
Monday 4 A.M.	closes in Hong Kong
Monday 8 A.M.	opens in New York
Monday 11 A.M.	opens in San Francisco
Monday 7 P.M.	closes in San Francisco
Monday 7 P.M.	opens in Tokyo

San Francisco closes on the West Coast, Asia is ready to re-open. Forex is a seamless, 24-hour market.

By comparison, the currency futures *exchange* markets in the United States, such as the Chicago Mercantile Exchange and Philadelphia Exchange, which will be looked at in chapter 4, are different markets. The CME opens at 8:20 A.M. EST and closes at 2 P.M., and the Philadelphia Exchange opens at 8:00 A.M. and closes at 2:30 P.M. Globex, introduced in 1998, is an overnight futures market available through the CME in Chicago. The CME Globex initially suffered from liquidity issues that eventually are being overcome with increased participation and more currencies traded.

Table 2.4 shows the 13 currencies traded on the CME and Globex.

The Basic Forex Transaction

For the benefit of those who have migrated over from the stock, bond, or commodity markets and are new to the forex environment, a brief review will escort such experienced stock/bond/commodity traders up to parity with the experienced currency trader, and together we can develop the online capabilities offered by forex markets detailed in later chapters.

Table 2.4   *The CME Trades These Currencies As Exchange Futures*

AUD	Australian dollar	FFR	French franc
BRL	Brazilian real	JPY	Japanese yen
GBP	British pound	MXP	Mexican peso
CAD	Canadian dollar	NZD	New Zealand dollar
DEM	German mark	RUR	Russian ruble
SAR	South African rand	CHF	Swiss franc
EUR	Euro		

The dollar is involved in 80 to 90 percent of all currency transactions in global forex trading and in most currency pairs, like the USD/JPY, is expressed like this in forex trading: One dollar will buy 103.45 yen. As the currency with higher value and also by convention, the dollar similarly reads USD/FFR, one dollar will buy 7.77 French francs, or USD/ITL, one dollar will buy 2,144 Italian lira, and so on, depending on the exchange rate of that moment.

There are the (four) inevitable exceptions, of course. Great Britain pound, GBP/USD, which reads $1.50 per pound; the new euro currency, EUR/USD, which reads $0.95 per euro; Australian dollar, AUD/USD, which reads $0.50 per Australian dollar; and New Zealand dollar, NZD/USD, which reads $0.60 per New Zealand dollar. The GBP, EUR, NZD, and AUD are all base currencies. Why? Well, in the case of sterling, also referred to as Cable, the GBP has historically been valued higher than the dollar. The euro started out life that same way, while simple tradition continues to be observed with regard to the other two. The NZD has the nickname Kiwi.

Although they make up only a fraction of forex volume, non-USD cross currencies are an important component of the forex structure. Cross currencies look like this: GBP/EUR, CHF/JPY, DEM/FFR, and so on. The ISO (International Standards Organization) sets the abbreviation standards used in forex markets, although brokers and journalists, among others, occasionally substitute their own shorthand. For example, DEM quite often turns up as DM; the Swiss franc's moniker, CHF, can be referenced as SF; and readers will run across others from time to time.

In every trade, whether USD or cross, there has to be a long and a short side. For example, a trader who buys USD/JPY is long the dollar and

short the yen. Which is to say, USD/JPY buys the dollar and sells the yen.
The size of a trade is established by "lot" size. Lots will vary, depending on
what the broker or dealer offers to his clients and what the trader chooses
to trade in his order. Of course, brokers have their own minimum requirements for lot trading. Brokers who cater to small investors will offer lots
as small as $25,000 and margins as little as $1,000, while brokers solicit-
ing larger investors may have minimum trades of $1,000,000, minimum
account sizes of $50,000, and margin requirements of $100,000. So margin leverage will vary among brokers, from as low as 1 percent margin (a
$1,000 account will buy a $100,000 contract) to as much as 10 percent
margin. Within the framework of the brokers' margin requirements and lot
denominations, it is the trader who elects the size of the trade. A trader can
specify a $500,000 lot trade in USD/IDR or $100,000 in EURO/JPY, as
long as the broker offers those lots. Typically, however, a trader can expect
to find lots that will be at least $100,000 and margins will run anywhere
from 2 percent to 5 percent. So on a $100,000 lot, margin could be, say,
$5,000. (Table 2.5 shows the author's survey of representative dealers' lot
sizes/margins, etc. [the appendix identifies dealers].)

Table 2.5   *Author's Comparative Survey of Five Forex Dealers*

	Dealer A	Dealer B	Dealer C	Dealer D	Dealer E
Minimum account	$10,000	$25,000	$2,500	$50,000	$10,000
Margin (day/rollover)	2%/2%	2%/2%	1%	2.5%/5%	2%/4%
Minimum lot size	$100,000	$100,000	$250,000	$500,000	$100,000
Spread average	5 pips	1–3 pips	3–5 pips	3–5 pips	5 pips
Commission	$19	$20	No	No	No
Volume	$150 m/day	$1 bn/day	$1 bn/day	$1 bn/day	$1 bn/wk
Free demo	Yes	Yes	Yes	Yes	Yes
Charting data	Yes	Yes	Yes	Yes	Yes
Regulated	CFTC/SEC	No	No	SFA	SFA
Online account report	No	Yes	No	Yes	Yes
20+ currency pairs	Yes	No	Yes	Yes	Yes
Interest on account	Yes	Yes	Yes	Yes	Yes

Dealing the Spread

In forex, there is an immediate cost in establishing a position. As an example where the dollar/yen is being bid at 103.40 and its ask is 103.45, this five-pip spread will define a trader's cost, as we will see shortly, as $48.35.

Bid and Offer

When a trader buys at the offered (asking) price on a spread, in this example 103.45, immediately he has established a loss on the trade that the size of the spread determines. The spread is the difference between 103.40 and 103.45, of course, and is a source of income for the market makers who use the spread for that purpose.

The higher price is the price that the dealer sells at and is his "asking price." So that means this higher price is the price that a trader can buy at from this dealer. The low price in the spread is the dealer's bid. Another way of saying it is that the bid price is what the dealer is willing to pay for a dollar/yen position at that moment. The dealer is buying and it is the dealer's bid. Therefore, the low price is where a trader sells to the dealer. The reason, of course, the trader has a loss when initiating a trade is that in order to liquidate a buy position, for instance, which is filled at the offer price, a trader would need to sell at the bid price, which in this case is five pips lower than the offer. Spreads will occasionally vary hour by hour with the same broker and same currency pair, due to market volatility, liquidity, or demand in a particular currency pair at a given time. Also, traders will learn that while some dealers use the spread to make their money, other dealers permit traders to negotiate the spread and take their commission on a per-trade basis. Throughout the world of forex, spreads can vary widely. Which dealer offers what spread format is a function of their banking relationships, the choice of client they wish to attract, and their own business model as dealers.

A Pip of a Spread

The value of a pip is determined by the specific currency exchange rate and size of the trading lot involved. In this example, because the yen has two decimal places in its rate relationship with the dollar, the value of one pip per $100,000 lot is found by 0.01 × $100,000/103.45. Each pip on this trade is worth $9.67. A five-pip spread therefore constitutes a $48.35 cost for that trade, which has to then be made up with a favorable currency move in the market.

The CHF is a four-decimal-place currency. Here is how its pip spreads are valued.

Currency Pair	Bid	Offer	Lot Size
USD/CHF rate	1.7540	1.7545	$100,000

To find the value of one pip on this spread with this exchange rate use 0.0001 × $100,000/1.7545 = $5.70 per pip. Five pips therefore total $28.50.

Later, we will look at the dealer formats that permit negotiating spreads and consider other ways to narrow the spread or reduce the cost of establishing a position along with the mechanics of fills. For now, suffice it to say that traders new to the currency markets will find that a dealer's spread is part of your evaluation and decision process for selecting an online dealer and platform to trade with, and establishing an entry position is a cost factor traders pay close attention to.

Spot Forex

Table 2.6 shows a typical spot forex transaction whose value settlement or delivery is two days out. A trader who will not want to either take delivery or make delivery of a $100,000 currency contact but who wants to hold a position overnight will leave instructions for his broker to roll over the trade. This may or may not add costs to the position, but it extends the settlement date another 24 hours. In this way, a position can be rolled over indefinitely.

The trader wants to buy USD versus the yen. His account with the broker on this day has a balance of $50,000. Because his broker requires

Table 2.6 *USD/JPY*

Bid	Ask	Account Balance	Margin	Lot Size	Stop Loss
103.00	103.05	$50,000	5%	$100,000	102.55

5 percent margin on lots of $100,000, he can buy 10 lots (not taking into account commissions or fees) of $100,000 each.

Being long the dollar, the entry price will be 103.05 yen. A $100,000 lot expressed in yen, therefore, is 10,305,000 yen per lot. He places a stop loss order below his entry point to protect against large losses. The stop loss order is at 102.55, which means the position will be closed if the market touches 102.55. Our trader is buying 10 lots of $100,000 each in dollars or $1,000,000. Our trader is selling 10 lots of 10,305,000 each in yen or 103,050,000 yen. Later in the day, the dollar climbs to 104.10 yen/dollar. The trader sells the USD to close out his position at that point. The USD long position netted a gain of 1.05 yen/dollar on a lot size of $100,000, or 105,000 yen. Opening position was to purchase 10 "dollar" lots of 100,000 in dollars. Closing position was to sell 10 "dollar" lots of 100,000 in dollars. Dollar account balance at closing was zero in dollars. So when you purchase or sell a position, the base currency will always be zero on settlement. Your profit or loss will be given in terms of the secondary currency—in this case, the yen.

Closing position was buying 10 lots—$100,000 of yen at 104.10 or 10,410,000 yen/lot. Opening position was selling 10 lots—$100,000 of yen at 103.05 or 10,305,000 yen/lot. Total profit was 105,000 yen/lot.

The same $100,000 lot bought more yen at the closing than it sold at opening. Since the trader had to sell only 10,305,000 yen/lot to open the position, and he was able to buy 10,410,000 yen/lot when he closed the position, he made a gain. To convert the yen gain into dollar value, the closing exchange rate was 104.10 and the opening exchange rate was 103.05. Difference (profit) was 1.05. Therefore, the trader's profit is 1.05 yen × $100,000 lot size = 105,000/104.10 or $1,008 per lot × 10 lots = $10,080. We can check this profit by taking 0.01 (pip) × $100,000 (lot size)/104.10 = $9.60/pip × 105 pips = $1,008 per lot × 10 lots = $10,080.

As we can see, this trader's $50,000 account leveraged his position to yield more than $10,000 in profits. Now let's examine the risk by looking at an alternative scenario. The trader expects the dollar to continue rising, and instead of selling at the profit illustrated previously, he holds the position overnight, but it drops due to a surge in the Nikkei stock market during the Asia session, when he was asleep. By the time he gets to his online account, his stop loss has been triggered and he is out of the position. Traders should note, setting stop loss orders does not in any way guarantee that your position will be closed at that order's level. Your stop loss order does become a market order when the market touches that level in trading. But markets move so fast that, among other reasons, your transaction could be completed much lower than the stop loss anticipates. Readers should note that a few brokers will guarantee to execute a trade at your stop loss order level, but absent such an agreement with your broker, there are no guarantees of execution on market orders at a specific price, which, again, is what a stop loss becomes as soon as the market touches its price.

Here is as good a place as any to stop briefly and describe the "up versus down" language of forex markets. We have seen that when the dollar gains value against the Japanese yen, the yen numbers in the exchange rate go up. So our trader sold yen at 103.05 in the previous illustration and bought yen at the higher level—104.10—and so the profit was 1.05 yen per dollar. That is all straightforward. But let's examine what those numbers represent. The trader sold 103.05 yen per dollar at opening and bought 104.10 yen per dollar at closing. That means the yen fell, even though the exchange rate numbers went up from 103.05 to 104.10. So when the yen's numbers go up, its value falls. Now back to the loss scenario, where we need to look at our trader's overnight position on the dollar yen. Here is his loss:

USD/JPY	Open	Close	Account Loss	Lot Size	# Lots
long	103.05	102.55	Rate 0.50	$100,000	10

Opening position was buy 10 "dollar" lots of $100,000 in dollars. Closing position was sell 10 "dollar" lots of $100,000 in dollars. Dollar account balance at closing was zero in dollars. Opening position was selling 10 "yen" lots of $100,000 in yen at 103.05 for 10,305,000 yen. Closing position was buying 10 "yen" lots of $100,000 in yen at 102.55 for 10,255,000 yen. Difference was 50,000 yen. Ten lots total loss is 500,000 yen. Converting to dollar value: 500,000/102.55 = $4,875 total loss. Checking the math: 0.01 (one pip) × $100,000 (lot size)/102.55 (exchange rate) = $9.75/pip.

There were 50 pips lost (50 pips × $9.75) or $487.50/lot × 10 lots = $4,875 total loss. Always protect your position with appropriate means, including stop loss orders.

Spot Rollover

This was a spot trade that, as mentioned, had a settlement date 48 hours forward. When banks that deal to acquire or transfer cash use the spot market, they either deliver or take delivery of cash on these value or settlement dates. Many investors, however, do not want to have to deliver or accept $100,000 lots of cash, so when they take a position in the spot market, they either close the position the same day to escape the cash settlement obligations of a spot forex transaction or continue rolling it over to a new value (settlement) date 24 hours forward in order to keep extending the settlement date until they wish to exit the trade altogether. For London-based transactions, spot deals not earmarked for settlement on the value date are rolled over at 10 P.M. Big Ben time. Traders dealing in spot need to know what is involved. Even some experienced forex currency traders are unaware of the process. They are at a disadvantage.

On Wednesday, May 10, a trader opens the following spot position:

Buy USD/CAD
Buy $1,000,000
Sell CAD 1,500,000
Rate 1.5000
Value date is May 12, Friday

Wednesday, May 10, the trader bought $1,000,000 spot against the CAD at 1.5000. Value date is Friday, May 12. When Big Ben strikes 10 P.M. on Wednesday night, the broker follows the trader's instructions and rolls the long dollar position over to TOM (tomorrow and next day). But at 10 P.M. London time, the Canadian dollar has moved to CAD 1.5002. At 10 P.M. the broker begins the following spot rollover procedure:

Sell $1,000,000
Buy CAD 1,500,200
Rate 1.5002
Value date was Friday, May 12

The trader was long the dollar and during the day the dollar strengthened from CAD 1.5000 per dollar to CAD 1.5002 per dollar. The liquidation of the position therefore reflects a profit, since the $1,000,000 when bought equaled only CAD $1,500,000, whereas the $1,000,000 when sold equaled CAD $1,500,200 that same day on liquidation. The profit, therefore, was 200 CAD at the exchange rate at the close of day. That means a market to market gain of $133.15 (50 pips × $9.75) in dollar value.

This transaction closed out the position taken earlier in the day and prevented the need for settlement with cash delivery requirements on this spot deal. Now to reestablish the trader's spot position for the next day, the broker simultaneously at 10 P.M. Wednesday:

Buys $1,000,000
Sells CAD 1,500,100
Rate 1.5001
Value date is Monday, May 15

There was a one-pip differential on the rollover and here is how it is accounted for. On any spot rollover transaction, if there is a difference in interest rates between the two currencies, then that will be reflected in the overnight "loan" that the broker just initiated. The new position is effective at the opening of the next day's banking hours. On this date, the United States has higher interest rates during this overnight period than Canada. Consequently, the USD/CAD rate for the new spot position (1.5001) is at a discount at the former spot rate of 1.5002. The new position, like the old, is long the dollar, and the new position with the one-pip premium reflects the dollar's prevailing higher interest rates. The long position nets a one-pip gain on the rollover, therefore 0.0001 × $1,000,000/1.5001 = $66.66.

In this spot forex position on a $1,000,000 trade, the gain was CAD 200 ($133.15) on the day's currency move, and then CAD 100 ($66.66) on the rollover premium to spot, due to interest rate differentials between the United States and Canada. Total gains for this day were $199.81.

Traders know in advance whether a spot rollover will gain or lose, based on this basic interest rate relationship between the currencies involved. If you are long dollars and the short currency has lower interest rates, you should gain on the spot rollover through the premium relationship of the dollar to that short currency. Spot traders keep these advantages in mind when they take their positions in forex, and it points up the value in keeping all aspects of currency valuations in front of you, such as interest rate differentials in the currencies you are interested in.

Eurodollars

Eurodollar is a very loosely defined term meant to apply to U.S. dollars deposited outside of the United States but earning U.S. rates of interest, such as on a T-bill. For instance, an Israeli bank that holds U.S. dollars and deposits them into an account in Israel earning U.S. interest has a "Eurodollar" account. They need not be deposited in European banks to be included in the category. The term, like many things in financial circles, has evolved and broadened as globalization has outpaced even language in some instances. By the way, this is a good time to note that Eurodollars should not be confused with euros. Introduced at an exchange rate of $1.17 per euro in January 1999, the new currency, as has been discussed, nose-dived to $0.90 per euro within its first 17 months. The reason? Well, throughout most of 1999 and early 2000, the United States had rising benchmark interest rates near or surpassing 6 percent, while the euro's benchmark rates stayed well below what the U.S. dollar returned. As a result, money flowed out of Europe into the United States to capture those higher returns on investments, and the euro headed south.

The Eurodollar market initially developed largely because U.S. regulations capped what U.S. dollars could earn in interest within the United States. Today, as many as 65 percent of all U.S. dollars in circulation at any given time are held outside of the United States, and even as interest rate restrictions have disappeared, money continues to accumulate in foreign banks and institutions. The Bahamas and Cayman Islands are large Eurodollar centers that offer tax advantages on interest income for Eurodollar account holders.

Still, as interest rate differentials began to get the attention of currency traders, new vehicles emerged to facilitate the capture of these capital flows. One important derivative that evolved has been the currency swap. Currency swaps are also used to hedge exchange rate volatility, but we want to look here at how swaps are used to capture interest rate differential advantages. With swaps taking 47 percent of forex transaction volume, traders need to have an understanding of them.

Experienced currency market hands know that some of the most influential capital flows affecting "their" exchange rates involve this movement of currency to capture interest rate differential advantages between countries. If country A has higher interest rates, Country B's currency will find a way to move out of B and into A. That occurs throughout the world's currency relationships and is a major component of rate valuations. The forex market sees a lot of trading in large quantities of Eurodollars seeking advantages based on interest rate differentials among the countries that can offer secure returns.

In 1998, the average size of both the spot and forward transaction was a little less than $5 million. The average size of a swap by contrast exceeded $30 million per trade. Besides spots and swaps, there are forward forex transactions, as well. Of the three types, most forex is traded as swaps, which are an exchange of one currency for another, and our friends the Eurodollars play a big role in motivating currency transactions (swaps) for interest rate benefits. Let's tie all of this together and examine a Eurodollar account involved in a currency swap. There are an abundance of different types of swaps, but for our purposes let's look at a simple one.

Plain Vanilla Currency Swap

As the name implies, a currency swap is an exchange of currencies between two or more parties. The plain vanilla currency swap we want to look at here is an agreement between two parties to exchange two currencies of equivalent value. A currency swap is actually traded as a surrogate for a currency future and for that reason has been reviewed by the Commodity Futures Trading Commission and the SEC, where they were ruled exempt from regulation as futures in the United States. There is an ISDA, International Swaps and Derivatives Association, which acts as an information and industry trade group.

Credit worthiness in this unregulated environment therefore is a priority concern, and participation is limited mostly to large banks or other financial institutions and corporations. Since swaps make up 47 percent of the trading volume in forex, traders should be informed of how such a large component of their trading market operates and why. Swaps do influence foreign exchange markets and exchange rates.

What motivates a swap deal? Well, basically, each holder of a currency wants to hold a different one.

What happens in a swap? An exchange of currencies, each of equal value between two parties.

What happens during the term of a currency swap agreement? Each party to the swap makes periodic interest rate payments in the currency received per the agreement. Depending on how day-to-day exchange rates move between the two currencies, these payments may be more or less than the day's exchange rate at the time of the swap initiation. Of course, exchange rate values on the actual date when each interest payment is due determine the real value of payments being made between the parties. So that represents a currency risk for each party. What happens to close the swap? Each party returns the currency to the other at the end of the swap.

Table 2.7 shows how two corporations might create and execute a swap agreement and why. First, let's take a look at the outline of the terms of their swap.

What motivates Corporation A in New York to enter a currency swap with a business in London? Well, Corporation A may have good U.S. credit in New York but does not qualify to borrow at the best prevailing English rates of 8 percent, yet it wants to finance the purchase of land in England.

What motivates Corporation Z in England to enter a swap with a New York business? Corporation Z has excess capital, and while it could earn the modest prevailing savings rate from a London bank, it could earn a higher rate of return—10 percent—from this American corporation wanting English pounds.

Corporation A swaps 1.5 million U.S. dollars for 1 million English pounds sterling and agrees to pay to Corporation Z counterparty an interest rate of 10 percent for a term of five years in pounds. The interest will actually be payable semi-annually for the term of the swap agreement.

Corporation Z agrees to receive $1,500,000 from A and to pay prevailing English savings interest in dollars semi-annually for the life of the

Table 2.7 *Two International Corporations Enter into a Swap*

Exchange Rate	U.S. Interest Rates	English Interest Rates	Term
GBP/USD $1.50	10%	8%	5 years

New York	London
Corporation A holds 1.5 million dollars.	Corporation Z holds 1 million pounds.

swap. For its part, Corporation A accepts the (lesser) prevailing return on its $1.5 million for five years because of its desire for English pounds.

Let's Look at This Currency Swap

What Corporation A gets out of this is the loan of English pounds at a cost of 10 percent, which it will use to buy some land in London. However, instead of using the 1 million pounds from counterparty Z to buy the land, Corporation A decides to instead put the entire proceeds into a London bank as interest-earning collateral for a loan of exactly 1 million pounds and use that borrowed money to buy the land. Corporation A has already lined up a purchaser for the land, a local business, which agrees to buy a purchase option for five years. In order to acquire the exclusive option to purchase the land, this London-based business agrees that for as long as it does not exercise the purchase option, Corporation A will get a payment from it every six months, which A applies to offset its interest costs to counterparty Z in the swap agreement. Corporation A also applies interest it receives on its loan collateral against the interest costs due Corporation Z.

Of course, Corporation A also collects interest on its $1,500,000 swap with Corporation Z. So Corporation A is receiving three income streams. It receives semiannual income from the option it sold for the sale of the land in London. It receives interest on its $1,500,000 loan to Corporation Z, and it receives interest from the London bank for its collateral on the 1 million pound sterling loan. If the local business does go ahead and purchase the land, the contract price allows A to make enough profit to cover the accumulated interest costs owed to Corporation Z from the swap plus the loan from the English bank, with a profit left over. Corporation A has its ducks in a row. So at the end of five years, Corporation A either has the expenses associated with the land purchase covered plus a profit, or it has the land. This is an acceptable risk to the corporation. At the end of five years, it also obtains the return of its collateral from the London bank and returns it to Corporation Z, fulfilling all the terms of the swap.

From Corporation A's Perspective

So very simply, from Corporation A's perspective, it had a profitable use for the 1 million pounds it needed to purchase land in London. It just did not have the English currency at an affordable interest rate. The swap deal fulfilled that need.

From Corporation Z's Perspective

Corporation Z receives $1.5 million and deposits it in a Eurodollar account that earns a much higher rate of interest than it could receive in a London account for the next five years and pockets the difference between that and the interest owed to Corporation A. By this agreement, Corporation Z pays out 8 percent interest for the use of the dollars for five years but receives a higher—10 percent—rate of return from the pounds it loaned to Corporation A.

In addition, Z gets interest from a Eurodollar account on the dollars it holds for five years. This interest rate differential motivated the currency swap for these two, now international corporations. Swap trades as a share of the greater forex market have grown from a 34 percent share in 1995 to over 47 percent in 1998.

Both parties find via rate differentials a profitable purpose in making a currency swap with minimal risk. There are, of course, an infinite variety of permutations to swap agreements. Many involve floating interest arrangements on one side and fixed on the other. Others involve buying a spot against a forward, and so on. Swaps, like the spot rollover, are in fact a form of forward that we will take up next.

Forwards

As we have seen, the $1.5 trillion per day forex market trades in relatively large lots, typically of over $1 million, so corporations, banks, and financial institutions in effect have substantial influence over capital flow and hence exchange rate valuations. Within the London interbank market, only 7 percent of its business involves private (nonbusiness) forex transactions. The BIS survey of 1998 shows that of $1.5 trillion of forex volume, 58 percent is in forwards (including swaps) and 42 percent is in spots.

This transaction involving the majority of forex trades is the derivative called a forward currency rate agreement. The forward, as we will see, is actually a combination of the spot rate and a currency swap, one at the beginning of the transaction, the other at the end.

Forwards, like many capital flow relationships, are driven by interest rate differentials, and traders who understand this derivative structure have a better understanding of why currency markets are influenced by interest rates as much as they are.

Unlike swaps, a forward can be liquidated by an offsetting purchase or sale during the term of the agreement, so it is in this sense very similar to an exchange futures contract traded on the CME and Philadelphia Stock Exchange, which we take up in chapter 4. The forward tends to be an agreement between a lender and a business. It actually has its roots in medieval times and has been documented in 17th-century Japan as well.

The reason for a forward exchange agreement is fairly straightforward. It insulates a businessman who is being paid in a foreign currency from exchange rate volatility between the initial date of the agreement and the payment of the invoice for his goods or services.

Let's say a U.S. businessman has contracted and invoiced $1 million in goods to a corporation in Japan, which will pay his invoice per its agreement in Japanese yen 90 days from now. We should note that if the invoice called for payment in U.S. dollars, there would be no need for a forward agreement.

The invoice amount is for 110 million yen, which, based on today's exchange rate of 110 yen per dollar, will get the U.S. supplier his $1 million. The $1 million proceeds are what the seller wants to guarantee. Both parties, however, know that the exchange rate will be different in 90 days from today's rate. But the Japanese businessman has no exchange rate risk since his sales and revenue are totally from domestic sources. The U.S. businessman, on the other hand, did some calculations and discovered that if the exchange rate falls to 120 yen per dollar, his receipts from the exchange of 110 million yen 90 days forward would be only $916,666—something he could not accept. His other calculations show that should the yen move the opposite way and appreciate to 100 yen per dollar, he would receive $1,110,000. Still, he will not take the risk.

He calls his bank, which tells him that the customer paying him the 110 million yen need not be involved in a forward exchange rate agreement, that he and the bank can do the deal themselves. The bank calculates a forward rate agreement based on today's spot rate of 110 yen and the interest rate differentials between the U.S. dollar and Japanese yen. The bank tells him that his 110 million yen payment can then be sold to the bank when it is received 90 days from now, and that the bank will buy the yen and sell the U.S. corporation dollars. So the forward rate agreement is an agreement between the U.S. corporation and his bank to sell yen and buy dollars at today's exchange rate of 110 yen per dollar. Here is the bank's calculation and how the forward rate is determined for 90 days out:

Spot rate × interest rate differential (eurodollar – euro yen) × days/360 × 100.

110 yen × (6.0% – 1/2%) × 90 days/360 × 100 = 1.5125

110.00 – 1.51 = 108.49

Forward rate agreement is 108.49

Because the United States has higher interest rates, those points (1.5125) were deducted from the spot rate of 110.00 to yield 108.49 or a forward exchange rate of 108.49. The forward points are deducted from the spot rate of the yen because the U.S. dollar earns a higher interest than the Japanese yen, and the yen's spot rate is discounted to reflect that.

At the new exchange rate, the business will then collect $1,013,918 in 90 days. At 110 yen per dollar, the transfer would have been $1 million. The U.S. business earned a profit on the forward transaction due to the prevailing higher U.S. interest rates as compared to Japan's.

Whenever the base currency, here the dollar, has higher interest rates than the second currency, the forward rate in the second currency will be discounted. This is why: The dollar with its higher interest rate, when held for 90 days, will earn more than the yen. In order to establish fair market value to both parties in the forward agreement for the exchanged currencies, the dollar's yen value is discounted. Indeed, its exchange rate is decreased an amount equal to the differences in interest rates between the two currencies. If the base currency, the dollar, has lower interest rates than the yen, the forward points are added to the dollar's yen value.

That is the formula just described and why a forward rate is virtually never the same as the spot rate. It also confirms that the forward rate for a currency like the USD/JPY is not a prediction of future exchange rate values. It is purely an interest rate derivative, based on the spot rate at the time of the agreement.

Q & A

Question: As a corporate CFO new to derivative forex markets, can I make an arrangement with a consultant to ensure that I get the best possible deal to facilitate currency swaps and currency forwards, and where can I access these professionals?

Answer: Absolutely. Like everything else, different banks will offer better or worse rates on forward agreements. The online Internet resource has an abundance of firms offering (free) consultation for getting the possible rates from the assorted money center banks making offers. I suggest your company seek them out. I have listed a number of them in the appendix of this book.

CHAPTER 3

Conceptual Blueprint for Maximizing Profits in Forex

A trader makes fundamental decisions in currency markets that are crucial to his success and profitability. For experienced stock, bond, or commodity traders who are new to forex trading, we want to outline, in a big-picture sense, how to go about making the right decisions in all aspects of their trading practices. At the same time, for participating currency traders we offer a review of their existing personal framework for trading forex. In the process, we will allow everyone to take a fresh look at his or her own "conceptual blueprint" for making profits in the currency markets.

Choosing a Market

Before you choose a dealer, evaluate an online trading platform, or implement a trading system—either your own or a software program you have purchased—you have to select a market to trade. Selecting a market may not be the most important or difficult decision facing a trader, but it is arguably the most fateful.

For many traders, a choice of which market to trade is never really much of a choice at all. Some may have had business links to a particular country and are familiar with its currency valuation. Others may have a cultural connection to a particular country, such as Canada or France, or perhaps have traveled there often and have acquired a familiarity and comfort level with it. Usually, a successful trader, via whatever route, arrives on a personal basis at a comfort level with the market he chooses to trade.

It bears mentioning that such a "comfort level," though an intangible in the world of candlestick charts and Stochastic indicators, is invaluable and needs to be appreciated.

Major markets like the Japanese yen or euro, with thousands of price changes per hour, mean there are more traders and greater trading flows, which is another way of saying that the USD/JPY and EURO/USD are liquid markets. Liquid markets offer the potential for profits all currency traders look for, and there are many others like the euro and yen.

With more liquidity, fewer trades are needed per at-risk dollar and that means lower trading (commission) costs. A highly liquid market attracting large volumes of investment flow also leads to a narrower, more efficient bid/ask spread, and that means the market has to move less in your direction to make the same level of profit. Some currency dealers boast of posting nearly 20 million prices a year on their online platforms.

On the other hand, markets such as the Argentine peso and even on occasion the Swiss franc and others can trade in an environment with very little price movement, certainly as compared to the majors'. Traders of those currencies can find themselves needing to exit their positions with less profit than they would like. Or worse still, having to "eat" a loss after being unable to find profit traction. So, a longer time frame fighting a slow market environment with less volatility and price changes translates into less profitability for your portfolio over the course of time. Net-net, the most profitable markets are also the ones that make trading easier and generate a higher return on your at-risk trading dollar. Confirming that your market has the elements necessary for profitability (price movement, volatility, and liquidity) is a prerequisite for every trader's conceptual blueprint for success.

Go to your online resource and take a glance at the charts of several smaller currencies, which highlight the rich variety of trading venues available to traders in the 21st century's online environment, and then perform a comfort-level check on your own preferred market if you have not already.

That very principle, choosing a market that facilitates trading currencies, is a theme that applies to other levels of trading practices. Find a market *trading system,* then a *dealer and trading platform,* and finally a *data source provider* that makes your trading easier, not harder.

An Overview of Forex Trading

We have seen how large institutions such as banks, multinational corporations, funds, and even central banks, all with deep pockets, are the major players in forex trading. The most important conceptual lesson to be gleaned from that knowledge is simple: Do not depend on the market to move the way your personal trading strategy needs it to.

Learn from the market every day and on every trade you make, and be prepared to adapt your short-term strategies to what the market is telling you. Use your total trading experience as a learning process and adjust your trading practices to accommodate the reality of the currency market environment you participate in. If you are a technician, for example, and market fundamentals seem to be driving currency movements, don't fight the market. It is a trader's job to find a way to "make the trend your friend."

Technicians Learning from Fundamental Traders

The following is excerpted from an April 14, 2000, *Wall Street Journal* article:

> Bank of Japan governor Masaru Hayami Wednesday sent his strongest signal yet that he is looking for a chance to raise Japan's interest rates, saying he would like to boost rates "at the soonest possible time." The dollar dropped to an intraday low within minutes after Mr. Hayami's remarks were reported Wednesday.[1]

This news item, which is not untypical of relationships between macroeconomic news and currency market valuations, is also an excellent example of the real-time news resources traders must have to stay ahead of currency moves.

We want to call on the Japanese yen yet again to reveal how the Japanese yen market in 1998 was one of those markets that closed the book on LTCM, a derivatives fund run by some of the most astute and sophisticated technical-model currency traders in the world.

Other large hedge funds, such as the Tiger Fund, also took big hits as the yen appreciated against the dollar, strongly contrary to their projections of a prolonged yen weakness. These large money movers had committed themselves to a market position that depended on the USD/JPY market acting the way their strategies wanted it to, and big as they were, the market unceremoniously trumped their positions. The yen strengthening in 1998 confirms that successful technicians need to integrate fundamentals into their trading practices. Market forces are liable to reveal themselves only after you have established your trading position, and you can be sure that, on many occasions, you will turn out to be on the wrong side of the market's move. The market trumps even the smartest and biggest market players time and again, so that is a lesson worth remembering. Successful technicians regularly rely on macro-fundamentals in their trading practices.

Fundamental Traders Learning from Technicians

Similarly, fundamental traders benefit from paying attention to support and resistance levels, moving averages, and Bollinger Bands, as well as other technical indicators of market price movement. Large institutional traders follow technicals religiously and take positions based on them. Need we say more?

Suppose you are a fundamental position trader, and fundamental analysis may be telling you a currency should be falling, but it nevertheless seems to be locked not only into a strengthening mode but also into a classic technical trading pattern. Swing traders, position traders, and other fundamental strategists should be open to learning from technicians. Simply put, fundamental traders should be prepared to use technical analysis in markets—learn from technicians and be ready to implement a trading strategy that is in sync with the market.

The euro is another example of a currency that baffled fundamental analysts for months and months. The euro's inauguration came amid such high expectations that it would compete with the U.S. dollar as the world's reserve currency and quickly become a *force terrible* on the world stage; thus, its market-driven devaluation seemed all the more unfathomable.

Currency market analysts seemed helpless to predict or even explain the euro's 25 percent decline during 1999–2000. In this environment, as the direction and the trend were one way—down—technical support and resistance levels for intraday traders proved to be an excellent strategy for both the short-term and long-term trader. Fundamental traders who kept waiting for the euro to "do what it is supposed to" lost the move for months in this currency.

The euro is, of course, something of a new model for international forex markets, in that it is the world's first zonal currency. There have been no other existing single currency models for traders to study and apply their trading systems to. The euro emerged needing to define its role in world currency relationships. One thing is for certain: Everyone is learning about this new currency from the same starting point, in the sense that it has a record to evaluate only as of January 1, 1999. And it was inevitable that more nations should join the European Currency Union, and sooner rather than later. As each new nation joins the ECU, the euro becomes a slightly different currency than it was before, so it is an exciting, ground-breaking phenomenon among currencies.

Choosing a Broker

The online currency market is evolving rapidly and in the event is developing new ideas and relationships between currency trading vendors and their clients. These innovations are developing so fast that many traders have fallen behind the curve of current knowledge and familiarity with trading venues and broker relationships, which, as a result, leaves them at a competitive disadvantage with traders who *are* current.

The same intense competition in the broader Internet environment that has led to massive price reductions, free ISPs, free downloading of software, and other free services or products of all kinds is just as pronounced and ubiquitous in the world of online currency trading, and no more so than in the explosion of online brokers and dealers.

For example, in many currencies, it has become expected that traders will be able to trade inside the traditional minimum five-pip spread, down to as little as a one-pip differential between bid and ask prices. Also, some dealers are offering to waive commissions on their customers' limit orders. Other traders are being given heretofore unheard of written guarantees of fill at the price levels of their stop loss orders, regardless of market conditions, and there are many, many other examples of brokers and dealers scrambling to offer advantages for *their* traders.

The competition for traders' affiliations is a real resource *for the trader,* and it will pay for us to stay alert to these new opportunities that arise quite literally day by day. These new venues, trading vehicles, and dealer/broker relationships, as we will see, improve trading practices and represent a valuable opportunity to increase profits. So it is impossible to overemphasize the importance of keeping current with all the technology, innovations, and promotional services that are constantly surfacing in the online currency trading world.

Trading Platform

Figure 3.1 shows one of the many new types of trading platforms offered by a dealer who invites bids and offers "inside the spread." In addition to providing traders with a look at pending bids and asks, this dealer format permits all limit orders to be filled at no commissions, whenever their limit orders are hit by other traders.

The screen to the right of the trading platform is an electronic version of the ticker tape, which shows all filled orders in the sequence they are entered. Subsequent to the last fills shown on the ticker tape at 106.91, there has been a lower "ask" offered at 106.90. The bid of 106.87 has remained the same so we have a three-pip spread on this trading platform.

Later in the day, we return to the trading platform to find the USD has gained slightly against the yen. Figure 3.2 shows a bid of 107.32 being entered into the platform by a day trader for a buy at the asking

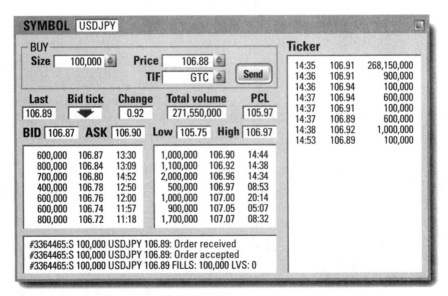

Figure 3.1 *A state-of-the-art online trading program for currency traders.*

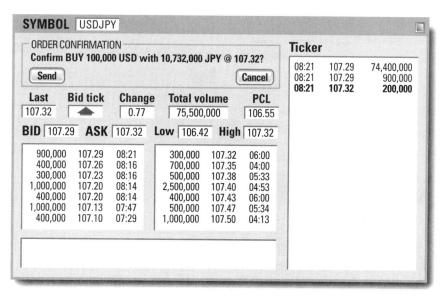

Figure 3.2 *An order has been entered at the ask, and the electronic dealer is requesting confirmation before executing it.*

price. He is being asked by the electronic dealer to confirm his order. Unexpectedly, the trading platform will come back with a confirmed fill, but at a lower price of 107.29. Why? Well, the executions of forex trade orders are so rapid, and the market can move literally before you can electronically get your order into the mix. That is what happened here. The electronic dealer automatically filled the order at the three-pip *better* price as the market moved in the few seconds it took to enter the order. Of course, the same can happen in the other direction, where a market order can be filled at a worse price just as easily.

The prices shown in the area to the left of the screen, below the bid and ask Level I area, is called the Level II information area, not unlike the Level II format for ECNs on the Nasdaq, which equity traders will be familiar with. Each price on the left is part of the pending queue of buy limit orders placed in the system, waiting to fill at the ask.

On the right, in the area below Level I, are the sell limit orders waiting to fill at the bid, if the market moves their way. Below the Level II area, the day trader sees his confirmation of the fill at 107.29 (see figure 3.3). The TIF box is "Time in Force" and has a minute selection menu where you can choose from 1 minute to 999 minutes for the duration

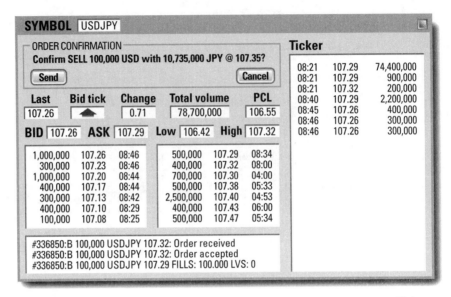

Figure 3.3 *Having bought at 107.29, the trader enters a sell limit order into the trading platform, hoping for a six-pip gain.*

the order is to be in force, as well as a Day Order option and the Good Till Canceled instruction shown on the screen.

Seeing a fill at a better price than he entered and still expecting the market to move to higher numbers, our day trader immediately enters a pending sell limit order at 107.35, expecting the market prices to go higher and earn him a six-pip profit. Figure 3.4 has the Level II display highlighting his accepted new sell limit order.

The market has now taken the spread down to 107.17/107.20, away from his pending sell limit order still in place. Our day trader prepares to cancel the limit order but will leave his executed buy at 107.29 in force, still expecting the market to come back his way. The online dealer will ask for the trader's confirmation before canceling his order. Our friendly trader presses a key on his PC and cancels his pending sell limit order.

Traders have an incentive to place orders inside the spread using this type of dealer's trading platform. For instance, another day trader wanting to buy at the narrowest possible spread sees the following online values:

Bid	Ask
106.91	106.94

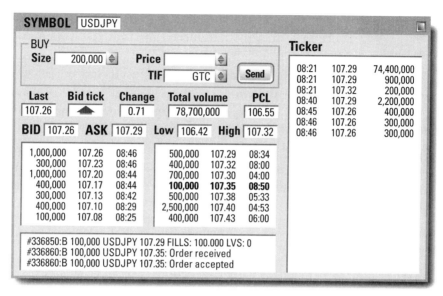

Figure 3.4 *The sell limit order is immediately displayed and highlighted in the Level II area on the right hand portion.*

Our friendly trader prepares to send in a sell limit order inside the spread at 106.92. The electronic dealer asks for a confirmation immediately before executing the order. Just then, the trader notices that the market has moved away from the pending sell limit order. The spread now stands at 106.87/106.92. The trader prepares to immediately cancel his trade. Now our friendly trader enters a new sell limit order priced at 106.89, two pips above the current bid price of 106.87. The Level III area of the traders' platform will show him that the 106.89 sell limit order was accepted, and it is highlighted in the Level II area on the right-hand side, with all the sell limit orders. Almost immediately, another trader buys at the sell limit price of 106.89. Why? Of course, it is one pip lower than the previous ask and only two pips above the bid. Because another trader looking to buy at the lowest possible price has an incentive to hit the new, lower ask price, it is more likely to be filled. Our friendly trader who placed the sell limit at 106.89 pays no commission charges whenever his limit orders are hit by other traders. It is in this way that trader-to-trader online formats use market incentives to generate narrower spreads, which means a more efficient market and, in this instance, lower commission charges.

The conventional wider spread ranges and former interbank dominance in setting the parameters for available trading prices in forex have been reduced by the technology that introduces trader-to-trader and inside-the-spread fills, and that results in a more level playing field for the non-institutional trader. Taking advantage of these innovations should be a major part of the online currency trader's blueprint for maximizing profits. Again, traders will have to stay alert to these rapidly evolving opportunities and be prepared to take advantage of them, lest they be at a competitive disadvantage within their market.

Here are some examples of the evolving dealer innovations being offered to forex traders:

- Using brokers' own proprietary ISPs, which protect their clients from glitches in commercial ISP service
- Trader-to-trader transactions, which permit spreads below the typical interbank norms
- Commission-free trading
- A waiver of commissions on any limit orders that are hit by other traders
- Initial account minimums of as little as $1,000, with 50 to 1 margin leverage, trading $100,000 lots
- Unlimited free demos with live trading formats
- Free use of charting, news, and other data with the opening of an account
- Voice *Squawk Box* contemporaneous feed from BIS and Reuters interbank dealer rooms, providing quotations from the top-tier market makers
- Guaranteed fills at the stop loss price ordered, even if the market gaps beyond the price

Order Entries

Profitable trading means that you have to make use of the resources available to you, and what can be more important than the instructions you give to your online dealer for execution of your trades? Knowing, for instance, that you can instruct an online dealer to execute a trade regardless of which direction the market may go, in advance of the market's move up or down, enables you as a trader to get in or out of positions before you know what the market actually will be doing, which for all of us is a large part of the time. Protecting losses or gains through stops and limits is integral to the strategy of every trader. These stops and limits, as well as many other order strategies, are a big part of risk management, which we shall examine closely throughout the pages of this book.

Market order will execute a fill at the best available price immediately and is the default order for most dealers.

Stop order will become a market order when a specified price level is reached. It can be used to enter or exit a position and reduces risk, although not perfectly. Markets may fall through a stop price level before a fill can be completed.

Buy stop order is used to reduce risk by specifying a price level to enter a new long position (or exit an existing short position). This permits a trader to create a market order if and when the market touches the specified price attached to the buy stop.

Sell stop order permits the trader to exit an existing long position (or enter a new short position). It becomes a market order as the market touches the specified price. The sell stop permits a trader in advance to get out of a long position (or enter a new short position).

Limit order specifies a worst possible fill price when executed. Unlike the stop price, where the market could surge beyond the specified level, the limit is an "or better" market order and guarantees a fill at the specified price or better. Because the limit price is not a market order, it runs the risk of not being filled under certain market conditions.

Stop limit order deals with two prices: the *stop price*, which initiates the order and converts it to a limit order, and the *limit price*, which establishes the highest or lowest fill price.

MIT, or market-if-touched order, is executed as a market order whenever the market touches the specified price level.

Improvement

A trader's predisposition for improvement is, on balance, the most important component in his conceptual blueprint for profits. We have reviewed the online currency environment, which is generating an ever-expanding menu of services and features that can enhance profitability.

But experienced traders have a valuable resource in the discipline established from their own trading experiences, and they should apply that same valuable framework to the online trading environment. For example, in currency markets—say, like the Japanese yen—the market may focus on interest rate differentials between the yen and another currency.

During 1999–2000, when the BoJ had a ZIRP, zero interest rate policy, and the U.S. Federal Reserve was raising its rates, expectations of either continued Fed rate increases or BoJ's ending of its ZIRP, based on statements coming from officials of the two governments, could capture the market's attention and would quickly be reflected in the valuations in USD/JPY.

However, the markets' focus could quickly shift from interest rate differentials to the U.S. stock market and comparisons with the Japanese Nikkei equity market. Whichever seemed to hold the most near-term promise would attract more capital flow, and that currency would rise. Next, this near-term equity growth focus would inevitably give way to worries about whether the United States' historic, consecutive 4 percent GDP growth record of recent years could be ending, causing a potential sell-off in the USD. Markets would move based on that scenario. Japanese elections might be the next blip on the markets' radar screen for influencing traders' decisions on how to value the USD/JPY. Would the U.S. Fed raise rates again? Would the Japanese economy slip back into recession? Focus shifts quickly and unexpectedly in currency markets, demanding traders' constant attention.

The point here is that profitable traders know the value of keeping current with their markets. And that same kind of attention is needed with regard to the online environment. It is really vital that traders adapt into their framework of online currency trading a habit of seeking out, on a regular basis, the opportunities that are developing literally day by day on the Internet. Executing one's trades more efficiently and profitably will be the confirmation of a trader's improvement. Pay attention, and be ready to take advantage of opportunities that can make your trading profitable.

Ever wonder how a trading system you have been fantasizing about would work in the real world? Access one of the many online resources that provide historical price data for currencies. You will find a selection of daily closing prices going back several years. You can call up any day's closing price with the press of a key.

With online historical data, we can go back and test strategies and get a real-world sense of how viably a conceptual trading system might actually trade in today's market. All without risking a cent.

We know the dollar and yen both appreciated against the euro after its introduction in 1999. Want to know quickly and immediately from an online resource whether the dollar strengthened more versus the euro in 1999, or was it the yen? You can call up an online "overlay" chart that will show you that the yen strengthened 25 percent versus the euro up until November 1999, while the dollar gained only half of that, 13 percent.

George Soros, the brilliant billionaire investor who correctly shorted the pound sterling in 1992, according to his chief investment strategist lost almost double that amount in the fall of 1998, amid the Russian default. According to the *New Republic* magazine, "Stanley Druckenmiller, the chief investment strategist at Soros Fund Management, estimated this summer that the Russian crisis had cost the Soros treasure chest close to $2 billion, the largest loss ever to hit the legendary group."[2] Soros, a role model for many currency traders, confirms for us, in a way that he would no doubt prefer to change, that as a trader's knowledge takes him to a higher level, he encounters stiffer competition.

Therefore, regardless of what level you trade at, improvement is the coin of the realm.

Q & A

Question: I am an experienced, seasoned stock trader, and I also have several years' experience trading with a voice broker format in global currencies. What do you recommend on a short time frame that will bring me to a comfort level trading currencies online?

Answer: The short answers are:

1. Use the online resources available to you. Start by checking the appendix in this book. You will find a reference source for all areas of online currency trading to check out.

2. There are proprietary software trading programs you can investigate. Software trading programs can give you buy and sell signals based on real-time prices. They can allow you to insert your own

trading parameters into the program and interact with real-time market prices.

3. You can also access historical data and back test trading ideas before trying them out with at-risk money.

4. You can arrange wireless and pager alerts based on instructions to dealers to implement your trading strategies.

5. Paper trading and demo trading are extremely useful for establishing familiarity with the new online trading environment.

6. Use charting to evaluate modifications to your trading system and entry or exit points for your trading program.

7. There are online educational formats that can extend your electronic trading knowledge into a level that will allow you to compete favorably with more experienced online currency traders.

Notes

1. "BoJ Head Intensifies Signal That Interest Rates Will Increase." *Wall Street Journal,* April 14, 2000.

2. *New Republic* (February 8, 1999).

4

A Close Look at the Exchange Futures Market

The $1.5 trillion-per-day forex markets we have been looking at are large indeed. They are known as OTC, over the counter markets. One of the underlying characteristics of forex, as I have just alluded to, is that in many respects OTC is not really a single market. In fact, *over the counter* is a term meant to imply "decentralized." So it should not be surprising, then, that in the forex's decentralized currency trading environment, a trader's relationship with an individual dealer will define a broad array of his trading parameters, and that this trading framework can vary from dealer to dealer. (See table 4.1, Forex Versus Futures.)

One practical confirmation of this multiplicity of markets in forex is the fact that at a given moment, prices do vary from dealer to dealer. If we could simultaneously monitor several dealers' trading platforms, we could see comparable but nevertheless different prices for the same currency pair at a given moment. As we have seen, if prices vary in forex OTC, then so, too, must their spreads. As one might expect, in a decentralized market you can find, in addition to varying bid/ask spreads, many dealers who nevertheless still only provide their clients with an essentially fixed spread (for example, five pips on the USD/JPY) all day long on their electronic trading platforms. So different spreads and prices among dealers are characteristics of the decentralized forex OTC market.

Also, as a trader, your margin requirements are, of course, completely at the discretion of your individual forex OTC dealer, as are lot (contract) minimums and size increments for trading. Hours you can trade will be different from one dealer to the next as well. A few dealers provide an

Table 4.1   *Forex Versus Futures*

Forex OTC	Exchange Futures
Price disparity	Uniform pricing
Contract trade flexibility	Fixed contracts
24-hour/5-day schedule	Scheduled hours
All 200+ currencies traded	Less than 25 percent of forex listings
Non-regulated	Heavily regulated
No arbitration format	Structured format for arbitration/mediation
Margin varies	Fixed margin parameters
Price quoting European style	Price quoting American style
Unlimited daily price moves	Exchange limited daily price moves

audio feed from major interbank sources such as Reuters and Telerate, so that their clients can listen in on the shouted bids/asks from the large two-tier interbank market, providing an invaluable window into these large markets' bid/ask prices in real time and in the process providing their clients with a unique resource with which to compare the prices they see displayed in front of them to the prices from a larger share of the forex market than they can access for trading themselves.

Comparing Forex to Exchange Futures Markets

So from this unstructured, unregulated currency trading environment called forex OTC, we can turn to an alternative currency market that is structured in ways the forex is not and in addition is well regulated. This alternative currency market is called an "exchange futures" market, and we want to understand how it functions and why it exists before plunging into strategies, technical analysis, and the meat of maximizing profits in electronic currency trading. One can surmise that a basic decision the trader must first make is which market to trade. Of course, some traders actually do trade both forex and exchange futures as part of their hedging or spread strategies. But for most traders, it will be one or the other, and this exchange futures/options market is quite different from forex OTC, as we are about to see.

Exchange futures markets developed, as we already know, in 1972 when the Bretton Woods exchange rate regime collapsed. The Chicago Mercantile Exchange was first to recognize the need for order and stability in the forex forward markets, which are the cash OTC equivalent to exchange futures contracts. In 1874 the CME was known as the Chicago Produce Exchange and had a futures exchange structure in place for commodities. Pork bellies, wheat, corn, and so forth had their delivery or "settlement" dates for these contracted commodities months apart, essentially because in 1874, when the CME was founded, it took that long to allow for farmers to get their products to market. Hence, when the Merc incorporated currency futures into its exchange in 1972, it used the same three-month settlement dates for currency futures that are still in place today. The CME is one of two exchanges in the United States that trades both futures and options.

The New York Board of Trade, NYBOT, through its Finex Exchange, is the other U.S. exchange that trades both futures and options. The remaining U.S. exchanges trade one or the other, but not both. The CBOT, Chicago Board of Trade, which opened its doors in 1848 and later merged with the Mid-American Futures Exchange, trades futures and is located very near the Chicago Mercantile Exchange. The Philadelphia Stock Exchange, Philx, trades only currency options. Worldwide, there are currently 10 global futures exchanges outside the United States where electronic dollar-based investors can trade in a wide range of futures or options instruments. The Hong Kong Futures Exchange has three "rolling forex" contracts, and the Brazilian Mercantile & Futures Exchange offers "customized" options. The variety of trading venues is not just geographical. Each exchange is its own unique futures trading environment.

U.S. Futures Exchanges

The Chicago Mercantile Exchange is the largest futures exchange in the world. In 1972, it broke new ground with the first exchange futures contract traded in the currency markets. Its day session opens at 7:20 A.M. and closes at 2 P.M. In 1998, its Globex 2 program inaugurated overnight electronic trading worldwide in currency futures. The Globex evening session starts at 2:30 P.M. and goes until 7:05 A.M. the next morning. The CME trades 15 USD-based contracts and a total of 59 cross rate pairs. It reported that for the months of January through May 2000, 12 percent of the CME's total volume (all contracts including agricultural, etc.) were entered electronically (see figure 4.1).

That represented a 117 percent increase from the same period of the year before. It is expected that electronic trading will eventually replace all open outcry pit trading in the currency markets. By comparison, the Globex 2 all-electronic overnight market registered an increase of 81 percent in contracts traded during 1999 as compared to 1998; in other words, 16.1 million contracts changed hands electronically in 1999, with volume up 81 percent versus 1998.

The New York Board of Trade's Finex Exchange (Financial Instruments Exchange) trades 25 currency futures and options contracts. Trading hours are 3 A.M. to 8 A.M., then 8:05 A.M. to 10 P.M. Its URL is *www.nyce.com.*

The CBOT, MidAmerican Futures Exchange, trades futures only. The Chicago Board of Trade began in 1868 trading commodities and engaged with the currency markets through its acquisition of the MidAm in 1986. The exchange trades six currency futures in a smaller-size format (half the size of USD/JPY, for example) than the CME.

CHICAGO MERCANTILE EXCHANGE

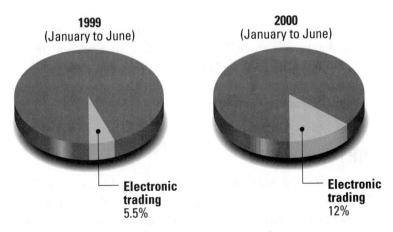

1999 (January to June)

2000 (January to June)

Electronic trading 5.5%

Electronic trading 12%

Figure 4.1 *Electronic trading is expected to continue capturing an increased share of futures trading at the CME.*

Hours are 7:20 A.M. to 2:15 P.M. Its 1999 volume was nearly 2 $^1/_2$ million contracts. Its URL is *www.midam.com*.

The Philadelphia Stock Exchange trades eight currency options contracts—like the MidAm, also of a smaller denomination than CME's contracts. Its trading hours are unique, 2:30 A.M. to 2:30 P.M. and it offers a customized option trading format, which permits traders to create their own expiration dates and exercise prices. Its URL is *www.phlx.com*.

Global Futures Exchanges

There are 10 international futures exchanges, mostly modeled after the U.S. format, which is to say, a SPAN margin system, a clearinghouse credit risk protection for investors, and the American system of price quotations. Virtually all are compatible with electronic traders.

The Budapest Commodity Exchange, BCE, was organized in 1995 and now offers seven futures contracts, with expectations of eventually expanding into options contracts. Morning trading hours are 10:30 to 12, then 1 to 4:15 in the afternoon. Turnover increased 30 percent in 1998 and totaled 8.4 million contracts overall. URL is *www.bce-bat.com*.

The Belgium Futures & Options Exchange, Belfox, located in Brussels, which began in 1991 and trades one currency futures option contract on the EURO/USD. Trading hours are 9:02 A.M. to 4:30 P.M. The Brussels Exchange URL is *www.bxs.com*.

The Brazilian Mercantile and Futures Exchange, BMF, trades two currency futures contracts and four "flexible" currency options contracts in Sao Paulo. Founded in 1986, its trading hours are 10 A.M. to 1 P.M., then 2:30 P.M. to 5 P.M. Its URL is *www.bmf.com*.

The Romanian Futures Exchange, SMFCE, (Sibiu Monetary Financial and Commodities Exchange) trades seven currency futures contracts and five currency options contracts. Trading hours are 9:30 A.M. to 4 P.M. Its Web site has listed leasing costs for a seat on its exchange for as little as $100/month. Its cyber name is Bursa Monetar-Financiara si de Marifari Sibiu. Its URL is *www.bmfms.ro*.

The Hong Kong Futures Exchange, inaugurated in November 1995, has a unique rolling forex contract format that, while not technically an exchange futures instrument, is noted here to call attention to the accommodation that commodity exchange markets are making to the worldwide interest in currency futures trading. Its URL is *www.hkfe.com*.

The Korean Futures Exchange, Kofex, was organized in 1996 and trades one futures and one options contract—the USD/Korean won. Exchange-wide, 1999 saw 1 million contracts traded on the Kofex. Hours are 9:30 A.M. to 4:30 P.M. Its URL is *www.kofex.com.*

The Moscow International Commodity Exchange, Micex, opened in 1999 trading 10 currency futures contracts electronically, including the USD/UAH (Ukrainian) and USD/KZT (Kazak.), among others. Its 1999 currencies volume was 1,719 billion rubles. Its URL is *www.micex.com.*

The South African Futures Exchange, SAFEX, is located in Johannesburg, South Africa, and opened in 1998. It trades a single currency futures contact, the USD/SAR (rand). Trading hours are 8:30 A.M. to 5:30 P.M. Its URL is *www.safex.co.za.*

The Tokyo International Financial Futures Exchange, TIFFE, trades a single futures contract electronically, USD/JPY. It opened in 1989 and hours are 9 A.M. to 11:30 A.M., then 12:30 P.M. to 3:30 P.M., then 3:40 P.M. to 6 P.M. Its URL is *www.tiffe.or.jp.*

Quoting Futures Prices

One of the most apparent differences between forex and exchange futures is the style of quoting prices. Exchange futures use the American style, as distinct from forex, which prefers the European-style quote.

Most worldwide currency futures contracts settle on a quarterly schedule: March, June, September, and December of each year. By way of illustration, on any given date in May, the futures settlement date for the nearest contract will be in June. Incidentally, the U.S. settlement dates are the third Wednesday of each contract month, with trading halted two days prior to settlement, not unlike the forex practice of settlement two days after a trade is executed.

Figure 4.2 shows the daily reports of currencies quoted in both the American and European styles. One is for the futures market, the other for the cash market. The forex OTC markets use what is known as the European style (foreign currencies per U.S. dollar), quoting 105.75 yen per U.S. dollar. Here is the formula for converting these forex notations to futures format: To derive the fractional number of U.S. dollars for one yen, which is the futures notation, when you only have the forex number of yen per U.S. dollar, simply take the reciprocal of the yen number. The reciprocal looks like this: $1/105.75 = \$0.009456$. As you can see,

Key currency cross rates

	Dollar	Euro	Pound	Peso	Yen
Japan	105.75	101.28	159.89	10.725	....
Mexico	9.8600	9.4429	14.908		.09324
U.K.	.66140	.6334		.06708	.00625
Euro	1.04420		1.5788	.10590	.00987
U.S.	....	.9577	1.5120	.10142	.00946

Source: Reuters

CURRENCY TRADING

EXCHANGE RATES

The New York foreign exchange mid-range rates below apply to trading among banks in amounts of $1 million and more, as quoted at 4 p.m. Eastern time by Reuters and other sources. Retail transactions provide fewer units of foreign currency per dollar. Rates for the 11 Euro currency countries are derived from the latest dollar-euro rate using the exchange ratios set 1/1/99.

Country	U.S. $ equiv. Mon	U.S. $ equiv. Fri	Currency per U.S. $ Mon	Currency per U.S. $ Fri
Argentina (Peso)	1.0008	1.0008	.9992	.9992
Australia (Dollar)	.6020	.6071	1.6611	1.6473
Austria (Schilling)	.06960	.07014	14.269	14.257
Bahrain (Dinar)	2.6525	2.6525	.3770	.3770
Belgium (Franc)				41.7965
Japan (Yen)	.009456	.009413	105.75	106.24
1-month forward	.009508	.009466	105.17	105.64
3-months forward	.009617	.009572	103.99	104.47
6-months forward	.009781	.009735	102.24	102.73
Jordan (Dinar)	1.4065	1.4085	.7110	.7100
Kuwait (Dinar)	3.2658	3.2648	.3062	.3063
Lebanon (Pound)	.0006605	.0006609	1514.00	1513.00
Malaysia (Ringgit)	.2632	.2632	3.8000	3.8000
Malta (Lira)	2.3326	2.3425	.4287	.4269
Mexico (Peso) Floating rate	.1014	.1013	9.8600	9.8725
Netherland (Guilder)	.4346	.4380	2.3012	2.2833
New Zealand (Dollar)	.4740	.4774	2.1097	2.0947
			.6194	8.55??

Figure 4.2 *Various newspapers carry the closing prices of currencies worldwide.*

the American style is units of USD per foreign currency: $0.009456 per one yen. The true value of this number is 9.456-tenths of the one U.S. cent. The futures number $0.009456, then, is simply the reciprocal of 105.75 yen per one USD.

Although the USD/JPY futures price is actually $0.009456, it is quoted on the exchanges and elsewhere more often in a shorthand version, $0.9456, so in practice the two zeros prefacing the whole numbers are simply dropped, and the shorthand number is read $0.9456.

In this case, to convert directly from the shorthand notation of futures dollars used in exchange trading, $0.9456, take the reciprocal of this value that accounts for the dropping of two zeros: 100/$0.9456. That reciprocal also yields 105.75. Remember, if the USD value you are working with is the true decimal notation for USD/JPY, $0.009456, the conversion to Japanese yen is achieved by 1/0.009456.

For currencies like the Swiss franc, the conversion is simpler. The forex notation for USD/CHF is 1.6284 Swiss francs per U.S. dollar. Converting that to futures notation is simply 1/1.6284, which yields the futures value, $0.6141. A Swiss franc at this forex price level is worth 61 and 41/100 U.S. cents.

We should remind our stock traders and other readers that the quarterly settlement prices, as we have already seen in forex forwards, are simply a reflection of interest rate differentials between the two currencies and not a market (or any other) prediction of currency valuations for a future settlement date.

For instance, exchange records show that on May 1, 2000, the USD/JPY cash forex spot rate on that date was 107.75, which is the American quote notational equivalent of $0.9280. The futures price quoted on May 1 was $0.9318, which is higher than the cash price and reflects the higher U.S. interest rate versus Japan. As the settlement date draws nearer (third Wednesday in June), the two prices begin to reflect convergence.

The spot forex equivalent of 107.75 ($.9280) and the futures price ($.9318) gradually converge, totally independent of the market swings in the daily cash valuations, so that on the June settlement date, forex and futures are the same.

We can refer to the June 2000 settlement date in our records to confirm these couple of things about futures and forex prices. The records show that the futures price for USD/JPY on the contract settlement date in June that day was $0.9445. So, number one, we find that indeed the futures contract actually traded at $0.9445 that day, not $0.9318, which was the futures settlement price actually quoted in the markets back on May 1, confirming that futures prices do not reflect future market valuation, they only reflect the interest rate cost-of-carry differential in the two currencies. Second, we can convert the June settlement date futures price of $0.9445 to a forex equivalent, which is 105.87 yen per dollar,

Table 4.2   *Cash Forex Price on May 1, 2000*

USD/JPY	Futures (Forex) Equivalent Price		Futures Price
107.75	$0.9280	<	$0.9318 (May) Cash Forex Price on June Settlement Date
105.87	$0.9445	=	$0.9445 (June)

Yen has strengthened since May 1. Futures price on settlement date are not equal to futures price back on May 1.

and that is indeed where the June 19 forex price traded on that date. So the futures and spot forex prices achieve convergence at settlement, confirming the reduction in interest costs, the closer to settlement we come.

Structural Distinctions Between Forex and Exchange Futures Markets

As we have seen, the structural pricing distinction between forex and futures markets is, of course, their differing real-price values. Cash forex is the price as of today, while futures are a price valuation based on interest rate differentials for a specific date in the future. The size of the contract differs between forex and exchange futures markets, too.

Unlike the flexible forex OTC relationships between trader and dealer, an exchange futures trader has a fixed contract amount that he must trade with and that is set by the exchange. He also has a trading schedule each day that he must conform to. Hours for the Chicago Mercantile Exchange are 7:20 A.M. to 2 P.M., Chicago time. During this day session, both futures and options contracts are traded at the CME. After 2 P.M., however, options effectively stop trading due to illiquid markets until the opening of the next day's session. But futures contracts do begin trading again at 2:30 P.M. until 7:05 the next morning. The CME's overnight session is all electronic.

Then, too, the currency pairs available are more limited than in forex. The CME trades 59 currency contracts in futures during the day sessions, 56 in its Globex 2 overnight sessions, and 12 options contracts, compared to over 200 currencies traded on the international forex markets.

Margin on a Futures Exchange

Experienced traders who have a familiarity with margin issues from their stock market perspective should familiarize themselves with how margin works in an exchange futures environment. Similarly, forex traders will find exchange margin somewhat different from their experience as well.

The CME has established a transparent margin format that virtually all futures exchanges follow as a standard for their own client accounts. The Merc's margin system is called SPAN, Standard Portfolio Analysis of Risk. Table 4.3 shows a representative snapshot of margin requirements

Table 4.3 *Margin Requirements*

U.S. $ Denominated Contracts	Initial Margin	Maintenance Margin
Australian dollar (AUD)	$1,317	$ 975
British pound (GBP)	$1,823	$1,350
Canadian dollar (CAD)	$ 608	$ 450
Deutsche mark (DEM)	$1,620	$1,200
French franc (FRF)	$2,025	$1,500
Japanese yen (JPY)	$4,212	$3,120
E-Mini Japanese yen (J7)	$2,106	$1,560
Mexican peso (MXP)	$2,500	$2,000
New Zealand dollar (NZD)	$1,485	$1,100
Russian ruble (RUR)	$4,500	$3,000
South African rand (SAR)	$1,755	$1,300
Swiss franc (CHF)	$2,160	$1,600
Brazilian real (BRL)	$3,500	$2,500
Euro fx (EC)	$3,240	$2,400
E-Mini euro fx	$1,620	$1,200

on any given day in the currency futures markets. Depending on volatility and other risk factors in a given currency environment, exchanges will review the SPAN formula and adjust its base margin requirements up or down as much as twice daily. These can vary considerably, so traders should be aware that their margin obligations can go up or down, based on the currency environment they are trading in. But the margin level, whatever it is, is based on an objective evaluation of market conditions and it applies to all traders equally.

Traders should inquire, during their initial discussions with a prospective broker, whether his firm follows SPAN *minimums* or whether it adds additional margin costs for traders. A few brokers do increase margin for certain markets, and traders should know this as part of their evaluation process in selecting an exchange futures broker. Because of exchange rules, when a trader establishes an account with his futures broker, his money is passed through immediately to a Futures Commission Merchant. The broker never has access to it. Your broker does, however, effectively administer profit and loss statements and the margin status for your account.

How Margin Works

If you enter a futures position in a given currency—say, the Russian ruble—you must have in your account at least $4,500 per contract. That applies to either long or short positions equally. For options, if you buy an option on the ruble, there is no margin requirement. Your premium payment for the option is all that will be debited in your account. On the other hand, if you sell an option, the initial margin requirement applies and your account must have a margin minimum of the full $4,500. Once the position is established, on subsequent trading days, your margin call requirement is reduced to the maintenance margin level—in this case, $3,000. If your account balance touches $3,000, due to a $1,500 loss or withdrawals or a combination of both in your account, then the broker, on instructions from the clearinghouse, will require a replenishment of your account balance back up to the initial margin requirement of $4,500.

Table 4.4 shows the standard ratios that the CME uses for determining the initial and maintenance margin levels for various currencies. Note that the two margin levels are fixed in a ratio. If volatility and risk factors increase in a market for a currency pair like the EUR/CHF, which has a 1.35 ratio, then the exchange may have the initial margin increased, which results in the ratio-dependent maintenance margin being increased as well. Both initial and maintenance margin levels increase an amount that stays in the same proportion to each other and that increases in absolute dollar terms. Note that for most currencies the ratio is 1.35. For the Mexican peso, the ratio is 1.25. Table 4.3 shows the initial margin at $2,500 and the maintenance margin at $2,000 per the 1.25 ratio. Referring to the table, the maintenance margin for the euro is $2,400. Apply the 1.35 ratio to the $2,400, and the initial margin of $3,240 is confirmed. That is how this ratio is applied. As you can see, the Russian ruble has a 1.50 ratio, which means the initial margin will be 1.5 times as great as the maintenance margin. Every trader, sooner or later, is impacted by margin issues, and the successful trader pays attention to his margin levels.

Table 4.4 *Standard Ratios*

Contract	Ratio
Agricultural	1.35
Forest products	1.50
Currencies	1.35
Brazilian real	1.40
Peso, Brady bonds	1.25
Interest rates	1.35
S&P / Barra-growth & Val.	1.25
Equity indices / QBI	1.35
GSCI	1.50
Russian ruble	1.50
S&P 500 / E-Mini S&P 500 / Nasdaq 100 / E-Mini Nasdaq 100	1.25

Another important distinction between forex and exchange futures trading is that market bids/asks are the same for all exchange traders, inasmuch as the exchange operates like a centralized, single dealer for all participants.

On exchanges like the Chicago Mercantile Exchange, there is no price disparity among traders bidding on the same currency pair and, as we have seen, the margin requirement is the same for all traders on a given exchange.

Regulation of Exchange Futures

All U.S. futures exchanges are subject to congressional oversight through the Commodity Futures Trading Commission and the Securities and Exchange Commission. The CFTC was authorized by Congress in 1974, in response to the new exchange futures market created two years earlier at the Chicago Mercantile Exchange. The exchanges themselves discipline member firms if necessary, and they have the authority to revoke membership, impose fines, and suspend trading privileges. The U.S. Congress has also authorized the National Futures Association, which shares oversight and regulatory responsibilities with the CFTC to investigate complaints in the exchange futures environs. The NFA staff is quite large, with over 140 field auditors and investigators overseeing all aspects of trading operations at exchanges in the United States. The NFA also administers an arbitration dispute format that does not require traders to hire an attorney, and an aggrieved trader need only prove unfair treatment, not legal violations of statutes or trading rules. Let's look more closely at the structure and regulatory framework that futures exchanges operate under in the United States.

The exchanges themselves (and in the United States, remember there are four exchanges trading currency futures/options) are certified by the CFTC and must operate under strict guidelines established by Congress and the Commodity Futures Trading Commission. For instance, the CME must have an independently incorporated clearinghouse that is responsible for balancing the exchange's contracts each day. The clearinghouse guarantees the financial integrity of trading operations at an exchange and oversees margin requirements of traders who have accounts and are trading on the exchange.

Clearinghouse Guarantees

As an example, suppose you enter an order through your broker's online trading platform to buy a September futures contract on the USD/JPY. On the CME that contract has a fill value of 12,500,000 yen. Each tick—in futures, the forex's "pip" is referred to as a "tick"—is worth $12.50. The broker's electronic platform submits the order to the open outcry pits on the trading floor of the Merc and, instantly, a seller is matched up to your buy order. But suppose, just for discussion purposes, that the counterparty to your trade is a floor trader who has been on the wrong side of multiple trades all week and has become extended. Then at the end of this day, he is unable to make good on his sell order to you; he is insolvent. Your buy order, which, let's say, appreciated $1,000 on the day, without the backing of the exchange clearinghouse, would be worthless. So the clearinghouse substitutes itself for the buyer's side of every sell order (the clearinghouse can use margin deposits to offset its liability on any potential defaults), and then, too, as in this case, it substitutes itself for the seller's side in every buy order, so that the bankrupt counterparty to your buy position is backstopped by the clearinghouse. In this way, every trade executed on the exchange is supported by the exchange's own clearinghouse corporation, and traders are protected from credit risk. In addition, there are clearing members of the exchange who are required to stand behind the orders cleared through them, from introducing brokers or other clients. The clearinghouse and clearing members must have the resources to effect this trade-executing protection, and also the clearinghouse is responsible for administering and collecting margin funds from all traders active on the exchange.

From Your PC to the Exchange Trading Pits

Beginning with your personal computer console's link to a futures broker, right on through to order execution and account reconciliation, the professionals associated with your exchange futures trading experience operate under a framework of certification and regulation that is unparalleled in any other market.

The broker's office associate who monitors your electronic order entries and answers your questions or discusses the nuances of order execution must be a member of the NFA and is accountable to both the exchange and the CFTC in terms of his professional relationships. The firm he works for will be an introducing broker, a status that must be certified by the CFTC and is also subject to NFA investigation should complaints arise. We have already noted the unusual restriction of your broker not being allowed to keep the money you use to open an account with him. Those funds are passed through to a higher level of exchange futures certification: a futures commission merchant. These FCMs keep client account money in a segregated account and follow strict procedures for its disbursement. A CFTC-certified FCM, in addition to having a membership with the NFA, must be a paid-up member of the exchange and is subject to exchange oversight, which is considerable. Some FCMs are clearing members, who, as just noted, match trades for affiliated clients and absorb some credit risk on behalf of traders.

Futures exchanges sell memberships that permit floor access to the exchange's open outcry trading pits, and members occasionally will offer their memberships for lease. The trading pits are populated by members of the exchange, such as large banks and investment houses, which trade either for their own accounts or on behalf of clients. FCMs will be trading for their affiliated brokers alongside smaller, individual floor brokers, known as "locals," on the floor of an exchange.

The world of exchange futures trading provides a structure and degree of credit risk protection unique in the financial markets and explains, in part, the attraction of exchange trading. Next, let's look at how to take advantage of the unique exchange structure for maximizing profit in electronic currency trading.

Q & A

Question: I am a reasonably experienced forex trader who is interested in trading exchange futures and perhaps options. How much of a disadvantage will I be at in terms of understanding exchange futures language, trade execution practices, and trading systems?

Answer: Once an experienced forex trader establishes a comfort level with the actual trading experiences in an exchange futures/options environment, all of his considerable knowledge and experience can be well leveraged in these markets. I encourage you to use electronic simulated-trading programs in combination with opening an account with an exchange broker and go over your issues with him before actually committing your money in a futures position. I am convinced that this practice and discussion will save you unnecessary losses during your initiation period with exchange trading.

5

Conceptual Blueprint for Maximizing Profits in Exchange Futures Trading

Experienced stock traders know how to incorporate a critical and important big-picture concept of their trading environment into their trading decisions and strategies. What moves stock prices? Earnings news, interest rates, sector growth, business cycles, technical indicators, and so forth. For those traders now entering the currency futures world for the first time, a first order of business should be to work on the same conceptual or big-picture perspective of the exchange futures market and reach a comfort level with that understanding of how futures prices work and a confidence that your trading framework can profit in this environment. Forex traders understand that exchange futures are a surrogate for forex prices, with an interest rate factor thrown in as a sweetener. So even though they may be now just starting out in currency exchange futures trading, they come with an understanding and grounding already in place that they can apply to this exchange trading environment.

For instance, the exchange futures price of the USD/JPY is higher than the forex spot price, not because investors expect the yen to gain long term versus the dollar, but because U.S. interest rates are historically (and at the time) higher than Japanese rates. By comparison, the GBP/JPY futures price is more closely valued to the forex price level. Why? You guessed it; the interest rate differential between the two currencies is much smaller. And where the U.S. interest rate is lower than another currency's—like, say, the Mexican peso's—the peso's exchange futures price is actually *lower* than the forex spot. So this conceptual understanding of pricing futures is a building block or starting point in the process of creating your conceptual blueprint for maximizing profits in currency exchange markets.

Figure 5.1's chart illustrates for us another important distinction in futures trading—gaps. This chart shown is for the three days blanketing a July Fourth holiday. The forex markets continued trading right through the holiday. The exchanges in the United States are, of course, closed. After having closed in the early morning hours of July 4, exchange traders wait for its opening at 7:20 A.M. on July 5, a span of over 24 hours, during which time the forex markets, of course, continue to trade. Therefore, on the July 5 opening, the exchange futures market's pricing level generates a gap in order to catch up to forex levels, which have been trading right through the American holiday during the previous 24+ hours. A close look at the chart will show other gaps as well. The CME's Globex format closes for an hour at 10 P.M. CST and then for a few minutes around 7 A.M. Trading does not go on during these closed time periods. So gaps in trading are part of the trading environment for futures markets.

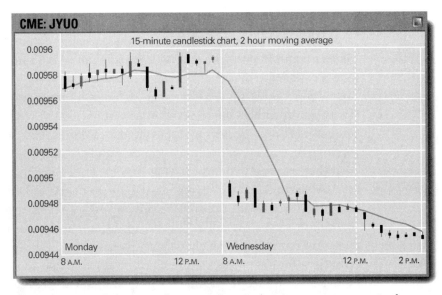

Figure 5.1 *Holidays (and overnight markets) generate gaps in futures prices, both in volume and price levels.*

Then, too, exchange options trade mostly on the daytime futures exchange time frame. That means that as the exchange closes at 2 P.M. (for the CME), the options market will essentially not trade until opening the next day at 7:20 A.M., some 17 hours later. During those 17 hours, the forex market may have moved considerably. The options pricing level then will be subject to a gap on opening, in order to catch up to its foundation of pricing premium value, the spot forex. So all in all, traders should keep in mind that the futures market is, at base, derived from forex price levels. The news that moves forex moves futures. If technical factors generate price movements in forex, the futures will follow and reflect those same factors.

Before entering a trade with an online broker, all traders want to know down to the last dollar what their position is going to cost, what is at risk, and how those profits or losses are going to be tallied. Forex traders as well as stock traders, each new to exchange futures markets, will want to reach a comfort level in this area before putting their money at risk in a trade, and so let's review what their real-time costs will be in exchange futures trading.

Margin Costs in Exchange Futures Trading

There is some similarity in margin policies between futures and stock exchanges because in both cases the available capital in a trader's account balance actually increases as margin requirements go down from the initial margin level to a smaller maintenance margin level. As far as the futures exchanges are concerned, when you *buy* or *sell* a futures contract on a currency through their exchanges, your account will be debited a like amount, regardless of whether you are going long or short the contract. That debited amount is very simply the current margin for that day, as set by the exchange. But unlike stock exchange transactions, there is no interest charged by a broker in futures margin accounting.

We can follow an accounting balance and compare exchange futures and stock exchange positions. In tables 5.1 and 5.2, we have assumed, for simplicity, an account opening balance of $4,212, which is just enough (not including brokers' or exchange fees, etc.) to open a futures position at current margin levels.

The CME futures contract for the Japanese yen, of course, is valued at 12,500,000 yen, or $125,000 worth of yen at 100 yen per dollar.

Table 5.1   *Comparison Between Futures Account Balances and Stock Traders' Account Balances*

	Futures Contract Purchase	Stock Purchase (100 Shares at $42^1/_8$)
Interest Charges	None	Yes (broker)
Initial Margin	$4,212	$2,106
Opening Account Balance	$ 0	$2,106
Maintenance Margin Level	$3,120	$1,263*

*30 percent of $4,212 market value of stock position

Table 5.2   *Account Balance Now Available for Additional Purchases*

	Futures Exchange	Stock Exchange
Account Equity	$4,212	$4,212
Initial Margin	$4,212	$2,100
Maintenance Margin	$3,120	$1,263
Next-Day Account Balance	$1,092	$2,949

Using $4,212 as the exchange margin requirement, the leverage, then, for a futures trader self-evidently far exceeds the stock trader's leverage. For exchange futures traders, the ratio is about 30 to 1, or 3 percent margin. For the stock trader, it is, of course, 2 to 1 or 50 percent. However, since we want to compare the real costs for trading, we need to compare $4,212 (which is the cost of establishing a futures position in USD/JPY) in a futures equity position with $4,212 in a stock equity position.

In so doing, we are in fact comparing investment dollars to investment dollars and identifying how margin applications differ per investment dollar between the futures and stock exchange systems. Put another way, yes, the futures exchange system has a more generous margin/leverage formula for investors. But, given that an investment dollar can choose to trade on either exchange, traders need to be informed on how margin reduces those available investment dollars differently on the two types of investment exchanges.

This is an important next step in identifying basic structural differences relating to trading strategies between a futures exchange and a stock exchange.

As you can see in table 5.1, after a trader opens a position, the exchange margin accounting procedures result in substantially less account equity being available to the futures trader as compared to stock exchange traders for the same amount of investment dollars. Starting with a $4,212 account balance, upon opening a position, the stock trader has half his investment available compared to $0 for a futures trader. Then the next day, when maintenance margin kicks in, the stock trader once again has nearly three times as much account equity as the futures trader.

To recap, the futures trader opens an account with $4,212 and takes a position that leaves him with a $0 balance on fill, while the stock trader has $2,106 in his account on fill. After the first day's trading, the margin debit against a futures trader's account decreases from the higher initial margin level to the smaller maintenance margin level, freeing up $1,092 ($4,212 − $3,120) in account resources for additional purchases. Similarly, the stock trader gets an increase in available equity from his exchange's maintenance margin levels.

In the previous example (table 5.2), when maintenance margins became operative, only $1,092 of an initial $4,212 position is available to the futures account holder, whereas in the stock exchange environs almost $3,000 remains available to the account holder for the same level of market investment—about $4,212. So in terms of investment dollars available in traders' account balances, it turns out that the futures exchange is far less generous than a stock trader is accustomed to.

Profits and Losses

Your online futures broker will post profits and losses in your account based on the established $4,212 asset value of a futures contract, which, as we have seen, is actually the margin assessed by the exchange for holding a futures contract.

Once more for review: Table 5.2 shows a trader who has bought a futures position and his account is debited the amount of the exchange's

Table 5.3   *After One Day's Trading*

	Futures Trader	Stock Trader
Opening Balance	$4,212	$4,212
Cost of Position	$4,212*	$2,106
Initial Margin	$4,212*	$2,106
Account Balance at Trade Execution	$ 0	$2,106
Maintenance Margin Level	$3,120	$1,263
Next-Day Account Balance**	$1,092	$2,949

*The initial margin is the cost of position in futures trading.
**Assumes no change in futures or stock value.

margin position for the yen, currently $4,212. If the trader had instead been short the contract, it would not have changed the margin requirements or the costs charged against his account balance for a single futures position, $4,212.

As we look at table 5.4, we see that the market has gone down, against the long position of our trader. Each tick eats $12.50 when it is against the yen, and as we monitor the trader's position intraday, we see that it has soon lost $1,000 or 80 ticks. It is not unusual for the yen to move more than 80 ticks in a day; in fact, it can be considered typical.

A glance at the margin levels again shows that the maintenance margin levels required for the yen are $3,120, which means that our trader will not be getting a margin call from his online broker as a result of a $1,000 loss on his contract. The stock trader whose stock went down $1,000, by contrast, does face a margin call as his account balance falls below margin requirements.

If a futures trader's losses do exceed margin minimums, the broker can, just as in stock trading, liquidate a position to get out from under a trader's losses if his client's funds are not forthcoming. If you never lose money as a futures trader, you will never have to face a margin call. However, since preparation and familiarity are the name of the game, traders will not want to be caught unaware of these differences in margin obligations between forex, stock exchanges, and futures exchanges. In exchange futures trading, there is no interest charge by your broker

Table 5.4   *The Effect of a Position Loss of $1,000 on Account Balance and Margin Requirements*

	Futures Trader	Stock Trader
Original Account Balance	$4,212	$4,212
Initial Margin Debit to Account	$4,212	$2,106
Maintenance Margin Debit to Account	$3,120	$1,263*
Next-Day Account Balance	$1,092	$2,106
Loss in Market	$1,000	$1,000
New Account Balance	$ 92	$1,106*

*The Maintenance Margin level is $1,263 for the stock trader, and his account balance falls below that level after a $1,000 loss in the market. Hence, he gets a margin call.

Summary

Futures trader's available equity is reduced. The $1,000 loss is deducted from second day's balance of $1,092. Account balance after $1,000 loss is $92. (Futures trader has no margin call.)

Stock trader's available equity is reduced. The $1,000 loss is deducted from second day's balance of $2,106. Account balance after $1,000 loss is $1,106. (Stock trader's account balance falls below maintenance margin requirement of $1,263, and he has a margin call.)

---

because he is not loaning a contract. When your account balance suffers a loss and the margin level is touched, the trader must bring his account up to the initial (higher) level, as opposed to the 30 percent maintenance level required by most stock brokers.

Finally, let's look at a futures trader (table 5.5) who starts with $20,000 in his account and who gets a margin call. This time he makes a multiple purchase of the same contract and suffers a greater loss—$8,000. After deducting the $8,000 trading loss, his account has a balance—$5,760—below margin requirements and not enough to meet the maintenance margin requirement of $6,240.

To sum this up, a stock trader will find this margin accounting procedure different in a distinct way from the system he is used to in equity

Table 5.5 *Margin Calls*

	Futures Trader (Purchase of 2 futures contracts)	Stock Trader (Purchase of 200 shares at $42^1/_{16}$)
Opening Balance	$ 20,000	$ 20,000
Cost of Position	$ 8,424	$ 8,424
Initial Margin	$ 8,424	$ 4,212
Account Balance at Trade Execution	$ 11,576	$ 15,788
Maintenance Margin Level	$ 6,240*	$ 2,527
Next-Day Account Balance	$ 13,760	$ 17,473

Position Loses $8,000 in the Market

	Futures Trader (Purchase of 2 futures contracts)	Stock Trader (Purchase of 200 shares at $42^1/_{16}$)
Account Balance	$20,000 – $8,000 – $6,240 = $5,760**	$20,000 – $8,000 – 2,527 = $9,473
Maintenance Margin	$6,240 (subject to margin call)	$2,527 (not subject to margin call)

*Two contracts ($2 \times \$3,120 = \$6,240$)
**Account fails below maintenance margin

markets. In stocks, maintenance margin is established as 30 percent of your original market position.

For instance, if a trader with a $20,000 opening balance is buying $8,424 of Microsoft, he can borrow 50 percent of that from his broker, establishing an account with a balance of $15,788. After that, if his position loses $8,000, he leaves an account balance of $9,473, well above the maintenance margin level of $2,527. So long as his account balance equals something more than 30 percent of the value of his original position (30 percent of $8,424 is $2,527), this stock trader's account balance prevents a margin call.

The Best Kept Secret in Online Currency Trading

TOPS, Trade Order Processing System, is the trading vehicle used by the CME to execute currency orders. This all-electronic network also has an interface for retail traders that many of us will want to take advantage of. First, what is TOPS and how does it work?

TOPS is owned jointly by the CBOT and CME and is used to manage, electronically, the large volume of trade orders that flows between brokers and the exchange floor, where the open outcry trading pits match buy to sell orders, and where the floor traders and floor brokers make markets for the futures contracts traded through the exchange. TOPS is, after all, the interface that enables brokers to offer electronic trading platforms to their retail clients, so that we can initiate orders online from our PCs. Without TOPS, there would be no online currency trading. TOPS, incidentally, is also the backbone of Globex 2, the 24-hour currency futures trading format at the Merc.

Traders who use online formats but who do not feel they need broker assistance in determining which trades to make, how to execute their trades, or for discussion of technical and fundamental indicators will want to consider installing a TOPS terminal that can integrate their PC with the exchanges trading pits directly. Why? Well, with TOPS, a trader can see the bids/asks as they come up on the trading floor and expedite his order execution, going directly from his PC to the floor of the exchange.

TOPS $2 Per Trade Costs

There is also another exciting benefit for electronic currency traders, however, that we want to note. The CME offers online traders the option of installing a TOPS terminal in their home or office, thereby giving them access to the floor traders' bid/ask spreads in real time *and eliminating brokers' commissions.* Using the TOPS terminal, traders, from their home or office PC, and seeing the bid/ask prices, can enter limit orders inside the spread and do the other things that this online access to real-time floor-trading data affords them.

Of course, the per trade costs go down dramatically, to as low as $2 per trade, avoiding brokers' fees altogether. There is a very modest monthly rental fee, as well as some minor installation costs. The Merc offers orientation classes that get a trader up to speed very quickly in the use of the TOPS equipment. I recommend that every day trader look into this option. Avoiding brokers' fees and getting the same bid/ask prices that the floor brokers trade from are real advantages that information technology generates. All in all, the TOPS format is one of the best-kept secrets in the exchange currency futures trading world.

An Online Trading Format

I know that all traders are keenly aware of the competition among brokers for our traders' affiliation. Brokers not only offer online demo trading platforms as one way to attract clients to their brokerages; they find sweeteners to add as well, such as charting, news, and data resources. This competitive environment is one of the resources that traders want to take advantage of. Charts, real-time streaming data, news, and so on are available, free, and online, for traders to incorporate into development of their blueprint's design for maximizing profits. Let's begin with a look at one of these online trading platforms.

Figure 5.2 shows an online trading format that provides realistic demo account trading experience. The trader selects a buy or sell transaction and quantity, using symbols for the currency contract and the month/year provided by the exchange and sends his order online to a broker for execution.

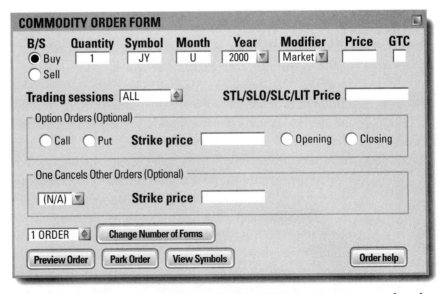

Figure 5.2 *This trade is to "buy" "1" "JY" (Japanese yen) for the contract "U" (September) at the market.*

Under the heading "Modifier" near the top of the platform, a trader selects the type of order he is instructing the broker to implement—in this case, a market order. For any order the trader wants his broker to carry over and maintain into the next trading day, he checks "GTC," good till canceled.

As we already know, exchange hours are limited and vary from one exchange to another as well. So, unlike the 24-hour forex market, traders have to pay attention to the specific hours an exchange is open for trading. Then, too, exchanges may permit trading in futures and options during one session but not options in another session. On the Merc, there are two trading sessions: One is the daytime session, in which both futures and options trade, and then there is Globex 2, where only futures trade electronically. Options traders find their market illiquid and are generally shut out of overnight trading at this time.

Making Mistakes on a Demo and Learning from Them

The purpose of a demo account is to flesh out mistakes it can elicit from your trading practices, strategies, and understanding of how the market works. In the event, you will improve your framework for applying your own personal blueprint for maximizing profits.

While we have the use of an online trader's platform here, whose use was designed specifically for demo applications, what better time than now to identify how a few conceptual mistakes can lead to losses but can then be helpful and instructive? These examples are simple for the benefit of stock traders just learning the exchange futures environment. But the big-picture message is important. Use demo trading to uncover your mistakes, whatever level you trade on, and without risking a dollar. Let's watch a former stock trader use the demo to practice his strategy in both the futures and options market at the CME.

In this review, we want also to look at how options orders are entered. (The abbreviations STL/SLO/SLC/LIT Price are not presently in use in the auditrade demo format.) At the bottom partition in this platform, we find choices available to a trader that enable him to select a screen venue for either spread orders or multiple orders (change # of forms). "Park Order" is, as the name implies, an opportunity for the trader to input his order, then wait until the market meets a special set of trading parameters before he executes it. "Symbols" created by each exchange are what the system takes off the platform and then interprets before converting them into trading instructions for floor brokers who execute the trader's order entry.

Our friendly trader enters an order for the purchase of a futures position "at the market." Note that the "all sessions" qualifier could be selected since it is a futures order and futures trade 24 hours a day on the CME. He sees a live price feed with bid/ask prices on the JPY futures contract. As of this moment, the spread on JYU0 is bid 0.9420 and ask 0.9425. The chart confirms that the market is neither volatile nor in a momentum trend, so the trader can expect his market orders to be filled near the bid/ask range.

Before execution, the trading platform shows the trader his order and asks him to confirm it before entering it into the electronic system. When the "submit" button is clicked, the order is sent for execution to the trading pits at the CME and confirmed for the online trader. He sees a fill at 0.9420. Our former stock trader immediately wants to enter a stop loss protection for the new futures position. He puts in a 150-tick stop loss order into the system based on the premium price.

Next, our trader's idea is to enter an option spread as a companion strategy to the long futures contract just executed. He selects a short put position as the first leg of a spread. He checks the live price bid/ask spread on options and finds that an out-of-the-money put with a strike price of 930 has a bid at 1.12 and an ask at 1.22, a 10-tick spread. He enters the 930 strike price, September contract, gets a request for confirmation from the online broker, and then accepts immediately a confirmation of order execution from the broker.

He finds an in-the-money put, at a 950 strike price, with a spread of 2.150 to 2.250, also a 10-tick spread. For the second leg of the spread, then, the trader enters a long put, on the same September contract, with a strike price of 950. Together, these two options create a bear put spread strategy, buying an in-the-money put and selling an out-of-the-money put. The underlying futures is, as we have seen, at 9440, so a 950 put is in-the-money.

The "View Activity" selection brings up the screen that will show his orders have been accepted and placed into a "Working Orders" status by his broker.

Shortly, they will automatically be filled as market orders. Indeed, within seconds, our trader learns that the online broker has filled the short 930 put exactly at the bid price noted a moment ago—1.12. The in-the-money put similarly was filled within the spread price of 2.20—in fact, right in the middle of the 2.15 to 2.25 live prices spread range.

The demo has a spread format that traders typically use for entering spread orders. It can be accessed by clicking the "change # of forms" button at the bottom of the screen and selecting "2 leg spread."

Our trader wants to protect his positions in this option spread by placing stop loss orders, just as he did on the futures contract but, in the case of options, below the option's premium price level. He does this by changing the modifier to "stop," and the information to place a sell stop on the 950 strike price put is entered. The trader elects to enter a sell stop price on his long put option, at 1.90, or 30 ticks below the premium price filled just moments earlier. Stops are an important tool traders should get in the habit of using to protect against potentially large losses in futures trading.

Then on to the 930 put, where a buy stop loss is similarly entered into the appropriate windows in this online trading demo. The price stop is set at 1.420, 30 ticks above the short fill price level of 1.120. This protects the position on the short leg of the bear put spread from a market decline. Remember, a put premium increases as the market declines. If you are short a put option, then a market decline costs you money, since you would be buying it back at a higher premium price. The stock trader has learned that option premiums move only a fraction as much as the underlying future price moves, so he sets his stop losses much tighter on his option premiums than on the future price level. Let's see if that was his first mistake.

Let's say, hypothetically, that the underlying futures price of the JPY begins falling on news of an unexpectedly bad economic report in Japan. Japanese exporters start buying the dollar and importers in Japan are selling the yen. This means that with the underlying futures price falling, the premium value of our trader's long put will increase, generating a profit. Conversely, the trader's stop loss on his short put could trigger an exit trade "at the market," enabling him to get out of his position before the market increases his premium losses.

Let's suppose that the market price level on the premium for this 930 September put option reaches 1.420. In other words, the market price in the underlying futures is declining (causing the value of his short put to rise) and triggering his stop loss. Wherever the prevailing market price is trading as his stop loss order comes down to the pits will determine the exit price in this leg of the bear put spread. Because this trader has sold the 930 option, as the value of the put rises, his cost to purchase in order to liquidate goes up, and that generates a loss on this leg of the spread. Conversely, of course, if the market rises, the premium value on this option would go down, and he could then buy the option at a lower price, creating a profit on this 930 strike price option.

Now with the hypotheticals out of the way, let's see what the market actually does. A quick glance at an online chart will show that the futures price level has indeed dropped to the 9370s. So the market, in fact, has moved against our trader's futures position, from 9420 to 9375, and this stock trader, perhaps spooked by the memories of bottomless trend days in the NYSE, decides to take the loss on his long futures position rather than wait for the market to bounce back, which, of course, it may do, or, on the other hand, it may never do.

Our friendly trader sees his short market order being entered. The online format instantly gets him a fill at 0.9378. The loss is 0.9420 − 0.9378 = 42 ticks. Since each tick represents $12.50, on the JPY futures contract, this position lost $525. This scenario shows why many traders prefer to get in and get out in day-trading strategies when trading futures contracts alone.

Futures markets can move 42 ticks in a heartbeat, and if you are on the wrong side of such a move without tight stop protection, it can be costly. One of the mistakes our demo trade review has disclosed is that the stop our trader elected to use on the futures contract was too low at 0.9290. Not wanting to absorb a potential 130-tick loss (9420 - 9290) of $1,625 on this contract, the trader evaluated the breaking news in the markets and elected to offset his long position by selling the futures contract immediately and getting out of this position with an acceptable loss of only $525. So the stop loss used to protect the futures was unrealistically low. Stops need to be like Goldilocks's porridge test: not too tight, and not too loose.

Liquidating Options

With the stops in place on the options, let's watch as the trader liquidates the two legs of his bear put option spread. Remember, he bought a 950 put and sold a 930 put. He checks the bid/asks on puts and finds that the 950 put is not being actively traded, while the 930 put is bid at 1.18 and asked at 1.26. He will enter orders to liquidate this spread and take his profit on this long put and his losses on the short put, and then hope that the net profits from his option spread offset the losses from his futures position, $525.

He gets a buy fill at the ask price of 1.31 for the 930 put. Because there were no active orders on the 950 put, he has to wait for his fill on it. When finally filled, it comes in at 2.40. Table 5.6 recaps this bear put spread.

The futures market price of the JPY fell 42 ticks, causing the premiums of the put contracts to increase. The long put position gained 20 ticks; the short put lost 19 ticks, for a net profit of $12.50 on this spread.

The conceptual blueprint of offsetting a long futures position with a bear spread is a commonly used strategy in exchange futures trading. However, as the demo account shows, this former stock trader's implementation was flawed. He needs to work on understanding the important relationship (Delta) between futures prices and option premiums. The demo account, however, served him well. It saved him from a potentially large loss and, as we shall see, will put him on the path to profits, when used wisely.

The relationships between premiums prices and futures, as well as strategies traders use to interact with each, will be an important part of our exploration of exchange futures trading strategies to take up next. For now it is enough to note the following:

The electronic trading format, along with real-time price and news data support, is an online resource vehicle for evaluating your strategic trading practices realistically and in terms of whether they will generate profits or losses. Together, we will flesh out a successful blueprint for maximizing profits.

Profits are the standard by which success is confirmed in financial markets. Traders will find that success in fine-tuning their strategies can be achieved through the use of demo trading and, most important, without cost. As we move along, we will develop software trading strategies, interactive charting, fundamental and technical analysis, and more, then

Table 5.6   *A Bear Option Spread*

Bought September 950 Put at 2.20	Sold at 2.40	Profit = 0.20 (20 × $12.50) = $250
Sold September 930 Put at 1.12	Bought at 1.31	Loss = 0.19 (19 × $12.50) = $237.50

test them with demo trading and historical back testing. Effective use of online trading vehicles, like this demo account, plays a pivotal role in developing the successful electronic trader's conceptual blueprint for maximizing profits.

Q & A

Question: How secure are margin deposits in an exchange futures account?

Answer: In the chapters following on exchange futures trading, we detail some of the extraordinary safeguards that the exchange clearing house provides in terms of securing margin and trading account balances. In a phrase, "They are very safe."

A Strategic Framework for Maximizing Profits

CHAPTER
6

Making Profits "Happen" in Currency Trading

Literally tens of thousands of currency-related sites are available on the Internet. Many of them offer software resources. Table 6.1 shows a rather incomplete outline of a few categories.

Upon reviewing search engine results from a few well-chosen word categories, it is not difficult to conclude that the most important online resource available to the currency trader is that software he has not

Table 6.1

Education courses in currency trading	Chat forums
Hedge fund strategies	Glossaries
OTC options	Live quotes
Risk management	Charts
Audio bid/ask feeds	Technical analysis
Exchange option pricing	Research
Live quotes	Exchange data
Currency market news	Forwards, swaps
Managed funds	Economics news
Fundamental analysis	Forecasting
Historical data	Simulated trading

found yet. This is simply one way of making the point that currency traders would benefit from developing a practice of continually researching the Web, for both new and existing sites, any one of which can bring a new, important perspective to their trading habits and framework. Apart from that, just tracking the ever-broadening spectrum of participants and resources in the online currency trading world will add to a trader's big-picture understanding of his trading environment. So, start today searching the Web for that most important resource, the one you have not yet used.

Fundamental Strategies

Beginning in this section, and especially in the next few chapters, we are going to highlight a variety of online resources and the contribution they can make in helping you develop strategies for successful—that is to say, profitable—electronic currency trading. In this, we want to make room as well for our partner in maximizing profits in electronic currency trading, fundamental analysis. It is part of our framework for maximizing profits from electronic currency trading to include fundamental analysis as a coequal partner in implementing profitable trading strategies. It is not really in dispute, insofar as we are aware, that fundamental analysis in fact does explain and account for currency price movements. But as we will see shortly, basic fundamental analysis tools need to be interpreted and applied in a timely and even contextual manner, and in this respect, technical analysis can often form a partnership with fundamental analysis in the successful trader's framework.

Those currency traders who use fundamental analysis might be excused for feeling ofttimes at a certain disadvantage in this new, highly technical online environment, if for no other reason than the abundance of charts, technical data, and other software resources available to online traders that emphasize technical analysis. The fundamentalist trader's sources of information seem to be so much more diffuse and scattered throughout the Internet, sometimes making it a chore just to locate the individual components needed for this fundamental analyst's framework. We are going to use the USD/JPY's price break, referenced in figure 6.1, to examine the unique approach the fundamental currency trader typically takes in first finding his online resources and then using them to develop his online currency-trading strategies.

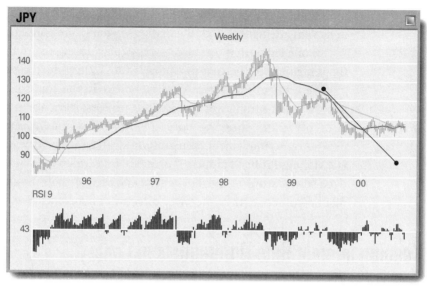

Figure 6.1 *Beginning in late 1998, the yen made a 40 percent gain versus the USD in one of the most remarkable currency actions in recent memory. (For an online chart, visit* http://book.theFinancials. com/chart.html?fig=6.1.)

Markets Rule

The Japanese yen, in little more than the space of a year (fall of 1998 to fall of 1999), gained more than 40 percent against the U.S. dollar. This price breakout action by the yen against the U.S. dollar was one of the more episodic periods in recent currency market history and is instructive for currency traders for a number of reasons.

One lesson we can learn is the fruitlessness of the sort of government intervention in currency markets the Bank of Japan exhibited in the 1990s. For instance, between 1995 and 1999, the BoJ intervened to sell yen in the forex markets 48 times, in its attempt to staunch the market's momentum that was taking its currency higher. It was in fact during the fall of 1998 that some of the most sophisticated currency traders we have, who, believing along with the Japanese central bank that the yen would weaken, were crushed. Some of their sophisticated studies used fundamental analysis to incorrectly predict yen weakness in the fall of 1998, when instead the Japanese currency was actually beginning a long-term bullish trend. LTCM, the Tiger Fund, and others suffered losses that ultimately would put them out of business. This market price breakout overruled the BoJ, which in only nine months, between June 1999 and March 2000, sold $70 billion' worth of yen in its vain attempt to check the market's demand for a stronger yen.

In one leg of that increase, in particular during the summer of 1999, the yen gained 15 percent in a move from 120 yen to 105 yen per dollar.

We want to revisit that currency move in the context of our fundamental trader's framework and, in the process, learn about the work that is involved in "sourcing" online software that fundamental traders depend on to implement their trading strategies. The title of this chapter is "Making Profits 'Happen,'" after all, and we know that even the most dyed-in-the-wool technician will acknowledge the relevance of fundamental components to the price direction of currencies.

Keeping Interest Rate Differentials in Context

The simplest, yet most "fundamental," component of currency pair valuation is the interest rate differential between two currencies. That said, how is a fundamental currency trader going to go about selecting the particular software package that provides the interest rate differential information *and analysis* that he needs? In your online search efforts, you will run across more than one Web site that uses a primer in fundamental analysis as a teaser to attract interest in their software product that uses fundamental analysis in currency strategies.

We want to identify what is relevant to fundamental perspectives of currency rates and then show the software charts and analyses that enable a trader to reach a decision on strategies, usually from multiple software sources. Obviously, plenty of data providers are available that can track the interest rates of both Japan and the United States. Getting that type of raw data is not a problem. What the fundamental trader needs, however, is much more than just raw bond prices, yield data, or balance of payments numbers.

The fundamental trader needs software packages that can provide context for understanding the impact of interest rates on currency valuations. That means, for one thing, that the policies of the two governments need to be kept up with. Details of the bond markets in each country need to be almost as familiar as the back of one's hand. We will need to access resources from many different online sites as we track the analysis procedures a fundamental trader would use in preparing for a summer rally such as the yen made in 1999 and, in the process, discover how fundamental analysis actually works and how it is integrated when sourced from so many disparate software packages.

A Little Background

In early 2000, the U.S. 30-year-bond began to rally substantially, driving its yield to historic lows, despite the fact that the Federal Reserve Funds rate was rising and GDP growth was robust. Inflation, though modest, was rising also. Strange things were going on in U.S. interest rate markets. The Treasury yield curve in the United States was both inverted and below the Fed Funds rate. Two things were responsible for this unusual and difficult-to-understand interest rate phenomenon in the United States. First, in the spring of 2000, the United States announced a multi-year Treasury buyback program that targeted some $30 billion in bonds during the first year.

Second, markets were beginning to anticipate new long-term, historic budget surpluses in the United States, and there was official talk of paying down the accumulated U.S. debt to zero, which would have meant that there would no longer be a market for U.S. long bonds. Why? Well, there would not be any bonds to trade; the U.S. Treasury would have bought them all back. That potential eventuality sparked a precipitous and huge demand for the long bond, driving its price up and its yield down, as we have said. That strong demand environment for bonds rubbed off on the 10-Year Treasury note as well, and so its yield accompanied the bond's tumble to unexpected lows. The whole experience raised considerable and unprecedented doubts about the historic benchmark role that U.S. Treasuries had played in valuing currencies.

All of a sudden, currency traders were wondering if they should be benchmarking the Japanese currency off other bonds in the United States. There was talk of U.S. Agency bonds such as Fannie Mae and Freddie Mac replacing the 30-Year T-bond. There was even speculation that high-grade, private corporate bonds might be needed as a substitute for U.S. Treasurys. So currency traders were perplexed, which generated some volatility in currency markets. The fundamental trader needed to be ahead of the curve on that debate, anticipating any possible change in status for the U.S. bond and its influence on currency exchange rates. The message from all this is simply that to be successful, our friendly trader needed software resources that could provide him with the data *and analysis* he needed to stay ahead of market forces.

A Fundamental Trader's Perspective

So this anecdote is a perfect illustration of why a trader, including a fundamental trader, needs to be constantly working his online resources. As events develop, be they studied by a fundamental or technical analysis framework, the trader who positions himself to profit from the always evolving influences on currency values is a trader who has made it his business to access the information and analysis that anticipates how those influences will affect currency values. The other traders will be left in the wash, if you will pardon a seafaring metaphor.

Interest Rate Nitty-Gritty

Interest rates, because they are a major factor in influencing currency values, as we have seen, get a lot of attention. One of the influences on interest rates is something called the national Current Account. If the U.S. Current Account is in deficit, that means American consumers are buying more goods than U.S. workers can produce, and foreign producers have stepped up to fill the demand.

Reference any of the online charts tracking the United States Current Account deficit and you will find accompanying explanations that note the distinctions between the Trade Deficit and Current Account deficit. The Current Account includes figures on the trade deficit plus foreign direct investment, portfolio flow, and government currency flow. U.S. Current Account deficit charts show that during the summer of 1999, the United States continued its pace of record-breaking deficits, which ultimately would approach 4 percent of the U.S. GDP. When a country's Current Account goes to deficit, that has an impact on interest rates, to be sure, but let's examine the complex factors a fundamental trader has to dissect in order to assess how a large Current Account deficit may also impact exchange rates.

"Fundamental Analysis Ain't 'Beanbag'"

In terms of currency flow, a large deficit in the U.S. Current Account means that a lot of U.S. currency has moved from U.S. hands into offshore pockets. Many of those foreign nationals with U.S. dollars (incidentally, as of the year 2000, two-thirds of all U.S. currency in circulation was held by foreign nationals) have no incentive, however, to sell dollars for their own currency on the basis of interest rate differentials. In 1999, domestic interest rates in Japan were below 1 percent, for example.

If U.S. dollar holders in Japan wanted to maximize profits from their dollars, they could deposit their U.S. currency holdings in offshore bank accounts, called Eurodollar accounts, as we discussed in earlier chapters. Since Eurodollar deposits involve no exchange of currency, those Eurodollar deposits do not immediately impact currency exchange rates. So for these two options, currency rates are not affected. We should note that in Japan, there is a traditional twice-yearly repatriation of profits to dress up corporate balance sheets, where dollars are sold for yen, obviously pressuring the yen higher against the dollar at those times.

A third option available to those holders of U.S. dollars who are not U.S. citizens would be to purchase U.S. bonds, stocks, or even U.S. businesses. This sort of transfer helps the U.S. economy while providing offshore investors with a reasonably high rate of return compared to other global investments. As U.S. interest rates rise, including Eurodollar accounts and U.S. Treasurys, they will attract more dollar flows back into the United States. So as long as U.S. dollars held overseas flow back into U.S. assets, in search of higher returns, because of the interest rate differential, the impact on U.S. dollar currency valuation tends to be positive and somewhat strengthening for the dollar, reflecting a worldwide demand.

So how these foreign-held dollars are disposed of will usually impact exchange rates only in an indirect way. Eurodollar deposits tend to support higher U.S. interest rates, which in turn support the dollar. The flow of dollars into bonds, equities, and so on supports U.S. economic growth, which supports the dollar. Bottom line? Since the Current Account must be balanced, *interest rates tend to be pressured higher, the more the Current Account deficit rises.*

If, say, Japan's interest rates are at rock bottom, as they were in the 1990s (Japan lowered its call rates to zero in early 1999, and, in fact, all through the decade of the 1990s, Japan had lowered its benchmark rates year after year), *the growing Current Account deficit in the United States tends to increase the value of the dollar vis-à-vis the yen.*

So, we can see, occasionally fundamental analysis is counterintuitive, and the successful fundamental practitioner has to keep current on all such nuances, as he selects from a group of software providers that specialize in this kind of fundamental analysis to help him do just that.

But suppose U.S. interest rates do not rise enough by comparison with other rates to attract enough U.S. dollars to balance its Current Account? Well, this is where the certainty of fundamental analysis surfaces. There is only one thing that can happen in that event: the U.S. dollar weakens. Holders of U.S. dollars who find other investments more attractive than U.S. bonds, stocks, and so on will sell their dollars and buy other currencies. As those dollars are sold, the worldwide value of the dollar diminishes, and a trader who has anticipated such scenarios with the help of his software analysis will be watching for opportunities to short the dollar and capture some nice profits.

In early 1999, our friendly fundamental currency trader wants to keep current with the cash flows from the record U.S. trade deficit, as he prepares his summer strategy for the USD/JPY. He is aware of the implications for U.S. interest rates from a growing Current Account deficit. He makes the connection from there that the interest rate differential, from a fundamentalist's standpoint, favors a strengthening U.S. dollar.

He has a number of charts and studies available from his software providers and we want to look over his shoulder and "see what he sees," as he prepares to take a position and then react to the summer move in the yen that we know is coming.

Offshore Influences

In the first half of 1999, we see a Japanese economy in a deep recession. An economy in recession has a couple of implications for currency flow; neither of them, as you might suspect, are good (for that country's currency valuations).

One is that money within the country that is available for investment is not going to yield a profitable return, so it seeks one of two recourses. Some, usually small, savers park their money in savings accounts. In Japan's case, it in fact has one of the highest consumer savings rates in the world. Indeed, the absence of consumer spending in the economy has been a persistent obstacle to its economic recovery all throughout the decade of the 1990s.

Then, also, those Japanese institutions and others who have large savings may turn to the other option, which is overseas investments. Indeed, at the beginning of 1999, Japanese nationals held a very large stake in U.S. government bonds. In order to invest overseas, of course, yen has first to be sold in favor of other currencies, which pressures the yen toward a lower value. Similarly, overseas investors are not attracted to domestic assets in Japan because of the poor profit outlook there. Furthermore, Japan, like many Asian economies, has long resisted foreign participation in its domestic economy, preferring instead to cultivate, through government policy, its foreign trade relations as a vehicle to "export" itself to economic growth.

In 1999, the United States was in its fourth consecutive year of 4 percent GDP growth as compared to Japan's recession. So the fundamental currency trader sees the big picture of economic growth in Japan and concludes that currency flow here as well again favors the U.S. dollar over the yen. But there is more the fundamentalist has to consider.

In the summer of 1998, the yen broke from 145 yen to 110 yen and then traded in a range between 115 to 125 up until June 1999. The fundamental trader has to be open to a possible price reversal back down to around 140. The Japanese government, which had intervened once in the currency markets at the 145 yen level, to strengthen the yen, was now reversing its stance and reacting with concern as the yen gained strength from its losses in the first half of 1998.

Japanese exporters take big losses when the yen gains. And the prospect of further appreciation of their currency would add yet more dents to their balance sheets. So government sentiment in Japan now was solidly in favor of no further yen strengthening. Japanese exporters who are always in the market selling dollars sought to aggressively staunch further yen strengthening.

In October 1998, the U.S. Fed Funds rate stood at 4.75 percent, and now, with signs of inflation re-appearing in the United States in the context of its historic, high-GDP growth, there were expectations of Federal Reserve increases in the near term. Indeed, by June of 1999, the Fed had begun its tightening program, which would extend all the way to June 2000 and a 6.5 percent Funds rate.

Figure 6.2 shows the Japanese equivalent to the U.S. Fed Funds rate, the BoJ's call rate, which in April 1999 effectively stood at zero. This ZIRP, or zero interest rate policy, would hold in Japan until August 2000. So with the aid of analysis available from yet another software resource, our currency trader sees U.S. rates on the increase, notices Japan's interest rate effectively at zero, and concludes with very little room for doubt that the underlying interest rate differentials once again favored a stronger U.S. dollar in the USD/JPY currency pair he trades.

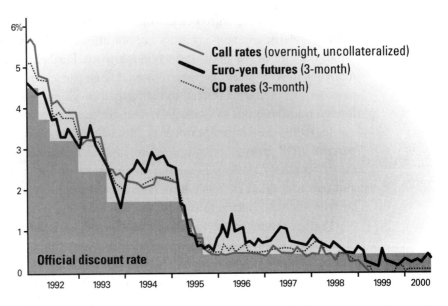

Figure 6.2 *The official BOJ "call" rate, which corresponds to the U.S. Fed Funds rate. It set a historic low of 0.50 percent beginning in 1995 and through January 2000, when it dropped even further to 0.25 percent.*

Other information streams among his other software programs were noting that Japan was quickly becoming the world leader in the value of its outstanding debt, due to its massive domestic expenditures and other spending programs to stimulate economic growth. At the end of 1999, Japan's debt would total $3.3 trillion, surpassing the U.S. total and making Japan the world's most indebted modern economy at 120 percent of GDP. The implication drawn by his software analysis was that a growing tax burden was looming in Japan's future, even if it should reach positive growth and emerge from its decade-long funk. Those new taxes would subtract from economic growth and hence discourage cash flow into the country from abroad—again, weakening the yen.

One of our friendly trader's software programs of fundamental analysis for currencies showed a chart overlay comparing the Nasdaq stock index against the Nikkei 225, Japan's major stock index (figure 6.3). Nasdaq would finish 1999 with an 80+ percent increase in its index. Although the Nikkei 225 did grow, its gains were dwarfed by this United States' "new economy" Nasdaq index, and so our friendly trader had one more marble in the pot supporting U.S. dollar strength against the yen.

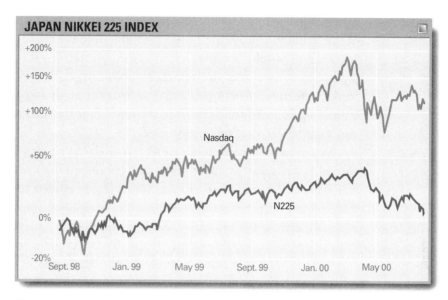

Figure 6.3 *Beginning in September 1998, through May 2000, the U.S. Nasdaq stock index out-performed the Japanese Nikkei by wide margins. (For an online chart, visit* http://book.theFinancials. com/chart.html?fig=6.1.)

Our friendly fundamental currency trader had accumulated all this analysis from several different software sources, which, taken together, pointed toward a weakening of the yen. But the yen had already incongruously strengthened from 145 yen per dollar to 112 yen in the summer of 1998. It then subsequently held those gains against almost the same backdrop of fundamental data and analysis that we have just reviewed. Overcoming the seeming absence of online software analysis, which would offer a different conclusion, he researched the online resource persistently for weeks, determined to get a balanced picture of the USD/JPY market environment before he committed to his strategy with at-risk dollars. That diligence paid off.

One of his purchases was a bargain. For $99, he obtained a year's weekly analysis of cash flows from a banking source in Japan. The BoJ, which was to gain its independence from the MoF in 1999, was providing $1 trillion a day in excess liquidity to the credit sector, but this liquidity was going unused. Japan's central bank faced a classic liquidity trap in the summer of 1999. The program's analysis also followed the so-called yen carry trade. This practice developed when Japan institutionalized its low interest rate policy to deal with the lost decade of low economic growth it found itself mired in during the 1990s.

Traders would borrow yen at the low interest rate prevailing in Japan and convert it to dollars, then deposit the dollar proceeds in U.S. banks, returning 5 or 6 percent. The bargain analysis pointed out an interesting counterintuitive risk to the upside for the yen that was astute and, as it turned out, quite prophetic.

As yen carry traders sold yen to buy dollars that they then invested abroad, a scenario that might develop, according to this analysis, is one in which the dollar could begin to lose value. Dollar holders in the yen carry trade would be pressured to sell their dollar holdings (and, conversely, buy yen), driving the yen higher. As momentum grew in favor of the yen, more dollar sellers would emerge, driving the yen even higher yet. The yen carry trade would become a dollar-selling stampede as yen-carrying traders sought to get out of their dollar positions in a falling USD market.

Another part of this bargain-basement software analysis pointed out that Japan's trade accounts were on the rebound as imports and exports began a sharp recovery in 1999, meaning cash flow into Japan was increasing.

In 1999, the price of the U.S. bond was falling. We know that as rates go up, prices go down, and short-term holders of U.S. bonds in Japan were selling their holdings, allowing them to repatriate the proceeds from their foreign holdings back into yen. Such buying of yen argued for a stronger yen, not the weaker yen that so many of the other analyses were concluding lay ahead in the short term.

Our friendly trader continued his software "shopping spree" on the Internet and found the "bluelight special"—a second software program that actually predicted yen gains in July 1999, just days before the yen surged. The analysis concluded, "Watch out for a collapse of the U.S. dollar," and referring to BoJ interventions, the analysis said, "If the forces from the Imperial Guard could not staunch the trend for yen strength, the risk of a break lower in the dollar is significant."

Our friendly trader had finally achieved the balanced portfolio of assessments he needed to evaluate his strategy. In addition, this "bluelight special" software program includes a technical analysis component to its analysis of a near term dollar price decline. So our trader had finally "partnered" fundamental with technical analysis, and he was prepared to make his decision.

Our trader is in forex markets, so he is not protecting his short position with either futures or options. He has to short the dollar with tight stops to protect against the dollar gains that so many of his software studies were suggesting. As it turns out, he hit the jackpot. The yen moved from 121 on July 24 to 105 on September 5, without so much as a look back. The lesson of this exercise for our friendly fundamental trader is to keep working and searching the multitude of online resources that are available to the online currency trader. Make these searches a regular part of your daily trading practices.

Today, the most widely appreciated and utilized asset of the online resource is the ability of the PC to store and retrieve information. This means that the online currency trader can archive historical price data and apply new trading systems to real-market price action over a short- or long-term time frame.

There are software programs available that archive 20 years of forex price data on all major currencies. What makes this capacity to store and retrieve data invaluable to the modern online currency trader is the ability to use that historical data and interface with a trading strategy that has not actually yet been used in the markets and test it against known trends and price environments within the historical data stream.

In plain English, the online currency trader can input a trading strategy he is developing and then test it against all available market records, without risking a dollar in the process. As one who has used both simulated and historical testing programs, I can tell you that their cost is made up many-fold in savings that result from trade system testing.

Q & A

Question: What is the single most important bit of advice you can offer the fundamental currency trader insofar as using the online resource to maximum advantage is concerned?

Answer: Use it or lose it! As we have shown in this chapter, the information a fundamental currency trader needs to be profitable is available online. It can take the form of news, software analysis, historical back testing of strategies, charting, or a combination of several of these. Remember, the most important resource a currency trader has is that online resource he has not yet found. Keep searching the Internet.

7

Forex Trading Strategies

The computer, or more precisely the PC, is providing contemporary forex traders with an enormous resource that, through diligence, can equalize the playing field among the participants in "our game"—foreign spot currency trading. As you know, in the past, large bank trading centers and institutional forex traders have held enormous advantages over the retail and small corporate currency trader, for instance, by their access to instant bid/ask price communication via their dealer networks. Many of these large institutional trading houses that serve as both dealers and market makers have long leveraged their spread-making and dealer relationships to the disadvantage of the smaller, "retail" forex trader.

Now, however, these same instant communication resources that have created a new and highly competitive IT environment in the broader economy have begun surfacing in the forex environment in the form of the online trading platform. It is revolutionizing forex trading. We have already seen such user-friendly innovations as trader-to-trader online platforms, where all retail traders have access to Level II, Nasdaq-like bids/asks, not just the posted numbers that we have traditionally been limited to in our trading decisions. Real-time data vendors, for their part, are now reaching out to the retail and smaller corporate forex trader as well.

Alan Greenspan, the U.S. Federal Reserve chairman, has said on numerous occasions that one of the more readily apparent and benefi-cent changes that information technology has had recently on business profitability has been the elimination of many structural redundancies and uncertainties in the business environment that he monitors so closely. The resulting efficiencies have been made possible by the computer. In congressional testimony, Greenspan has said that the computer chip has played a major role in reducing and to a large extent eliminating many business uncertainties that in the past had to be built into the structure of all business models, forcing them to hire extra personnel, purchase extra inventory, or make many other expensive accommodations to this lack of timely information about their own markets. That same sort of structural realignment in business marketplace relationships has been just as evident in the cash forex trading environment.

We see more dealers now offering traders an ability to post prices inside-the-spread, a real cost-per-trade savings benefit brought right down to the level of every forex participant. These online innovations can only continue to equalize relationships among institutional and retail traders.

Expanding Opportunities

This ongoing expansion within the online forex trading environment is a dynamic phenomenon. In the event, a more "equal opportunity" online environment within our forex markets is already attracting many new participants and is expanding the breadth of market participation in what was already the world's largest financial marketplace, forex. These new participants in our markets will need to quickly familiarize themselves with the same online technical resources being utilized by their competitors if they are to actually implement winning trade strategies based on electronic information. For our part, we do not want to leave anyone behind, as we welcome those who have been trading stocks, commodities, or bonds into our forex markets.

Online is definitely where it is at. Instant bid/ask recognition and access to the same trading information that banks and other large market makers have long enjoyed are indeed now creating a level playing field for all currency traders. That means greater potential profits for the retail and small corporate trader. The day is not far off when we will see a completely equal accessed playing field throughout the foreign currency cash markets.

As that day gets closer, each trader must remember that he will, alas, only be acquiring equal *access*. Once in the door and competing "in the same room," so to speak, with the big boys, only those traders who are maximizing the opportunities newly available to them from these newer online services and information formats will be in a position to compete successfully against those big trading houses. In this section we want to focus on these contemporary online resources that are just now becoming available to the individual trader so that we can help him maximize their most profitable use to the advantage of all.

Getting Comfortable with Trading Software

Figure 7.1 shows one of the more exotic software programs, which provides detailed daily trade recommendations for 15 major currency pairs. This particular data/analysis software provider, being London-based, highlights the global character of the new online trading environment. Precise intraday trading recommendations for each currency pair are made at the start of each trading day from London. An archive of all previous trading recommendations and whether they have profited or lost money is a part of the overall software data package available. Competition among software vendors forces this kind of transparency

CURRENCY TRENDS

	London opening	Trend	Entry date	Entry rate	Trend reverse	L/T trend reverse	1st resist	2nd resist	1st support	2nd support
EURO / USD	0.9160	Euro sell	July 12	0.9488	0.9184	0.9349	0.9184	0.9225	0.9140	0.9085
STG / USD	1.5055	£ sell	Aug. 16	1.5010	1.5042	1.5043	1.5070	1.5140	1.5042	1.5015
USD / YEN	109.05	$ sell	Aug. 16	108.54	108.79	107.35	109.60	110.00	108.79	108.25
USD / CHF	1.7065	$ buy	July 12	1.6363	1.6878	1.6642	1.7125	1.7195	1.7025	1.6940
USD / CAN	1.4815	$ buy	July 31	1.4836	1.4799	1.4821	1.4840	1.4880	1.4799	1.4750
STG / YEN	164.15	£ sell	Aug. 16	162.91	163.64	161.48	164.50	165.25	163.64	162.85
EURO / STG	0.6085	Euro sell	July 12	0.6270	0.6106	0.6214	06.106	0.6135	0.6060	0.6025
EURO / YEN	99.82	Euro sell	Aug. 2	99.95	99.92	103.34	99.92	100.34	99.45	99.00
EURO / CHF	1.5630	Euro buy	Aug. 11	1.5528	1.5498	1.5554	1.5660	1.5700	1.5600	1.5554
EURO / SKR	8.3700	Euro sell	Aug. 4	8.3980	8.3967	8.3645	8.3750	8.3967	8.3645	8.3450
EURO / CZK	35.385	Euro sell	July 28	35.565	35.460	35.757	35.460	35.757	35.315	35.225
USD / ZAR	6.9350	$ buy	Aug. 16	6.9725	6.9530	6.9320	6.9530	6.9950	6.9150	6.8800
USD / SING	1.7180	$ sell	July 27	1.7345	1.7305	1.7318	1.7200	1.7250	1.7155	1.7115
AUD / USD	0.5875	Aud buy	Aug. 16	0.5888	0.5837	0.5879	0.5885	0.5940	0.5855	0.5837
NZD / USD	0.4515	Nzd sell	July 24	0.4625	0.4555	0.4622	0.4525	0.4555	0.4500	0.4465
FTSE	Ftse long @ 6398 since Aug. 14				FTSE CLOSE		6475.5	FTSE TURNS		6393

Figure 7.1 *An alternative to the conventional chart-based technical analysis study. This software version of a chart study is provided in spreadsheet format.*

and is a boon to the forex marketplace, making it easier for traders to evaluate the applicability of certain trading signals to the particular currency market they trade.

Referring to figure 7.1, on this day London trading opened at 9 A.M. as the USD/JPY traded at 109.05. Shortly after the opening in London, the forex market began selling the dollar and the trading system soon recommended "sell the dollar." A trade *entry point* was immediately made at 108.54 as the market continued selling off the USD/JPY.

This particular software system calls for an exit if the market reverses and so a *trend reverse* call, or exit price, was listed in the daily bulletin, 25 ticks higher, at 108.79. That level is also the first support level. A lower second support level is 108.25. The online analyst's first resistance level is 109.60, with a second resistance level listed at 110.00.

Because of the competition I referred to earlier, traders can get a charting signal system reduced to this sort of tabular format, which enables them to quite easily establish their trading strategies from a spreadsheet data format provided with their software package. Here is the summary of this intraday trading action and how this system performed.

The market opened at 109.05 and traded down through the first support level of 108.70. This signaled a trend reversal from the previous day's move up to 109.05, so a "sell the dollar" alert was given at that point, with the market falling. A short trade in the USD/JPY was filled at 108.54. If the market were to reverse again and trade back *against* the position up to 109.60 (the initial resistance level), the program then ultimately would call for an exit trade there, with a 106-pip loss at that level (109.60 – 108.54). But if the market trades *with* the position, the program signals a buy stop all the way down to 107.35, for a profit at 119 pips, or $1,487.50. The market subsequently only traded as low as 108.13, permitting a small profit protected by the use of trailing stops.

Technical analysis has come a long way with the help of our increasingly competitive trading environment. Technical analysis promises to become an even more popular tool for the forex trader. The online revolution in forex trading is an environment unto itself, and one of the most productive aspects of online trading is the interactive relationship between charting and technical analysis, which holds the promise to increase the productivity and profitability of every currency trader. Let's develop and utilize this most important aspect of online currency trading, *forex charting and technical analysis.*

Moving Averages—Simple, Exponential, and Momentum

We already know that a simple moving average (MA) is, by its mathematical structure, a trend-following chart analysis indicator. Its value lies primarily in evaluating historical trading patterns.

The exponential moving average, by contrast, weights its data line toward the most recent price patterns and so increases the applicability of the MA tool to the most current price levels. In terms of a trader using a moving average to help anticipate price direction, the exponential incarnation of a moving average has been a step forward from the original, simple moving average.

Momentum is a big part of technical analysis. Basically, of course, momentum is the velocity (rate of change) of prices. So if we as traders can anticipate that prices will evidence a strong increase or decrease from their current price trend, then we would presumably have an advantage over the market. The momentum line is constructed in a straightforward mathematical way. Today's closing price is subtracted from the closing price of 20 days ago (or some other time line). If the market is lower today, a negative price is generated and vice versa. A rising momentum line from a negative (below center line) start would constitute a buy signal.

In theory, the exponential moving average should be of use as a momentum indicator. It should be. But experience teaches us that a simple momentum line on a chart is a trend-following indicator and provides no price leading value whatsoever. So a momentum line's usefulness, *by itself*, as a price predictor is extremely doubtful. The same is also true for an exponential moving average chart. The exponential moving average and the momentum graph are improvements from their original parentage, the simple moving average. They are, by themselves, however, inadequate as stand-alone trading tools in real markets.

That brings us to *oscillators*. An oscillator is a technical analyst's charting tool that uses exponential moving averages to anticipate momentum in a pricing environment. An oscillator, unlike simple MAs or simple momentum lines, can be quite useful to forex traders in our unique, sometimes volatile, trading environment. Basically, oscillators can provide a short-term warning that an existing momentum trend may be ending.

Making the Most Out of MACD

One study that forex traders will find attractive for a number of reasons, which we will get into right away, is the Moving Average Convergence Divergence chart study. This was introduced to the financial markets in the 1960s, primarily for stock market analysis. But since the advent of, and seemingly geometric increase in, forex trading value, brought on by the breakup of Bretton Woods in 1973, "techies" (as technical analysts are affectionately called) have applied it with more than a little success to the currency markets.

The MACD chart is an oscillator that uses exponential moving averages quite generously. In fact, there are three exponential moving averages (EMAs) in the MACD study, and we also will look at an additional histogram that makes MACD a very facile and interesting study to use in forex trading. Because it is an oscillator, we know that it is designed to move above or below a center line. That is the nature of oscillators. Unlike some oscillators, though, such as the Relative Strength Index, which we will examine next, the MACD has no upper or lower boundaries. But let's get on to how this technical analysis study is constructed, which is quite fascinating.

The MACD calculates two momentum values. One is a 26-day EMA; the other is a 12-day EMA. For you math buffs, the slower 26-day MA is subtracted from the faster 12-day MA, and that difference is plotted as the MACD, or fast moving average line (see figure 7.2).

Next, this study plots an EMA of the MACD line itself on a nine-day period, and this new line is called the *signal* line, which is a slow moving average. In practice, this construction follows the currency prices very closely and serves as a coincident indicator, as distinct from momentum and moving average plots, which are all lagging indicators.

So this new MACD analysis meets one of the most important criteria of technical analysis: It can help the trader anticipate trend changes in currency prices. It is also, as we will shortly see, an excellent indicator of overbought and oversold conditions. It is applied very successfully in identifying exit or entry positions. Indeed, the MACD is one arrow in the technical analyst's quiver that should be understood well and referenced regularly.

Tracking Prices with MACD

A glance at figure 7.2 shows the MACD lines at the top of the daily USD/JPY. A cursory view would show that the two lines generally seem

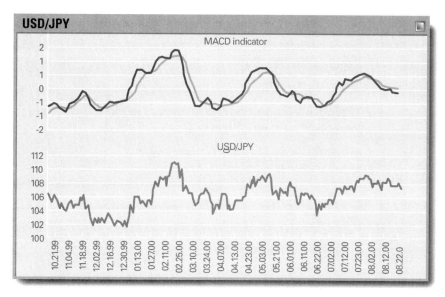

Figure 7.2 *The MACD technical analysis study. The heavy line is the MACD line itself; the lighter line is the signal line.*

to follow the trend in prices shown. But there is much more that the MACD analysis has to say. Let's look closer.

The heavier line is the faster MACD line. Remember, that line plots the difference between the 26-day and 12-day moving averages of the printed prices. The second line is the signal line, and it is a 9-day exponential moving average of the MACD itself, and so it will be a slower line.

The bolder MACD line, in November, made a move down and across the signal line, accurately anticipating a trend change to lower prices as compared to the previous two-month neutral trading range. Subsequently, as we can see, USD/JPY indeed moved down from 105 yen per dollar to about the 102 level. MACD signals are stronger the deeper into a bullish or bearish zone they are. So in this case, because the MACD lines were only slightly below their zero line in the index, the bearish signal we have discussed was appropriately only a mildly bearish trend change indicator. In fact, as we can see, the price of the USD stayed around 102 for the entire month of December.

The MACD lines next move in tandem to the extreme upper portions of their range during January and February and from those high environs, the MACD crosses its signal line and moves sharply lower around Febru-

Table 7.1

Reading the MACD	The MACD Is Saying
When the MACD crosses the signal line	Trend change alert
When both lines are in the extreme upper or lower ends of their ranges	Overbought/Oversold
When the MACD crosses over the signal line at the top or bottom of its range	Sell signal

ary 20. Notice the fast MACD line moved down and below the signal line from the upper reaches of the range, implying a strong trend change signal, which in this case would be a sell signal for the USD.

Indeed, prices moved lower, from 111 yen to 106 yen, in the first leg of their move down the chart. Another point to emphasize is that any time the two lines move in the extreme of their range, as they did here, they are signaling an overbought (or oversold) condition.

In March and early April, the MACD makes a couple of shallow crossings from a mildly negative chart environment. In this more or less neutral chart territory, crossing moves are not considered to be strong signals of impending price direction changes. Later, though, from a moderately high price environment in the middle of May, the MACD signals a change in trend from a rising price level to a falling move. The market price levels follow these MACD signals from 110 yen to 104 yen, as you can see.

We need to draw and emphasize some conclusions about MACD signals.

There is an overview perspective when you use any technical analysis study for trading position signals that needs to be brought up here. No single technical analysis or study can be relied on *by itself* to consistently predict price trends, changes in direction, or break-outs. All incarnations of technical analysis studies need reinforcement before a trader commits to a cash-at-risk position in the markets. That being said, the MACD is one of the better studies in technical analysis for currency markets. And there is more. Look at figure 7.3.

Some software programs provide a MACD format that incorporates something new, which helps to visually represent the convergence and divergence characteristics of the analysis. Figure 7.3 shows the bar formation for a histogram based on the MACD calculations from the prices in the chart body.

The bars on the bottom of the chart are a visual representation of the convergence and divergence of the two MACD lines in relation to each other. This visual representation simplifies greatly the relationship of the two lines that generate MACD signals. When the bars are above the center line, the MACD line would be above the signal line. When the bars go below center, the MACD would be dipping below the signal line.

As the MACD line moves away from the signal line, in either direction, the histogram bars grow longer. If the bars are growing up above the center line, the MACD is rising. If the bars go down below the center line, the MACD is crossing below the signal line and signaling a down move on the price scale.

This feature permits an interesting and easy visual representation of the proximity of the two, which are ofttimes difficult to discern lines in the body of the chart. The histogram makes buy and sell signals extremely easy to read. When the bars move from negative territory, as in figure 7.3, and cross the center line, that represents a cross of the MACD line from under to over and above the signal line in the body of the chart. That is an implied bullish signal. There are strong and weak

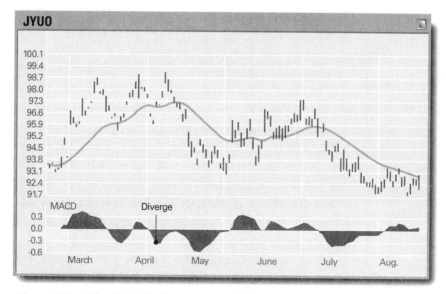

Figure 7.3 *The MACD histogram adds significant clarity to this technical analysis study.*

buy signals that are important to distinguish, and we will discuss them as well. For now, let's track a price movement using MACD.

This format for the MACD is far superior to the two-line representation, for reasons that will be apparent. For instance, when the MACD value is toward the top of its range, signaling an overbought condition, it is more plainly represented in the histogram (see far left of chart bottom).

Isolate the month of March in figure 7.3 on the chart and note that the MACD line crosses over the signal line from above and then, a short time later, crosses back again, this time from below. It is very difficult to pick up with clarity those important signals on the line charts in figure 7.2. But look how clearly that action is represented on the bar histogram in figure 7.3 (note the far left portion of the bottom of the chart beginning in the last half of March). So clarity is invaluable not only in charting pictures, but in decision making. This histogram contributes clarity to both and for technical analysts is an invaluable resource in their trading strategy evaluation.

Remember, the more the two lines diverge from each other in the figure 7.2 format, the higher the bars will rise from the center line. The closer the two lines are to one another, the shallower the bars will appear. When the histogram crosses from one side of the line to the other, this signals that the MACD is crossing the signal line. So putting that all together will enable us to employ the histogram to track price movements and identify price trends with great ease.

A useful divergence signal is apparent from this bar histogram format, which traders also need to be alert for and pay attention to in their strategy evaluations. The yen made a major price move down, starting in the last half of April and lasting until the middle of May, as shown on the chart. (Note: We are using a software program that can invert the price scale, enabling us to monitor price changes in terms of strength and weakness of the yen). The MACD study shows a divergence in its indicator that is important to the interpretation of the MACD analysis. Look at the chart in figure 7.3 once more.

Immediately preceding its move down, the yen made a gain from 104 yen to nearly 101. Now look at the histogram at the bottom of the chart for the same time frame.

While prices were going up at the end of April, the MACD histogram was showing a clear move down, below the center line. This divergence between the MACD histogram and prices is in itself a strong sell signal. In fact, had a trader courageously followed this signal, he could have shorted the yen against that move up and then profited nicely from the ensuing four-week move down that occurred as the yen, after topping out at 102 yen, slid all the way to 107.

You will notice that at the trough of that yen move down, the histogram made a cross precisely as the yen was recovering. That particular signal is reinforced by the depth of the oversold condition that built up during May, just preceding the histogram cross. So from that new buy call at the bottom of the yen move in the middle of May, almost until the beginning of July, the MACD histogram accurately maintained a bullish trend position. Following the MACD histogram from there, we see that another prescient trend change was predicted during the last week in June, when the histogram accurately signaled another MACD cross and a sell signal at that time.

Relative Strength Index

Momentum oscillators such as the MACD, which have a near-term weighting from their exponential moving average components, are studies that can be very helpful to forex traders. Let's look closely at another of this genre, the Relative Strength Index (RSI).

Forex traders who use technical analysis will, as they become more familiar with RSI, find how easily adaptable and perhaps even indispensable to their trading strategy framework it becomes. It is no risk to predict that many traders will find the RSI an important strategy-enhancing tool.

RSI was developed in 1977 in reaction to a couple of the deficiencies in existing technical analysis studies of that time. For one thing, chart studies involving momentum oscillators were generating too many false buy and sell signals. Then, too, there was no momentum study that offered a price range structure so that price trends could be put into a definite scale perspective of overbought or oversold. The Relative Strength Index filled both of those gaps for technical analysts, and it has been going strong ever since.

The RSI measures currency price strength of a given currency against its own past price performance. So the "relative" in Relative Strength Index refers to a price comparison of a currency with itself, its own price history. The index has absolute levels of 0 and 100, plus a center line. Above or below the center line is a bullish or bearish trend indication. When index levels cross over 70, an overbought condition is implied.

There are also divergence and "failure swings" that can be identified with the RSI. Devotees enthusiastically swear by the support and resistance indicators that the RSI chart itself generates, often when the raw chart price data shows nothing at all.

What Does the RSI Do?

The Relative Strength Index incorporates exponential moving averages in its construction, thereby weighting its index toward the most recent data. The RSI measures a ratio between closes on up days against closes on down days. More precisely, it adds the increases on up days for a specific term of the index, such as 14 days. It then adds the losses on down days for the 14-day period. The formula then divides the average increase in prices on up days, by the average decrease in prices on down days. It makes a further mathematical adjustment for smoothing so that the index as a whole is more stable and, in its result, produces a technical analysis study that tends to anticipate price trends.

Figure 7.4 shows a chart of the USD/JPY with an RSI index at the bottom. One of the first characteristics of the RSI we want to note is the

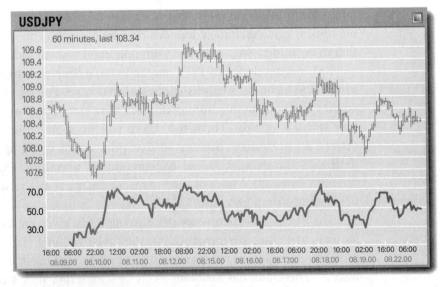

Figure 7.4   *The Relative Strength Index (RSI) is one of the best trend anticipating technical analysis studies for currency markets.*

center line—the 50-line value. A reading above 50, as we said, is a bullish trend, while a reading below 50 identifies a bearish trend. A big-picture review of this chart shows that when the index is below 50, prices are indeed falling, and when the index stays above 50, prices maintain a bullish level. Strictly speaking, however, signals are not supposed to be read from any single technical analysis source like the RSI.

Implications of the RSI

I like to view the RSI as an *implied* indicator. A level above 70 *implies* an overbought price condition. A reading below 30 *implies* an oversold condition. A word of caution is needed here. Should a trader react to a price trend that finds the RSI over 70, for example, he could find himself shorting into a bullish market, something that is not for the conservative investor. As with the MACD, in terms of signal generation, users of the RSI would benefit from a confirmation source outside of RSI itself. But having said that, I will now point out some pleasant and profitable surprises that will accompany your gaining a comfort level with the RSI.

Looking at the RSI on this two-week chart in figure 7.4, we can see that although the currency is volatile and moving within a two-yen range in this 15-minute chart, the index itself is relatively free from false signals or "head fakes." The software package that provides this chart allows the trader to input any time period for the exponential moving average. Here, I have chosen a 14-day time frame. Many packages come with a standard 9-day moving average for short-term studies, whereas a few have no capability for modifying the time period input. In selecting a software program, you need to place a premium on flexibility in these software formats, and traders want to remember to consider the larger subject of formatting flexibility as they go about choosing their technical analysis software programs.

As noted, we can use any time input, but the 9-day period and 14-day period are the most popular with short-term currency traders. Of course, if you are charting from a 10-year time span and are a long-term or intermediate-term forex trader, you need to use a 60- to 90-day or even longer time frame with the RSI. Intermediate charting profiles, such as, say, a two- to three-year chart, may use a 30-day period in the RSI configuration. It pays to experiment with all technical analysis software, so that the one you choose can be adapted to the particular currency market you wish to trade in, neither giving off too many "head fakes" nor missing price trends altogether. Technical analysis is as much art as science sometimes.

One tip to keep in mind, if you move from a 14-day to a 9-day period: Many technicians recommend switching to an 80/20 split on the index as signal references, instead of the 70/30 we use with the 14-day format. But here again, your first priority is to get a software program that allows you to modify the configuration, then back test it with historical data and charting and see for yourself which configuration is most appropriate to the forex market you trade.

The second thing we want to take notice of in figure 7.4 is the strongest call an RSI analysis can make, a divergence. Prices, at the far left of the chart, are in a steep downward move of one full yen over a six-hour time span. By contrast, the RSI index is in an upward slope, diverging from the price trend. This is a signal that a price trend reversal is imminent, and sure enough, it was. The yen bottomed at 107.50 and immediately rose to 108.80 in a short 14-hour time period.

The RSI can be an enormous benefit (and profit maker) for a forex trader. Let's look at the far left-hand side of the chart over the 8/09 date. Leave out the divergence factor in this chart. Just focus on the RSI itself. The RSI had dipped sharply below the center line and touched the 30 index level, an oversold implication. Within minutes of this implied signal, the price jumps from 107.50 to 109.50.

The RSI follows the first leg of the price move up, piercing the 70 line and almost off the chart on the high side. It maintains a line generally above 50, implying a bullish price environment, and then crosses below the 50 center line and moves toward the 30 line, accurately anticipating a fall in prices by just a few hours, touching the 30 line as the price move bottoms at 108.30.

This is where the RSI earns its keep, so to speak. On 8/18, the index again touches the 70 line, implying an overbought price environment well in advance of the imminent price plunge. The RSI correctly anticipated the next down move in prices by 12 hours.

As we follow the RSI toward the end of this chart, it once again touches the 30 index oversold line and then watches as prices rebound from there. A trader could have used this basic RSI signal during this time frame and made nothing but profits on each trade.

We will expand our review of MACD and RSI analysis later on. For now, getting familiar with technical analysis applications you may have used in stock market applications, but applying them now in the forex market, is something that I think all readers here can see is a must on any forex trader's "to do" list.

Q & A

Question: What is the single most important thing I can do to sort out the various technical analysis software products on the market in order to decide which works best in the market I trade?

Answer: There are an abundance of software providers who will offer a free trial of their products. Take advantage of these offers, and back test their trading systems against the historical record of prices in your market. Then use the simulated trading venues that are available, and test the system against current market-price movements in real time. I guarantee, you will save money both in the short term and long run.

CHAPTER

8

Trading Strategies in Exchange Futures Markets

Traders who risk their money to profit in currency futures markets have one thing in common. They all believe they have a strategy that can best the markets, which, of course, really means, best other traders. Trading is competitive, and markets can only be made when a buyer and a seller with different strategies meet and agree on a trade. Both, alas, cannot be right. The buyer believes the market will go higher, while the seller is convinced the market is headed lower, at least in the near term. Whichever way the market price does indeed go, one will be proven right and the other wrong. Another thing that all traders have in common is that we each know the market will at some time or another force us to modify or even abandon the strategy and framework we thought we could rely on. We all will be looking for new answers because of trading losses. So we know, then, that avoiding losses is an important component of every trading strategy. Once large losses are booked, much time and resources have to be invested in getting back to ground zero. Anticipating changes in market trends, with an eye for avoiding such losses, has to be incorporated into all our trading frameworks. Exiting a losing position early is an important part of strategies that traders will want to bear in mind as we review strategies for exchange currency trading. That is defensive trading, yes, but it is also "survival" trading: "We live to trade another day."

Trends

The marvel of currency markets, when viewed with a big-picture perspective, is that from these thousands of individual price decisions that traders participate in, a direction emerges. Charts are a wonderful resource for representing that big picture. Trends are easily discerned and verified by the use of charts. Draw a line, such as in figure 8.1, following the closing prices on a chart being evaluated. In this example, the prices are daily, but they could be weekly or monthly just as well.

These directions in exchange futures prices have two basic factors that make up a dynamic of currency trading we want to call attention to: trends and duration. If your strategy can correctly identify a trend (direction in currency futures prices), up, down, or sideways, then obviously you stand a reasonable chance to profit from that trend. Then, too, when once a trend is defined, if your strategy can reasonably anticipate its duration, profits will accumulate and maximize, and, as we noted earlier, just as important, losses will be minimized. Accumulating profits *while avoiding large losses* is the ultimate confirmation of a successful strategy.

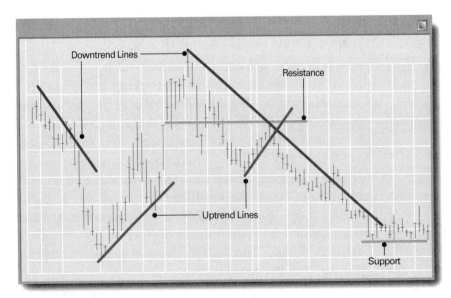

Figure 8.1 *The four basic elements of charting applications important in exchange futures technical analysis: uptrend, downtrend, support, and resistance.*

Some traders develop their strategies based on market trends that are short term (day trading or less than a month). Others use a strategy that projects intermediate-term trends (less than three months), while still other traders implement long-term (three months or more) strategic judgments of market trends, based on their own personal mix of technical (and/or fundamental) analysis.

Look at figure 8.2, and see how these trends become apparent. From March 1990 all the way through to March 1995, yen exchange futures contracts were in a major up-trend. A single futures contract purchased at the trough of that trend (early 1990 at 0.6250) and then sold at the peak would have yielded $75,000 in profits. That is maximizing profits. Here is how it worked.

A move in early 1990 from the low of 0.6250 to 0.6251 is one tick. In CME futures trading, one tick on the yen futures contract is worth $12.50. The total five-year move on the yen futures contract went from 0.6250 to 1.250, finally reaching its apex in March 1995. An equivalent move in forex terms (remember, futures are the reciprocal of forex) would be from a low of 160 yen in 1990 to a high of 80 yen in 1995. A

Figure 8.2 *The yen, as traded on the exchange (CME), has a remark-able record of trader-friendly volatility and long-term trend moves, making it one of the most popular currencies traded on world currency exchanges.*

long-term position trader who caught this move could purchase one futures contract, at a margin I suppose back in 1990 of about $1,000, then hold his position and for five years never look back.

Notice, too, that from its peak in 1995, the yen made an almost mirror-image turnaround, promptly falling in four years to almost where it began five years earlier. Exchange futures traders who wish to short a futures contract can do so just as easily as when purchasing, which is to say at the same cost—the cost of margin. So our trader, who caught the up move, could also have had a long-term strategy to catch the down move, which totaled nearly $70,000. For the decade of the 1990s, a profit of $145,000 from the purchase and sale of one futures contract with an account debit on only $1,000 is what I call maximizing profits.

Support and Resistance

A common theme in technical analysis (TA) and also a building block that links virtually all TA strategies is "support and resistance." This will be familiar ground for online stock traders, who will be happy to find that they can very readily transfer their technical analysis strategies and expertise, produced from years of successful stock trading, to currency exchange futures markets.

As we know, the price level known as *support* is where buying pressure has overtaken selling pressure and market prices are driven higher. Support is, very simply, a level that price trends resist falling below, thanks to buying interest out-battling sellers.

What about resistance levels? What are resistance levels and why do they exist? Well, simply put, resistance is the price level where traders have in the past cumulatively sold positions, preventing (at that time) a further rise in prices, resulting in a price move that stays at or below this resistance level. So *resistance* is a price level that price trends resist rising above, as buying pressure has given way to selling pressure, marking a price peak, from which price levels then declined. Eventually, when prices re-approach a resistance level, sellers may again emerge predominant, forestalling once again an upward breakout in price levels, which an up-trending market tries to generate. So resistance shows where sellers have definitively chosen to sell a currency and have in the past won the battle with buyers, resulting in lower prices or, at the least, a halt in a rise of prices. Where buyers finally do trade more than sellers, the resistance level then will be broken.

These technical support and resis-tance levels play an important role in trend evaluation. In an up-trending market, such resistance levels must be broken, typically as prices stabilize briefly, near a resistance price target, before continuing a move upward.

For technicians, a price chart is used to provide confirmation that a currency futures trend may be ending, beginning, strengthening, or weakening. The inability to break a resistance level, for instance, can by itself predict a change in market price direction from up-trend to side-ways, or reverse, and head down.

When support or resistance is convincingly broken, what had been the resistance price level then becomes a support price level and vice versa. After breaking resistance to higher price levels, price movement often takes a rest and retreats back down to that old resistance level and then consolidates at the new higher support level. Whenever a market trades sideways for a prolonged period, after breaking a resistance level on the upside, the likelihood is that this will be a reconfirmation of up-trending market increases for a very common-sense reason: More traders have invested at the new, higher plateau of prices, and chances of a retrenchment below the new consolidated price support level becomes much less likely, creating a predisposition for higher price movements. So trend lines and the role that support and resistance plays is followed closely by strategic analysts and is a conceptual "building block" for vir-tually all technical analysis.

Utilizing Software Strategies

Online currency traders new to the exchange futures market will quickly learn the value that electronic resources offer them and the advantages they have over traditional phone-based futures traders. But like all tech-nology-based advances, as more and more exchange futures traders become electronic traders, the benefits tend to equalize, because, frankly, online traders will ultimately predominate both in number and prof-itability. So it is inevitable that exchange currency traders will utilize online resources more effectively or even, one might say, more profitably, and we will simply displace older forms of exchange currency trading. So, net-net, the exchange currency markets belong to the informed, up-to-date, and most online-oriented trader, and that leads us to software. Software and services are exploding all over the Internet.

A trader buying a proprietary trading system is paying for buy, sell, or hold signals, which are usually based on technical analysis. There is an abundance of such proprietary software available, so let's look at one system's record, on a real-market basis.

Technical analysis is based on the belief that repetitive price patterns not only exist but flourish in financial markets. TA is a study of those patterns, for the purpose of identifying predictive price patterns or trends, from which traders will develop strategies and earn profits.

Moving Average and Oscillator

Two of the most ubiquitous components in technical analysis are the moving average (MA) and the oscillator. A moving average by itself cannot predict price trends. But a combination of two moving averages can provide a forward indicator of breakout or support levels, as, for instance, when the short-term moving average crosses the long-term moving average.

A simple moving average is a mathematical summation of closing prices for a specific number of days. A 20-day simple moving average is the total of 20 days of closing prices divided by 20. On the 21st day, that closing price is added to the total while the first day's is subtracted, and the average once again is divided by 20 days. So one can see that a simple 20-day moving average like this one is a mathematical representation of market prices over 20 days. It identifies very well a price trend but only after the fact, so it is known and used as a trend-following indicator. In the past, some credence has been given to generating buy and sell signals from a moving average. For instance, if a closing price moves above a 20-day moving average, that would be a buy signal, and conversely, if a closing price falls below a moving average, that would be a sell signal. Unfortunately, in the real world, closing prices are crossing over moving averages rather frequently, and historical back testing confirms they are without much predicative value. So as exchange futures traders, we start out from the proposition that moving averages are useful trend indicators but not predictive.

An exponential moving average is a modification designed to offset the slow signal generation of the simple MA just described. The exponential moving average places greater emphasis on the most recent two days. The most recent (first day's) closing price gets typically an 18 percent weighting while the next (second day's) previous closing price gets an 82 percent weighting, thus bringing the moving average more closely in line with recent price movement. As such, an exponential moving average can be useful as part of a strategy for determining when to exit or enter a market. For example, if an exponential moving average is going down, it could be time to unwind a long position. Even so, remember that the exponential moving average is still essentially a look backward; it is short-term weighted and should not be used by itself as a predictive tool.

An oscillator is yet one more tool of the technical analyst that is designed to address the problem of too many buy/sell signals being generated, especially in a sideways, choppy market. It is considered to be a momentum tool and a signal generator based on underlying market momentum. What an oscillator does is plot a line along the bottom of a price chart, based on the difference in today's closing price and a closing price, say, 20 days prior. If today's closing is lower than 20 days ago, a negative number is generated, and if today's closing price is higher than closing 20 days earlier, a positive number results. A zero line splits the oscillator graph, permitting a negative or positive value for each day. Technicians believe that oscillators have value as momentum indicators and can be leading indicators for price changes. A positive value for momentum reflects an up-trending market, and so a buy signal would be generated from positive values.

Proprietary Software Strategies

Figure 8.3 shows a chart produced by a software program that provides a trader with daily updates, showing most recent support and resistance levels on various currencies. The one shown here has a variation on the support and resistance indicators: solid resistance at 9770, first resistance at 9499, major support at 9292. The data at the bottom of this chart shows a slow Stochastics Oscillator, which currently reads "oversold" for this currency level.

Our friendly currency trader can select from a plethora of software data providers and technical analysis studies. Among them are software systems listed in table 8.1.

For the yen price level shown in figure 8.3, all the long-term indicators show sell; all intermediate-term indicators show sell, and four out of five short-term technical indicators show sell (only Bollinger Bands show hold). First, let's look at long-term strategies using technical analysis.

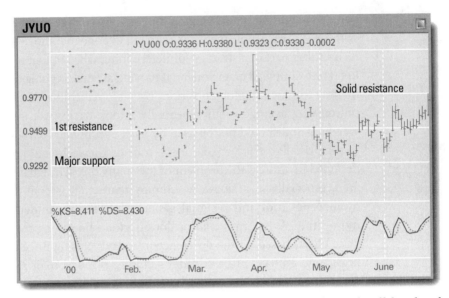

Figure 8.3 *Proprietary software trading systems provide all levels of information. Traders have to pay attention and evaluate what is important to their personal trading decisions and what is "noise."*

Table 8.1

Short-Term Indicators	Long-Term Indicators
40-day commodity channel index	60-day commodity channel index
7-day directional indicator	Price vs. 50-day moving average
10-day moving average	20-day moving average
20-day MACD	50-day MACD
20-day Bollinger Band	50-day parabolic time/price

Long-Term Strategies

In describing these strategies, traders will benefit from a real-world discussion of which strategies really work and produce profits, and which are predisposed to losing money and therefore need to be modified or discarded altogether. In the real world of trading, many times our reliance on a specific technical indicator is indeed discarded, causing our whole framework of trading for the moment to be thrown up in the air. Similarly, a software system with a strategy for buy and sell signals may need to be modified to be effective in the specific currency market it is applied to. In other words, when evaluating the software that provides trading signals and entry/exit points, be prepared to evaluate it critically, for adaptability to the markets you trade.

I cannot think of a better way to start a review of strategies than to review one that produces just such a frustration. Many technical studies use both moving average and oscillators, and the first one we want to look in this chapter is called the Commodity Channel Index (CCI). We first want to take our own advice and consider that every technical indicator may not be suitable for every market, and we also want to raise the possibility that some studies that are supposed to generate a sell signal, for instance, in a particular market environment, may actually be better used in a different way, such as a hold.

The Commodity Channel Index is just such a technical tool. The CCI is a technical indicator that compares current price to a moving average. Normally, the moving average is 20 days, but for long-term trading, a 60-day moving average is used. This index mathematically normalizes an oscillator that is designed to anticipate the beginning or ending of market trends. It does this with an index range of +100 to –100 as its primary indicator and signal generator. The index can either be displayed at the bottom of a price chart, with a zero line splitting the index, or as a line overlaid against the price bars. An index level over +100 is a buy signal and –100 is a sell signal. When the index crosses back over the +100 or –100 level, that becomes a signal for a buy or sell position to be liquidated. We will see that the Commodity Channel Index program needs to be modified for the yen exchange futures market, so that a liquidation signal occurs when the index crosses zero, not the neutral territory barriers of +100 and –100.

A long-term position trader has to have a long-term moving average for his base of trend identification. But using the 60-day moving average as part of the CCI introduces major difficulties for a choppy market in the short term, which make it ineffective unless modified. Otherwise, the trader would be moving in and out of markets too rapidly, contrary to his long-term strategy.

Figure 8.4 charts the indicator as a line alongside the price bars and one can see that, on a real-world trading basis in a choppy market, the signals being generated simply have no potential value in this market as

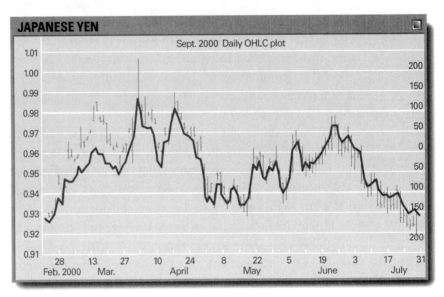

Figure 8.4   *The Commodity Channel Index fails the signal predictor test for the yen exchange futures market.*

a component of a long-term strategic trading system. The CCI misses the big up-move in February and again in early March, then moves in and out of short positions in April and May. Let's track the signals a long-term CCI generates in such a real market.

As noted, the CCI calls for a buy whenever it crosses +100 in a rising market. When the index subsequently falls below +100, the long position is then liquidated. If the market continues to trend down, a sell signal is not generated until the index falls below −100.

From February 20 to March 30, the yen contract gained 500 ticks (well over $6,000), and the CCI indicator was trailing the trend, barely breaking its own zero line for most of that time. It was not until March 31 that the CCI finally broke the +100 line to signal a buy. Unfortunately, the index breaks below +100 almost immediately, signaling a liquidation of the long contract. Then as figure 8.4 shows, a few weeks later the CCI breaks +100 again, only to drop below it virtually the next day. So the $6,000 up move was completely missed.

As the market free falls, starting on April 17, a trend-anticipating signal should have been generated, calling for a short position that would have produced a $6,000 gain. But again, unfortunately, the Commodity Channel Index does not cross −100 to signal a short position until the down move has essentially been spent. Then it crosses above and below the sell signal line several times, producing no profit and even missing a second up move beginning May 20 and lasting through June 25. The up move was a 450-tick trend worth $5,500. The index never made the long call. Data from the software itself, in table 8.2, traces the precise CCI signals and the profit and loss accumulation for this market. This market had a potential gain of over $17,000 in three trend moves, all of which were missed by the CCI trading program.

Now let's modify this software program's signals so that a position, once signaled by crossing a +100 or −100 line, is maintained until the index crosses the zero line, and see the changes in profit and loss accumulations. This time, let's apply the CCI to a decade-long market trend.

Figure 8.5 shows the CCI signaling a buy in December 1991, almost two years into the bull market for the yen. One of the characteristics of this technical indicator when used as a long-term strategy is its penchant for giving late signals on important market trends. As we can see from

Table 8.2

Date	Entry Action	Price	Date	Exit Action	Price	$ P/L
3/31	Bought	1.0065	4/3	Liquidate long	0.9819	($3,075)
4/17	Bought	0.9846	4/18	Liquidate long	0.9801	($ 562)
5/1	Sold	0.9409	5/4	Liquidate short	0.9477	($ 850)
5/8	Sold	0.9402	5/11	Liquidate short	0.9429	($ 337)
5/15	Sold	0.9342	5/19	Liquidate short	0.9576	($2,925)
6/1	Sold	0.9398	6/2	Liquidate short	0.9414	($ 200)
7/12	Sold	0.9341	7/13	Liquidate short	0.9344	($ 37)
7/14	Sold	0.9372	7/20	Liquidate short	0.9386	($ 175)
7/21	Sold	0.9279	7/28	Liquidate short*	0.9200	+$ 987

Total number of trades: 9

Average days/trade: 3

Total losses: ($7,174)

*Oversold signal

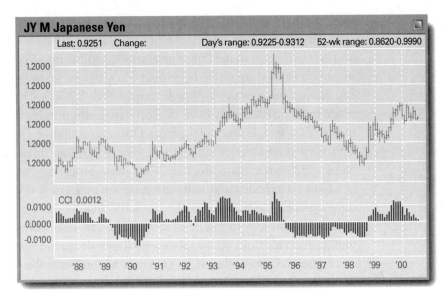

Figure 8.5 *The Commodity Channel Index needed to be modified and adapted through back testing for the yen futures market. This index's moving average has been changed from 20-day to 60-day.*

figure 8.5, the CCI lags a major up-trend in the market, which begins in March 1990. The index did not reach a buy signal (+100) until December 1991. What is even worse, it will make a liquidation call on the buy just two months later, as the index fell below the +100 line and back into neutral territory shown at the bottom of the chart, while the market continued onward and upward. So, of the advance the yen futures made from 0.6250 to 0.8000, the CCI indicator caught none of it. In fact, after the buy signal (December 1991), the market actually traded on net down and at a loss before the CCI liquidation signal got the position out of the yen in March 1992.

The next signal from the CCI was another buy, this time in August 1992, but here again, the index fell back into neutral territory two months later, thus liquidating the long position in a yet developing bullish yen futures market, just two months after signaling a buy.

Profits so far have been negligible. It was not until January 1993 that the CCI indicator stayed long the yen, giving its practitioners the chance to participate in the yen run up for most of the year. It caught a second move—the rise in early 1995—but on balance, of the $75,000 in profits available from a single futures contact in this five-year bull move by the yen, this technical indicator captured only a fraction of it when used as the software recommended. The need for a benign modification is quite apparent from the retrospective chart. Once a buy signal was generated, in December 1991, had the software program maintained the signal until the index had re-crossed *below zero* in a down market, the CCI would have captured almost all of the $75,000 profit from that point on.

So a simple adaptation of this indicator would be to hold a position once signaled, until the index falls back *through the zero line,* rather than back into neutral territory, between the +100 and −100 lines. When implemented in this way, the CCI captures nearly all of the $75,000 increase of this bull move. I need to point out, however, that when reviewing this modification to the short-term chart in figure 8.4, we find that the Commodity Channel Index still fails to serve the trader well.

A conclusion we need to draw from this analysis is straightforward. Only if you can endure the short-term deficiencies of the CCI and are focused on a market strategy that is truly long term—say, over three years—can the CCI can be a useful resource to factor into one's trading strategies. Should a trader rely on it solely for confirming a strategic software trading system? Not without evaluating it against a real-market environment. Back testing is a resource traders should utilize as part of an evaluation process in all their strategic trading practices.

Short-Term Strategies

A futures trader who prefers a short-term trading framework is no doubt among the majority of traders in exchange currency markets. Indeed, it is in the compressed framework of day trading that the online resource is most compelling. Five-minute trades are really only practicable when a trader has access to real-time pricing data, news, and charting. And, of course, the ability to change stops and entry/exit positions instantaneously is the kind of trading environment the electronic medium was made for.

One of the central ingredients in a trading environment that a short-term trader must have is volatility. If prices are not moving, then it is literally impossible to profit in the futures market. A long-term trader will find enough volatility in even a relatively flat market over a period of several months so that his strategic framework can operate and achieve profitable trade execution (see figure 8.5).

Volume is often considered the proxy of volatility. In bull markets traders look for volume to increase on rallies, peaking at their tops, before decreasing, sometimes dramatically. The same is true for bear markets, with volume expected high near the trough of a bear run, just before moderating. Volume and especially volatility are such integral components for any trading system that virtually all software trading programs include data on them.

Bollinger Bands

A charting system that many software trading programs include is called Bollinger Bands. Bollingers provide a visual image of these market influences that volume bars along the bottom of your chart can miss. Bollinger Bands are essentially a trading envelope, constructed to capture about 95 percent of all price data.

These bands expand or contract as market volatility increases or decreases, because of a mathematical formulation known as standard deviation. Simply put, Bollinger uses two standard deviations from the moving average for both an upper and lower band, and because these bands are mathematically tied to volatility in the price movements along the moving average, the bands narrow in times of quiet price action and widen in times of broader price fluctuation. Therefore, Bollinger Bands have characteristics of trend lines, with this added advantage of their automatic adjustment for volatility, thus providing a predictive feature in their use.

As the bands widen during periods of market volatility, the Bollinger chart will very often identify prices moving away from one line in the band and toward the other. When the price range is between the center line's moving average and, say, the lower band, in a bearish trendline, many traders will buy at a price target on a moving average line when prices break up through the moving average, then sell as the price touches an upper band target for a short-term gain. Before we track such a strategy, here are three characteristics of Bollinger Bands, when used as part of a strategic trading system:

1. Sharp price movements tend to occur after bands tighten.
2. When prices top outside the band, and then top inside the band, the move may be close to being spent, and a reversal is often anticipated.

3. If a move starts from one band, then crosses the moving average, there is a tendency for prices to continue in that direction and touch the other band.

In figure 8.6, when a price tops out against an upper band at signal #1 and subsequently crosses the moving average, it tends to then reach the lower band before re-touching the upper band. The intraday chart in figure 8.6 is an excellent reflection of this Bollinger Band characteristic. Find signal #1 on July 30 on the chart as it touches the top at the upper band, then subsequently crosses the moving average before reaching (breaking) the bottom band at point #2.

So this Bollinger has established both a trend signal and a price target by this move. A short-term trader would sell at the moving average price of 0.9200, then buy at the lower band target of 0.9190, for a $125 profit off this five-minute trade.

Notice from price signal #2, with the trend reversing and once again crossing upward through the moving average, a buy at 0.9195 would then position this trader for a sell at the target price on the upper band. This bullish trend carries through the price target all the way to 0.9220.

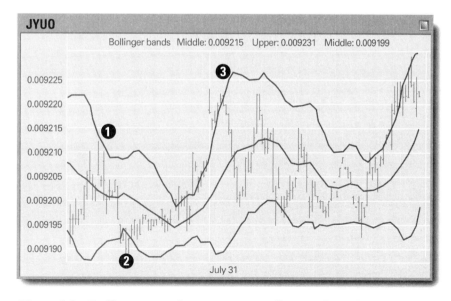

Figure 8.6 *Bollinger Bands prove an excellent technical analysis tool when applied to the Japanese yen exchange futures market.*

With trailing stops, a buy stop would lock in a profit at 0.9210, for a 15-tick gain on another five-minute trade. Using this system for price signals and price targets, the Bollinger Band is generally correct as seen in the rest of the chart in figure 8.6.

As in all system signal charts such as Bollinger Bands, it is always recommended that two or more charting signals confirm every buying or selling strategy, before you risk resources in the markets.

Q & A

Question: Do I have to back test and evaluate every trading system signal generator according to the market I trade and my personal strategic framework, or can I go with the proprietary system I purchase as is?

Answer: I think we all know the answer to that question by now. By all means, use every resource available to review and test a system you purchase against every market scenario you can use in your evaluation. In the process, not only will you be more aware of the nuances of applying your proprietary trading system, but you will be alert to its specific advantages as well as to any caveats in implementing a trading strategy when your trading resources are at risk in a tough market environment.

CHAPTER
9

Option Trading Strategies

One of the first goals that traders should set for themselves in creating an option strategy is to arrive at a familiarity and comfort level with exchange currency options. They will find options to be a tremendous resource that can both protect them against large, unexpected losses and generate profits for them with an equal facility. Futures and option traders are always cautioned with a worthwhile caveat that considerable risk is associated with these derivative trading vehicles. Since risk is part of the environment of exchange currency markets, I will add my own admonition to the usual one—managing risk while maximizing profits is what distinguishes successful traders from the pack.

Forex traders seldom seem to venture into the world of over-the-counter options in the spot cash trading environment, and although stock traders are more exposed to the options trade in their equity market, by and large those traders who use options as a fully coequal vehicle in their trading practices are relatively few and far between. Here, as we flesh out the framework for maximizing profits in currency trading, we want traders who trade exchange futures to open up their "options," if you will excuse the double meaning, and take a serious look at employing exchange futures currency options as part of their daily trading strategies.

Options Are Derivatives

We recall that Orange County, California, lost nearly $1.5 billion in the late 1990s, due to some poor investment strategies that used derivatives. As a result, for a short time, the name "derivatives" carried a derisive connotation among much of the public.

The public and professional acceptance of derivatives has gradually changed now, as people begin to understand that derivatives, far from being a synonym for unreasonable risk, are in fact a useful trading vehicle that investors at virtually every level of engagement in financial markets can successfully integrate into their trading strategies. Yes, options are a *derivative*. So are futures. So, too, are many business contracts.

A home purchaser who writes a contract making his purchase of the property contingent on getting a loan approved by a bank has written an option. The contract to purchase, therefore, has value only as a derivative. Looked at this way, one can see that the value of such a "loan-contingent offer" to purchase a home is derived from (and contingent on) the decision of a bank to approve a loan application. So, yes, derivatives are a useful and actually quite necessary part of virtually all financial markets, in one way or another. As in the case of a home purchase, derivatives (and options) facilitate markets and make transactions more efficient.

Reasonable Uses of Currency Options

We want to confirm in this chapter the assertion that options, when used prudently, can be a reasonable and profitable component of exchange futures trading strategies, and traders should feel comfortable using them as part of their own framework for trading currency futures, either on an as-needed (contingency) basis or as a routine in their trading habits.

We want to briefly introduce to the forex trader and uninitiated stock trader the nomenclature and environment of the option, as used in currency exchanges, so that we can then move quickly to concentrate on developing strategies, both here and in later chapters, for maximizing profits among as many traders as possible. Remember, options should be understood as a resource to both limit losses and expand profit opportunities in the unique environment of exchange currency markets.

As we all know, the buyer of a call option has purchased a right, but not an obligation, to *purchase* a futures contract at a predetermined price. He pays for this right in the form of a premium that, in a market-determined environment, will predictably gain or lose value, depending (contingent) on what the underlying futures price does.

Option Prices

There is a "time value" component to an option's price that one does not find in the underlying futures contract, and we want to look at how an option premium is actually priced and in the process begin to uncover, quite literally, a multitude of opportunities to use options for maximizing profit in our trading strategies. Let's look at the unique pricing structure of an option premium and affirm the principle that this stranger may well be just a friend you haven't met yet.

As in many markets, there is a shorthand use of numbers. As you will recall, the Japanese yen futures contract is expressed as 0.9269, even though the mathematical number is actually 0.009269. Similarly, option strike prices are shortened for convenience in notation. An option's strike price will be written as a 94 put, instead of 0.9400 or 0.009400. Premiums on options also are similarly shortened for notational convenience.

I want to purchase a put, which gives me the right, though not an obligation, to *sell* a futures contract for a specific price on or before the contract's expiration date, should I exercise the option. I can exercise an option any time if it is an American style. If it is a European style, then it can only be exercised at its expiration date. The put's strike price at 94 (0.9400) is ITM (in-the-money) because it is higher than the current futures price level of 0.9269. If I should exercise the put, I would acquire a short position in the underlying futures contract at a market price of 0.9400. I would then buy an offsetting futures contract at the lower market price of 0.9269 and pocket the profit. If I sold the option rather than convert it to a futures contract through exercise, I would receive the premium's market value at the time of sale.

Remember, the American-style option can be exercised any time before the expiration date, whereas a European-style option can only be executed at contract expiration. The ability to exercise an option and convert a call or a put into a futures contract underlies the premium values of exchange currency options. Their value ultimately derives from the futures contract they are written against.

Let's say that right now the market is trading the September futures contract on the yen at 0.9269. I hold a 94 put that I have purchased, two weeks earlier, paying the premium price of 1.35. At the time when I bought the put, the September futures contract on the yen was trading at 0.9369, exactly 100 ticks higher. Because the futures market fell, the put's premium increased. Today's put premium price at the trade is 1.95. The profit, then, is 60 ticks or $750. Let's look at table 9.1 to see the interesting relationship between option prices and futures.

Things to Notice About Option Pricing

The first thing to notice about option premiums is that a call's premium decreases in value as its strike price increases, while a put's premium does just the opposite (see table 9.1). The call premiums are larger than the put

Table 9.1 *Underlying Futures Price Is 0.9269*

Calls

Strike Price	Contract	Premium
91	September	2.20
92	September	1.50
92.50	September	1.24
93	September	1.03
94	September	0.64

Puts

Strike Price	Contract	Premium
91	September	0.51
92	September	0.81
92.50	September	1.05
93	September	1.34
94	September	1.95

Table 9.2 *Characteristics of Options Prices*

92 Call	1.50
92 Put	0.81
Difference	0.69
Add the strike price	0.9200
To the difference	0.0069
And it equals current futures price	0.9269

premiums up until a moment the strike price exceeds the futures price (when the calls go out-of-the-money [OTM], and the puts go ITM).

Take the option price for an ITM call and subtract from it the option price of a put with the same expiration date and strike price, and you will find that the difference, when added to the strike price, will equal the underlying yen futures price (see table 9.2).

Another interesting feature about options prices is that if you know one option price—say, a put—and do not know the corresponding call's premium, you can subtract the known option's price from the futures price and obtain the corresponding option's premium (with the same expiration and strike price) (see table 9.3).

Time Value/Intrinsic Value

The premium price is set by the market, of course, and, as I said, is directly tied to the futures price. A put's premium of 1.95 is a function

Table 9.3 *Characteristics of Options Prices*

Known put's strike price	0.9300
Less futures price	0.9269
Difference	0.0031
Known put's premium	1.34
Subtract difference	0.31
Identifies unknown call premium	1.03

of the underlying futures trade of 0.9269. How? Well, the strike price is 94, or 0.9400. The futures price at the time the short trade was initiated was 0.9269. The intrinsic value of the 94 put today is the difference between the futures price and the strike price, 0.9400 – 0.9269 = 1.31. The premium is 1.95. Subtract from the premium the intrinsic value of the put, which is 1.31, and you get a difference that is the time value of the premium or 0.64 (see table 9.4).

Time value is really a catch-all term that includes not just the wasting asset of time-until-expiration, but volatility, interest rate differentials, and other factors. It is really everything that affects a premium's price other than intrinsic value. As an option approaches expiration, its time value also approaches zero. Whenever an option is OTM, it, of course, has only time value in its price.

Options are known as wasting assets for a good reason, and the time value component of an option's premium shows why. Remember, option premiums can continue to rise in price right up until their expiration, if the underlying market dictates it. But in a theoretically stable futures market price environment, an option premium would decline a little every day until the time value equals zero at expiration. On contract expiration, if the option's strike price is at-the-money (ATM), its value is zero. If it is ITM, it has an intrinsic value precisely equal to the difference between its strike price and market close on that day.

The intrinsic value of an option can be determined at any time, in the case of the put, simply by subtracting the market price from the strike price of the put. Therefore, any put's strike price that is equal to or below the market price is OTM. Refer to table 9.4.

Table 9.4 *Market Price of Underlying Futures Contract Is 0.9269*

Put Strike Price	Time Value	Intrinsic Value	Premium Value
90	0.30	0	0.30
91	0.51	0	0.51
92	0.85	0	0.85
93	1.03	0.31	1.34
94	0.64	1.31	1.95
95	0.38	2.31	2.69

In-the-Money/Out-of-the-Money

The intrinsic value of an option increases as the strike price rises further into the money. On the other hand, time value *decreases* as a proportion of the premium the more ITM an option goes. For those options that are OTM, time value *increases* as they get closer to the market price level, obviously because there is an increasing likelihood of their becoming ITM and exercisable. A popular trade strategy that uses this component of time value is one that sells options that are deeply OTM. The rationale is that the market is less likely to reach such an option's strike price level, where it could be exercised. The option seller receives the premium value as a credit to his account, and he hopes the option eventually expires worthless. These "naked options" must be watched closely, since there is theoretically an unlimited risk should the market catch up and move past the strike price.

Using Options

Let's use a put option in a futures trade and begin to explore how options complement futures strategies. A futures contract has excellent leverage, as we have already shown, but we will see that an option contract has even more. A forex move of 107.52 (equivalent of 0.9300 in futures notation) to 108.69 (0.9200) is a 100-tick move in futures. At $12.50/tick, that is a $1,250 profit if you are on the short side of that trade.

Your account would be debited a margin requirement when initiating such a short trade, an amount that is currently $4,212 on any single futures position. Let's compare shorting this futures contract to purchasing a put.

Our friendly trader wants to buy a put with a strike price of 93 when the market is trading at 0.9284. That means his put is ITM. The premium he must pay for this option to sell a futures contract on the yen is 1.12, or $1,404. He sees that he can purchase three 93 puts for exactly the cost of a single futures position, $4,212. So he does that.

The market promptly falls to 0.9184, and he offsets (sells) the long profitable put position. The online broker flashes back to him that the premium he received from the sale of his three puts was 1.72/put, or a total credit to his account of $6,450. The gain to his account therefore was $6,450 − $4,212, or $2,238. Let's review this transaction and compare it to a short futures position in table 9.5.

Table 9.5 *Comparing Futures Profits to Options Profits*

Purchase of One Futures Position

Account Debit	Market Move	Net Profit	Risk of Trade
$4,212	100 ticks	$1,250	Margin (but unlimited)

Purchase of Three Puts

Account Debit	Market Move	Net Profit	Risk of Trade
$4,212	100 ticks	$2,238	$4,212

I said that options can limit unexpected losses. This has been a perfect illustration of why. The option buyer's risk is limited to the cost of his puts, while the upside potential gain is substantial, since the market could fall theoretically to zero. There is a lot to be learned from this single example of comparing a put option trade to a short futures trade.

Greeks

As we see, for a trader who wants to commit to a move in a currency market, the option can protect that trader against downside losses, as compared to an outright futures contract position. It also, as we have seen, increases the profit substantially. These are important advantages in any trading strategy. So can we put to rest the fear that options are risky? Used this way, options are far less risky than futures. Of course, the trader pays three commissions on his puts purchase, since the trade needed three options to double his profit on the trade compared to the futures position. Why is that?

The answer is "Delta." Delta measures the option premium's rate of change compared to the rate of change of the underlying futures contract. In other words, when you examine a rise or fall in an exchange currency futures contract, you notice immediately that option premiums gain or lose value proportionately, not tick for tick with the futures price. There is a way to mathematically predict that proportion. It is named for a letter in the Greek alphabet, Delta.

Delta

A rule of thumb for an option's Delta is that an at-the-money option will increase at a rate 50 percent as fast as the underlying futures price, and its Delta therefore is 50 percent, which means the premium on the option—for example, a 94 put with a 0.9400 futures market price level—will increase or decrease 50 percent the rate of the market itself. (A put's Delta will range from 0 to –100 percent, where a call's Delta ranges from 0 to +100 percent.) If the futures price climbs to 0.9500, the premium on the 94 put, let's say it was 2.00, will decline 50 ticks to 1.50. This, of course, is a theoretical formula. In the real-world trading environment, as a price moves from 0.9400 to, say, 0.9500, a 94 put moves from an ATM status with a 50 Delta to an OTM status, with a correspondingly lower Delta, perhaps 40, and therefore a smaller ratio of premium decrease to futures increase. So the more out-of-the-money an option is, the lower its Delta goes.

A call option's Delta works exactly the opposite. As a futures market price increases, the call goes further ITM, causing the premium and its Delta to rise. Eventually, when a call option price travels deep into the money, it will actually move in premium price nearly in equivalency with the futures market price. Also, let's not forget to mention that a put's premium increase is theoretically capped because a futures contract decline must halt at zero, while a call's premium is theoretically unlimited to the upside because a futures contract can rise to infinity (theoretically).

So the Delta, because it is a constantly changing number, is useful primarily for short-term premium evaluation. As should be apparent, it is a particularly useful resource for establishing hedge positions. Let's track a trade involving an option, but instead of comparing an option to a futures contract, we will use this option as a hedge against a futures position.

Using Options As a Hedge

For instance, a trader wishing to take a Delta-neutral position in the market might sell a futures contract at, say, 0.9200, then buy two ATM calls with strike prices of 92. Hence, his market position would be perfectly hedged in terms of its Delta. That means, theoretically, the increase or decrease on one side will be offset by a decrease or increase by the other side of this spread position.

Why would a trader do that? Well, one reason he would is that quite often liquidity is greater among the futures contracts than it is in the option bid/ask spreads. In fact, it is often the rule rather than an exception that a move down in the futures market will *print* lower prices in futures contracts immediately, but options' bid/ask spreads will lag and show no posted trades whatsoever for as long as several hours at the start of the CME's trading day. A trader who has a Delta-neutral position (like the one in table 9.6) in a declining futures market could offset his short futures, take a profit, and give the market a chance to recover. If the market indeed climbs, his option position—two calls—will move back close to their original, purchased premium value, meaning his hedged short futures position will have given him a profit while never having to offset his two calls. If the market does not retrench, the option may have to be offset, nullifying the gain of the short futures contract. The options are a hedge because had the market gone up, against the futures contract, the two calls would have gained value (equal to the futures because they were Delta-neutral) and protected against an outright loss in his short futures position. Remember, if no trades are printed on the 92 calls, any stop-losses he may have placed on the calls would never have been activated by the online broker.

Table 9.6   *Existing Position Hedged Futures Strategy (Opened the Day Before)*

Short futures contract at 0.9200	Two calls strike price 92 premium at 2.00

Next Day's Opening of CME at 7:20 A.M.

Futures market falls to 0.9120 on open	No bids/asks printed on open (even though theoretical premium falls to 1.60)
Trader takes profit of $1,000	Two calls' strike price 92 premium (not printed)
Offsets short futures	No options bid/ask traded on 2 calls
Futures market rises back to 0.9200	Two calls' premium rises to 2.00
On close	Marked to market—no change in premium

In this scenario, the short position produced a $1,000 profit, while the two calls produced no profit or loss. But many scenarios for constructing an option hedge are based on Delta, and traders will want to familiarize themselves with all of their incarnations.

These Delta points, in addition to the premium ratio, can also be used as a reference for the probability that an option will finish ITM. ATM options with 50 Deltas have a 50 percent mathematical chance of *finishing* ITM. Then, too, as the option gets close to expiration, the Delta values of ITM options will tend to increase, all things being equal. Traders will want to keep Delta numbers in front of them as they create option/futures strategies for their own portfolios.

Selective Use of Software Data and Strategies

Software programs typically generate a lot of information. *Selective* use of all the data available to the online currency trader is important. To try and use all the data provided to you would be overwhelming and ultimately very confusing.

Look at figure 9.1. This software program offers a "theoretical" pricing model for options traders. It tells you the price level an option at a given moment should be. It allows you, the trader, to input the basic factors that make up a premium's price. One factor is the difference between an underlying futures' and the option's strike prices, which we know is the intrinsic value component of an option premium's price. You can choose a software program that gives the Greek values, including the Delta numbers that we have been talking about, for any option/futures combination you wish to input.

As table 9.7 shows, volatility and price levels impact Delta. The lower the market volatility (for ITM options), or the narrower the spread between the option's strike price and the market price, the higher the Delta. Rising prices mean rising (call) Deltas.

Falling prices mean rising (put) Deltas. Delta is only one of those "Greeks" that describe an options' unique pricing value. Changes like these in the value of an option's Delta are measured in another formula called Gamma.

In addition, this software program inputs market volatility, interest rate differentials between the USD and yen, whether the option is a call or put, and the number of days remaining until expiration. It uses the

ONLINE OPTION PRICER

Underlying price	0.9300	**Days to expiration**	20
Volatility	15.00	**Interest rate**	6.33
Strike price	0.93		
Pricing model	Black-Scholes ▼	**Option type**	Put ▼

[Calculate]

Theoretical value	1.15	**Delta**	0.4948
Gamma	0.1217	**Vega**	0.0865

Figure 9.1 *This program does a theoretical pricing model and "Greek" valuations according to the input from the trader based on current market conditions. Notice the Delta on the ATM is nearly 50, as it should be.*

Table 9.7 *How Volatility and Price Levels Impact Delta*

Time value declines	Delta increases
Volatility declines	Delta increases
Underlying futures price declines	Put's Delta increases
Underlying futures price declines	Call's Delta decreases
Underlying futures price increases	Call's Delta increases
Underlying futures price increases	Put's Delta decreases

Black-Scholes pricing model, which is an industry standard, and an accepted mathematical formula that puts all these factors together and spits out the theoretical price value of an option.

Look at Everything; Use Only a Little

Theoretical pricing software like the one shown enables a trader to determine if the market is overvaluing an option or undervaluing it. If it's overvalued, you might consider selling the option, There is, of course, a body of opinion among option traders that believes that the market itself is the best judge of valuation. But anyway, this sort of information is out there, and the exchange currency option trader will find plenty of vendors giving you the opportunity to buy their particular mix of data with which to implement your personal trading strategy. So remember, be selective.

Gamma

Gamma is a measure of an option's exposure to the underlying futures' price movement. It is a number between 0 and 1, can be either positive or negative, and each point movement in the Gamma value will equal a corresponding rise in your option's Delta. If the Delta, or rate of change in the premium relative to the futures, has a high Gamma reading, then, for instance, a call's premium will rise in price more quickly in a rising market. It will also fall more quickly in a falling market. In different market environments, some options will have low Gammas, in which case the premium price change will be slower than the same option at other times in other markets. That is important for a trader to know, and it can impact his trading decisions significantly. For instance, if the Gamma is high, and our friendly trader has an ATM option—say, a long call—the market suddenly turns higher. With a higher Gamma, our trader knows the premium will be moving strongly apace the underlying market's move. He can let it run.

On the other hand, if the Gamma is low, in the same market move, his option premium will lag the underlying's climb, and it may be prudent to close out his profit earlier in the run up.

These are theoretical values for comparative purposes, not an actual market illustration. That said, notice how the Delta increases (table 9.8) as its option goes further into the money. The Delta actually changes slightly with every tick increase or decrease. However, when initiating a position, one can anticipate approximate premium changes vis-à-vis the futures contract.

A Gamma reading of +0.1000 (10 Delta points) means that for each point move in the futures, the option's Delta will move up 10 points. Let's say a futures contract on the yen moves from 0.9200 to 0.9300. That means a 92 call's Delta, which is at 50 presently and whose Gamma is +0.1000, would move from 50 to 60. If the Gamma reads 0.3000 (30 Delta points), the Delta on the 92 call option would have zoomed from 50 to 80 on the same future move of 0.9200 to 0.9300.

Table 9.8 *Delta Increases*

Futures Price Starts at	Call (92 Strike Price) Option Premium	Delta Now at
0.9200	2.00	50
Futures Price Rises to	Call (92 Strike Price) Premium Rises to	Delta Now at
0.9300	2.50	75
Future Price Rises to	Call (92 Strike Price) Premium Rises to	Delta Now at
0.9400	3.25	90

As you get familiar with Gamma readings, you can interpret a high or low Gamma and anticipate how much your option's premium is likely to respond to unexpected market moves. Gammas are the same for both puts and calls and will tend to be high numbers when the strike price is near the money. When options go deep into or out of the money, their Gamma numbers, or Delta points, typically head lower, and these then become less sensitive to market moves than options with strike prices closer to the market.

A Gamma number answers the question, "How great is my option's exposure to market change?" A low Gamma tells you that the Delta (rate of change of the premium) is not highly sensitive to futures price changes. You may want to look for another option with a higher Gamma that will participate more in the market move. For instance, the closer to expiration an option goes, the lower its Gamma will fall. If you are in a long-term position, and your option is close to expiration, you can therefore maximize your market profitability with the option you hold by rolling it over to the next farthest out contract month with the same option strike price and benefit from that one's higher Gamma. Take one more look at figure 9.1, which shows the Delta, Gamma, and Vega for a 93 put on the yen, ATM. Notice that the Delta, which the software program just calculated, is only barely below the formula's 50 reading where ATM option theory calls for it to be. Let's price in a 100-tick increase in the yen futures (seen in figure 9.2) and see what the put's Delta shows. The Gamma shows a number that projects a 12-point

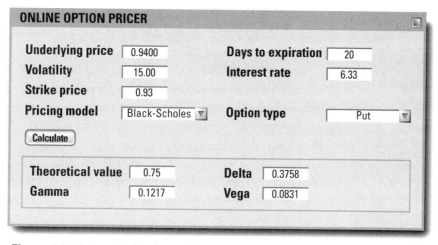

Figure 9.2 *New Delta from the same 93 put but with a futures price that makes it out of the money. Its Delta dropped to 0.37 from nearly 0.50 as a result of the 100-tick move up in the underlying futures market in the yen.*

increase in Delta for every 1 cent (100-tick) move in the futures. Sure enough, the option pricer identifies a new Delta, now 12 points below the previous ATM reading in figure 9.1.

There are many option-pricing software formats. Some include other Greeks such as Pho, Theta, and Vega. Readers should review the information that programs like these provide and determine which ones they feel they would be able to use and which they would not.

Other Greeks

Four others that options traders often pay attention to in evaluating their options strategies are: Theta, Omega, Vega, and Pho. We want to mention those other Greeks briefly. Theta measures the decay of an option's price due to erosion of its time value. The closer to expiration an option gets, the higher its Theta number becomes, meaning it loses more time value each day. Remember, every option has a time value component in its price. At-the-money and out-of-the-money option prices are made up entirely of time value, and Theta becomes a useful management tool for those options.

The Vega number is the increase in the option's price that occurs for a one-point increase in volatility. Let's suppose a volatility chart for the yen is currently yielding a 15-percent volatility level. If the call premium is 3.00, and the volatility goes up one point, the Vega number defines how much the premium will rise. With a Vega number of 0.15, the 3.00 premium would rise to 3.15 for a 1-percent rise in volatility. So Vega measures an option's sensitivity to a change in market volatility. There are others, but of all the Greeks, by far the most important and useful measure for evaluating option pricing is Delta. Traders will help themselves by reaching a comfort level with these important measures of price movement in their option positions.

Option Spreads

One of the most popular option trading strategies in use on exchanges is the option spread. Option spreads are basically a combination of two or more options, with or without futures, created to take advantage of a specific market movement yet protecting against losses. Bull spreads are constructed to profit from price increases. Bear spreads do just the opposite. Let's look at a bull call spread.

If the market moves higher—say, to 9450—the premiums of each of the two calls will both increase. We know from the Delta review we have done that the 92 ITM call will increase more than the 96 OTM call. Therein lies the basis of the construction of a bull call spread. The long ITM call increases more in an up market than the short OTM call, and the differential in their price movements will create the position's profit. Let's see how it works.

Intraday Option Trading

The net gain for this position was $277.50. Compare that to the cost of the position (table 9.9), which was a net ($3,125 – $937) $2,188. A 100-

Table 9.9 *The Cost of Establishing an Options Position*

Buy 92 call at 2.50	Account debited $3,125.00
Sell 96 call at 0.75	Account credited $937.50

Table 9.10 *New Underlying Futures Price at 0.9450*

Bought 92 call at 2.50	Sold 96 call at 0.75
Now at 3.03	Now at 1.05
New call value 3.03 × $1,250 = $3,787.50	New call value 1.05 × $1,250 = $1,312.50

Let's Do the Math

92 call sold for $3,787.50	96 call bought for $1,312.50
92 call bought for $3,125.00	96 call sold for $937.50
Profit = $652.50	Loss = $375.00

tick move occurs intraday nearly as often as not in the yen futures market, and so this position produced a not untypical 12-percent gain for this trader intraday, while significantly limiting risk of loss in a market decline. Margin applications vary depending on the market, but generally, on this kind of a spread, margin will be very small, if any. Software programs will include graphs that visually identify and project a profit and loss scenario for a spread strategy, based on current market conditions.

Figure 9.3 gives our friendly trader an online screen with 42 strategies to evaluate within the context of the overall market perspective he chooses. Selecting a neutral strategy opens up another screen with a choice of 14 strategies in figure 9.4. Figure 9.5 provides a risk projection and a graph to visually define profit and loss potential. This trader found the yen at 0.8300 and projected a bear spread graph. As you can see, he has a net credit to his account (not including margin) though his profit will be limited to $625 when the yen stays below 0.8300. His loss risk is similarly limited to $625 and occurs when the yen moves above 0.8300. These P/L projections are all valid "at expiration."

It is useful to point out here that our friendly trader took his bear spread position with the intent of trading these options, not holding them to expiration. In fact, he traded the position intraday. Most options are initiated and then are subsequently liquidated prior to expiration. The prolific calculations that traders are bombarded with from data providers such as we see in figure 9.5, which describes profitability while assuming that traders will hold a position to expiration, have limited value for the

OPTION STRATEGIES

BULLISH		BEARISH		NEUTRAL	
Limited risk	**Unlimited risk**	**Limited risk**	**Unlimited risk**	**Limited risk**	**Unlimited risk**
Buy call	Buy underlying	Buy put	Sell underlying	Long straddle	Short straddle
Bull call spread	Covered call write	Bear call spread	Covered put write	Long strangle	Short strangle
Bull put spread	Sell put	Covered short	Sell call	Long iron butterfly	Call ratio spread
Covered long	Call ratio spread	Put ratio backspread	Put ratio spread	Short iron butterfly	Put ration spread
Call ratio backspread	Synthetic long	Short collar (fence)	Synthetic short	Long iron condor	
Long collar (fence)	Long covered combo		Short covered combo	Short iron condor	
	Long price repair		Short price repair	Long call butterfly	
				Short call butterfly	
				Long put butterfly	
				Short put butterfly	
				Long call condor	
				Short call condor	
				Long put condor	
				Short put condor	

Figure 9.3 *The 42 strategies one program offers, mostly on exchange currency futures options.*

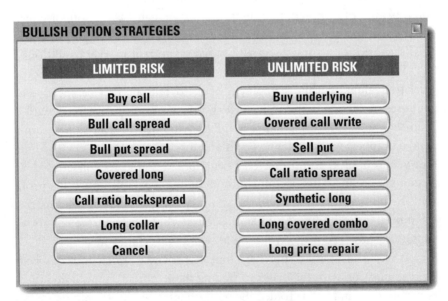

Figure 9.4 *Fourteen strategies offered by a program under a bullish market framework selected by the trader.*

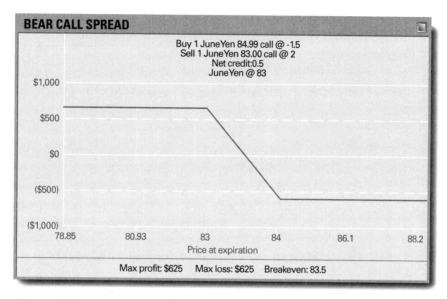

BEAR CALL SPREAD

Buy 1 June Yen 84.99 call @ -1.5
Sell 1 June Yen 83.00 call @ 2
Net credit:0.5
June Yen @ 83

Price at expiration

Max profit: $625   Max loss: $625   Breakeven: 83.5

Figure 9.5   *A program that plots a profit-and-loss graph to evaluate the strategy a trader is planning on using before it is implemented using his at-risk money.*

intraday and short-term trader. Now let's look at table 9.11, which tracks the bull call spread in table 9.9 and identifies the loss from holding a bull spread in a down market.

Even though the market went down, against the bull call position of the spread, the loss was only on net, $287.50. The maximum potential loss, of course, for the position is the difference in the premiums of $3,125 less $937.50, or $2,187.50. That would occur if the market plummeted, sending the premium on the 92 call to zero. In the event of such a market tumble, of course, the short 96 call would expire worthless, guaranteeing the full credit for our friendly trader.

The reason option spreads like these are so popular, or at least one of the reasons, is that before the 92 long call would lose all premium value for liquidation, the trader would presumably have time to offset and take some of the value in the option before seeing the premium plunge to zero. That being the case, the real risk in such a spread is much narrower than the potential loss, at least in relative terms. Once again, we see upon examination that options are risk mitigators rather than risk generators.

Table 9.11   *Underlying Futures Price at 0.9350*

Now Falls to 0.9250

Bought 92 call at 2.50	Sold 96 call at 0.75
Now at 1.97	Now at 0.45
New call value 1.97 × $1,250 = $2,462.50	New call value 0.45 × $1,250 = $562.50

Let's Do the Math

92 call bought for $3,125.00	96 call sold for $937.50
92 call sold for $2,462.50	96 call bought for $562.50
Loss = $662.50	Profit = $375.00

Q & A

Question: Currency futures options have something of a checkered reputation. Can you lay this issue to rest once and for all? Are exchange options risky or are they prudent?

Answer: I am very pleased to answer this one. And like any good economist, I will say, "On the one hand they are risky, and on the other hand they are prudent." Seriously though, we are going to take an in-depth look into the use of options later in the book, and we will answer this question directly and explicitly for you. Good reading!

CHAPTER 1

Closing the Deal: Profit Is the Name of the Game

All of us, regardless of whether we are speculators, intraday, short-term position, or long-term hedge traders, would like to establish cash flow from our trading strategies that gives us the opportunity to continue trading and generating profits. In other words, "nobody likes to lose." One thing, however, needs to be said about "losing" in currency trading. What is that? Well, when a trader sustains a substantial loss from a single trade, that kind of loss can put him into a big hole, from which he then has to spend considerable time and resources climbing out. Whether in fact he ever does recover or not depends strictly on one thing: his ability to generate future profits.

Stock market traders moving over into our currency markets may be familiar with analyses concluding that during the past 100 years, whenever any Dow bull market transitioned into a bear market, investors History concludes that those losses were so large that on average they took eight years for investors to recoup. As anyone who has fallen into a hole can tell you, even when you get out, you are then only back to where you started.

There is a reason for calling this sort of history lesson to readers' attention. It is believed that the majority of currency trades are in fact losing ones, and we need to insert into chapter 1 of each of our personal strategy books a new title, "Avoiding Losses."

Some who suffer large losses never do get back to square one. George Soros reported a loss of $2 billion during the Russian financial crisis of 1998. Julian Robertson's Tiger Fund went from an equity of $20 billion in

1998 to $16.5 billion in 2000, before liquidating. And, of course, the famous LTCM managed fund lost upward of $1 billion during the 1998 Russian financial crisis before declaring bankruptcy through the intervention of Alan Greenspan and the U.S. Federal Reserve.

Amid the excitement and anticipation of our own daily trading experiences, it is sometimes easy for any of us to lose sight of the important lesson that once losses are booked, the only way to recover from them is to turn your trading around and begin to trade profitably. Profits, at the end of the day (or at the beginning) are the name of the game

Drawdowns, as they are known in the currency trading world, are a part of every currency trader's experiences, and so here we believe that the path of least resistance on the road to profits is a road that encounters the fewest losses. In fact, we like to assert that, truth be told, minimizing losses is really a fundamental requirement of successful trading. So the first thing we must do in discussing how to close the deal and lock in profits is to discuss how to trade in a way that preempts losses.

Being Detail-Oriented

Currency traders are a high-quality, hardworking, intelligent group of people. It is no surprise to them, therefore, that the most successful traders in their midst are detail-oriented people. As you go about acquiring the volumes of information necessary to be a successful trader, you will conclude that paying attention to detail is a hallmark of a profitable currency trader.

Being aware of new developments in the field is also a handmaiden of attention to details, since so many of the new resources in currency markets are micro-oriented, not major, big-picture improvements. Because I personally believe that simple illustrations offer the most productive insight and contribution to the study of our markets, I want to call your attention to figures 10.1 and 10.2.

The chart in figure 10.1 uses the Relative Strength Index, which we introduced to readers in chapter 7. A look at the RSI index on the bottom of this chart shows a strong buy implication on September 1, as the index is sharply falling below its 30 index line and into an oversold territory. That is an important signal to the short-term trader. This RSI signal is based, as most are, on the 14-day moving average component of its index.

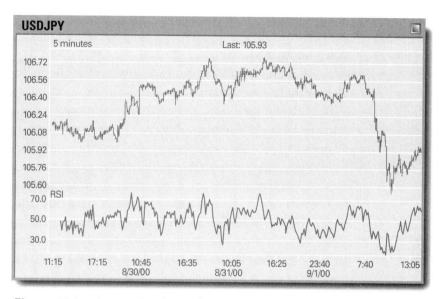

Figure 10.1 *A standard 14-day RSI study on a 5-minute chart. Notice the sharp drop in the RSI index on September 1.*

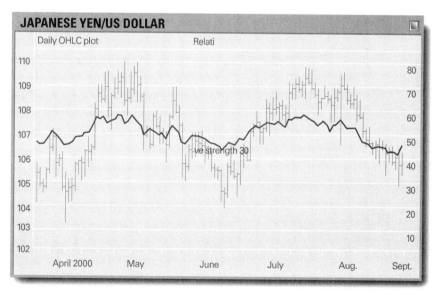

Figure 10.2 *RSI as a line overlay against the prices. Notice the RSI index does not fall to 30 on September 1.*

Charts Are Full of Details

As we know, oscillators like the RSI use exponential moving averages within their framework. Recently, many software programs have begun offering traders a flexibility that enables them to change these moving averages to suit their own particular trading framework. For instance, a short-term trader would typically use the 14-day moving average shown in figure 10.1, but the longer-term trader might use a 30- or 40-day moving average. The longer-term moving averages smooth out those shorter-term price fluctuations, so as to eliminate what traders call market "noise." *Noise* is a term we use to identify whatever data streams and other information are peripheral to the trader's focus. Such noise is something that all traders seek to minimize. The long-term trader is generally not interested in a lot of buy and sell signals from the RSI that a shorter-term trader acts on. He wants to look at longer-term price trends, and he discounts short-term moves like the ones shown in figure 10.1. A 30-day EMA is one way to discount short-term spikes in an RSI study.

Now let's look at the chart in figure 10.2. This RSI has a 30-day moving average built into it and, as you can see, this time the RSI is not generating an oversold condition on September 1. In fact, it barely touches the moderate 40 index line, which is a nonevent for the RSI.

Our friendly short-term trader has subscribed to a charting provider that permits customized EMA lines in his RSI studies. Our friendly trader is about to have a detail that he has overlooked generate a loss from a trade. He has not yet noticed that the chart he is using for this day's trading has mistakenly been set to the 30-day moving average on his RSI parameter. Using the modified 30-day RSI, he is never able to see the oversold/buy signal as the price drops like a rock on September 1. His last trade was a sell at 106.70, which he took from the standard 14-day RSI the day before. Missing this detail on a RSI chart study cost him 60 pips on the intraday move September 1—a loss that he must now make up through gains of 60 pips before he can begin to generate the net profits he had targeted for this week.

Lowering the Noise Level

Under the pressure of time and the ubiquitous market noise that we all have to contend with, traders are well advised to work on a method to frame their sources of information in a way that makes it easier, rather than more difficult, to get an accurate picture of what the markets are doing. Avoiding losses starts with building a data source network that clarifies the information you depend on to make your trading decisions.

What it simply boils down to is this: The trader who can "close the deal" consistently is constantly scrutinizing new potential online resources. Selecting a new charting service can give you a flexibility your old charting source did not have if it allows you to adapt the charts' format to your own specific trading needs. But it is important to use such new resources with an eye for the details so that we avoid errors and losses. These are just a couple of small ways to polish your trading practices, and incidentally, attention to detail also has the salutary effect of preventing losses that can occur from misinterpreting charting and charting-related studies.

Discarding old formats for new ones is the currency trader's version of "creative destruction," a phrase coined by a famous 20th century economist, Joseph Schumpeter. Mr. Schumpeter believed that a dynamic, growing economy inevitably generated "gales of creative destruction" that displaced old models for doing things with newer, more modern formats, which in turn created great advantages through higher profits.

A timely and effective utilization of online resources such as those mentioned earlier can play a major role in capturing profits for you. For instance, a growing number of different incarnations of trading alerts are available to online currency traders. Time is a scarce, and hence in-demand, commodity for all of us. Balancing our trading obligations and time on our PCs with other responsibilities is a real challenge for us all.

Online Price Alerts

If you are a long-term position trader, you can arrange to have alerts e-mailed to your PC mailbox with end-of-day prices, based on the parameters you have entered into the program. This e-mail resource is a simple, usually free, format that keeps you informed of end-of-day exchange rates. If, however, you often need a trade closed or opened at a certain price level when you are away from the PC (such as on your way to the dentist or driving to the store), then this format is not for you.

For the short-term trader, there are alerts your online broker can send, based on your instructions to him, which, when activated, will fire off an instant intraday, e-mail message to you with the price information you specified. You may even have a real live person pick up the phone and call you, alerting you to the price level that you may want to trade from.

With the wireless Internet breaking new ground literally day by day, it is not surprising that our cell phones with Internet capabilities are being utilized by online currency brokers. If you are a fundamental trader, you can access breaking news scrolled right from your cell phone. If you are a technical trader, you can also receive support/resistance price levels, buy/sell indicators, and other technical analysis price break signals directly from your cell phone, with a capability for you to type in instructions or call your online broker with your orders in response.

The trader's online environment is one thing that is constantly evolving as new resources become available almost literally by the minute. These changing resources are available to facilitate closing the deal. Those online resources are ones that a trader can take advantage of if he is paying attention and if he is invested in this notion of being detail-oriented in his trading practices.

Entry Points

Every trader has to first enter into and then exit out of a trade position. Those entry and exit prices establish profit or loss. Conceptually, all traders believe our every move is optimizing either an entry or exit trade. That is to say, we believe we are buying into a market at the optimum, or at least near the optimum, low, and we just as surely anticipate selling our long position at the optimum, or at least near the optimum, high just before the market heads south. Of course, the human condition has long been known for convincing itself that "what ain't so is what we know for sure." More often than not, unfortunately, we do seem to be somewhat more imperfect than that conceptually pure perspective we create for ourselves as traders. But, to the everlasting credit of our species, we nevertheless and invariably continue to pursue such conceptual perfection, while managing to convince ourselves that complete and perfect success is only a matter of the next trade away. In that spirit, we want to help our readers along the path to ultimate (financial) salvation.

Using the Right Charts

Look at figure 10.3. We have included three studies in this chart so that we can have a tripartite reinforcement of a simple buy or sell signal and then evaluate the substance of the trade based on what the market actu-

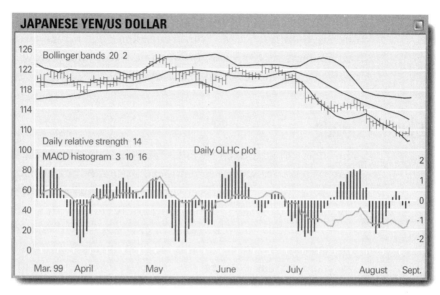

Figure 10.3 *A confluence of four separate signals, all implying a stronger dollar.*

ally did, rather than what we hoped it would do. In the process, we expect to learn some invaluable lessons that can translate into maximizing profits or, more aptly, instruct us on how best to close the deal on our trades and lock in those elusive profits that we might otherwise miss.

For starters, figure 10.3 is a daily chart. Dailies are used most effectively for an analysis of intermediate-term trading strategy. The daily chart of the USD/JPY provides a (approximate) six-month review of price action. For day traders, a daily chart would not offer them much help in evaluating intraday moves, except, thanks to the candlestick format used in this chart, perhaps in the macro sense, where the currency pair's opening plus its high, low, and close are recorded. The daily chart does not show, for instance, the intraday spikes or ticks that the day trader needs to discern in order to make his trading strategy effective. Nevertheless, a daily chart does provide a much needed perspective on the longer-term trends that can play into a day trader's judgments about where and when to enter or exit a trade.

For the most part, the daily chart, then, is used primarily by the intermediate-term trader. A speculative position trader may well be an intermediate-term trader who takes a position based on his trend expectation for prices that leads him several weeks into the future. Such a trader may enter a position with the expectation of exiting it as much as one full month later. We want to use once again the yen's gains during the summers of 1998 and 1999, to help us evaluate how best to maximize an entry move (or an exit move).

Bollinger Bands

The chart in figure 10.3 includes, as one of its three studies, a technical analysis resource we have mentioned before, Bollinger Bands. These are one of the most effective, yet simplest, technical analysis studies a currency trader can use. The Bollinger study starts with a moving average and to that adds an upper range line, which is two standard mathematical deviations removed. That is balanced by a lower EMA line, similarly two standard mathematical deviations removed. The construction of this trading range is such that over 90 percent of all prices are contained within the boundaries of this envelope.

When a price moves outside of the envelope in the upper range, that is taken as an overbought price environment and implies a sell signal. Conversely, when a price moves outside of the lower envelope, it is taken as an oversold condition and a buy signal. On the daily price chart, where each bar includes the day's open and close, the Bollinger Band study adds one other component that contributes to the evaluation of a market strategy. First we ascertain whether the price *closed* outside of the Bollinger envelope. If a daily price closes outside of one of the two bands, it reinforces the buy/sell signal for that date. Put another way, if a price *moves* outside of the bands of the Bollinger study, that is an implication of a price trend change. If, however, a price also *closes* outside of the Bollinger envelope, an exclamation point has been added to its buy or sell signal.

Two Old Friends, MACD and RSI

We have chosen to include, with the Bollinger study, two of the best technical analysis studies currency traders can also use in their trading analysis, the MACD and the RSI, which we reviewed earlier in this section. Taken together, these three overbought/oversold indicators, along with their buy/sell signals, represent a highly reliable and useful resource that currency traders can employ with some confidence in their at-risk trading strategies.

In this exercise, we want to locate a date on the chart where all three studies are signaling the same price direction and market environment. Following those indicators, we want to see how we would fare in the context of the by-now-familiar USD/JPY move of 1998 to 1999, from a short-term trader's standpoint.

In figure 10.3, we actually find a confluence of four signals from the three studies, each indicating the same price direction for the dollar in the summer of 1999. Starting with the week prior to July 26, our first signal for the U.S. dollar finds the MACD histogram bars plunging into the lowest area of their range, signaling a severely oversold condition with a buy implication.

Reinforcing that indicator is the RSI index, which is touching its 30 line, a clear signal #2, implying an oversold market price for the yen. Notice that the dollar has fallen from the 120 price level earlier in the week, to about 116 on July 26, a serious short-term price drop for the dollar against the USD/JPY. So on the face of it, these two indicators suggesting "oversold" are certainly reasonable.

Signal #3 is the Bollinger Band envelope in the top half of the chart. The bars close outside of the lower band, signaling again yet another oversold/buy signal, all within days of the other two just noted. If our friendly currency trader felt unusually conservative that week, he might have waited for one more signal suggesting that he should buy the dollar against the yen. He did not have to wait long.

On August 1, signal #4 surfaces as the MACD crosses over the zero line and moves strongly up, which is *against* the trend of USD/JPY prices, as they persist in a down mode. This divergence, where the MACD indicator opposes the price action, as we recall from chapter 7, implies that we should ignore the price direction and follow the MACD divergence indicator. MACD divergence trumps price action.

Tracing the actual market prices from the week preceding July 26, 1999, when the yen was at 120 per dollar, the U.S. currency plunges, with nary so much as a look back, all the way down to 105. It would be months before the dollar even tested the 110 yen level. Our friendly day trader who bought the dollar against the yen at 116 essentially was not ever likely to recoup his losses. Depending on how many contracts our trader bought, each expecting the dollar to gain against the yen, his loss could have totaled in the tens of thousands of dollars from the summer's unexpected fall of the U.S. dollar against the yen in 1999, and in spite of four separate, and usually reliable, technical analysis signals to buy the dollar.

There is not a trader in the world who has not had the experience of entering a position in a currency market, on the long side, just as the market peaks and heads sideways (or down) for the next several cycles, thus frustrating his confident analysis of those components of the market that seemed to virtually assure him of a spectacular bull run in his favorite currency.

Similarly, I am sure we all can recall at one time or another seeing the market rise, just the way we expected it to, *after* (unfortunately) we exited a long position, thus denied by an "unreasonable" market of the deserving and much sought after windfall profit. So entering or exiting a position in sync with the market's timing priorities rather than our own is, of course, what permits profits to travel from "that other trader's" portfolio and into ours, which is, after all, where we believe it rightfully belongs. There are ways to accomplish this and also minimize losses that we want to highlight and that we are confident will in fact protect traders from substantial losses in their own trading. Let's get going.

Entry Orders

Entry orders seem to dictate not only whether, but also how, we get to the point of "closing the deal" on a currency trade. If we enter expertly, we only have to choose how to capture the profits in an exit strategy, a nice problem to have. If we enter poorly, though, we are left with a decision of how to lose as little as possible. So entry execution strategies are important, and let's focus on them.

Market orders are the most efficient and sure way to enter a position in the currency markets. Getting a fill at the market's best available price for you to buy or sell your position is what a market order will deliver for you. Contrast that with, say, a *limit order*. Buy limit orders, as we know, are placed below the current price. If the market comes down and touches your buy limit order's price but then immediately reverses and takes prices higher, you stand a fairly good chance of not being filled.

MITs, or *market if touched* orders, are preferable to buy limit orders, at least in my opinion. In a falling market, when the price touches a buy MIT order, regardless of what the price does in the next few minutes, the order will be filled at the best possible price.

For entering a position, a *stop limit order* is one of the more flexible and useful trade execution orders a trader can employ. What the stop limit order does is list two prices. In the case of a buy order, for example, the buy's stop price (entered below the current market price) establishes that the order is to be executed when the market falls to the stop price level. The second price, the limit price, prevents the order from being filled at a higher price than the limit specifies, which could happen if the market abruptly reverses. Look at table 10.1 for an illustration of the stop limit order.

If a short-term trader sees a market with shallow price swings, he does not want to end up being filled with a buy order at the high end of a narrow swing. Our friendly trader's purpose for having a buy stop limit order is to catch the market in a short-term fall, where a buy can establish a low position. But he does not want to buy into a head fake market move, where the market price initially falls but then rises again immediately. So he uses the stop limit order as illustrated in table 10.1. Let's review our short-term trader's relationship to this market action and compare it to three other options for entry into the markets we looked at earlier. Our trader's *market order,* of course, would have been filled at 115.87. A *limit order,* on the other hand, would not have been filled at all, as the market reversed immediately and exceeded 115.80 (ask). A *MIT order* placed at 115.80 would have been filled at 115.87.

Table 10.1   *The Stop Limit Order*

Forex market USD/JPY currently at 116.00 (ask).

(The day trader sees this as the high for the day.)

Trader enters a buy stop limit order as follows: Buy stop at 115.80; limit at 115.85.

Forex market falls to 115.80 (ask).

The online trading platform is alerted as the market's "ask" reaches the buy stop's 115.80.

(Bid is 115.75.)

Forex market, however, reverses and abruptly rises to 115.87.

(Bid is 115.82.)

The online platform is unable to execute the trade at 115.87, as it exceeds the limit attached to the buy order, even though the buy stop was triggered at 115.80 (ask).

The short-term trader succeeded in one sense, because by using the buy stop limit entry order into this market and not being filled, he avoided giving up seven pips to the market. This was a discretionary decision on his part, because he felt that the market would not subsequently rise higher than the 115.90 range.

It is important to remember that how you enter a position impacts your profits in a rather direct way. An evaluation needs to be made prior to entering your online order, concerning how important it is to get your fill at "this" time and at "this" price. Usually, hindsight determines the wisdom of such decisions. Still, a trader goes with what is in front of him. Determinations must be made. If the market should rise immediately after touching the 115.80 level and is in fact beginning a strong run up in prices, the market order, even at 115.87, would have been the preferred and most profitable choice. The same is true for the MIT selection. Yet if the market bounced back down to 115.80 or lower, as the short-term trader was expecting, then the protecting *stop limit order* would have served the trader well. So net-net, we all make determinations based on probabilities to the best of our abilities, and we all sooner or later recognize that even with traders, the market rules. The key to long-term profits is, of course, knowing those probabilities and then also utilizing all the resources available to us so that we can maximize our chances for success.

Now let's do an evaluation of what our friendly trader should have used in the way of market entry orders to prevent the losses he subsequently suffered by buying the dollar during this near-historic plunge in dollar value against the yen in the summers of 1998 and 1999. Let's say that our friendly trader bought the dollar at 116 on July 26. Here is what happened. The market was priced at 115.90 and came back to 116.10 on July 26, intraday, before resuming its downward trend again. Our trader placed his entry buy order with the market at its high for the day at 116.10.

Remember, our trader got multiple buy USD signals from his technical analysis study sources and made the decision to buy the dollar in the summer of 1999. Our friendly trader, like all traders, can enter the market flat-footed or cautiously. Let's see what happens. (Remember, we know in advance that the dollar is not going to strengthen, but actually weakens significantly against the JPY.)

We know that neither an *MIT* nor a *market order* would have helped him. These entry orders would have been filled and his losses would have begun to mount from the first minute in his buy position, as the dollar plunged.

A *buy stop limit order* would not have had a chance to prevent his fill. A buy stop at 115.80 with a limit at 115.85 was the wrong order entry strategy at the wrong time. This market trend was not a shallow-swing price movement but a long-term deliberate decline in prices. It fell a little each day. So, in all likelihood, the buy stop limit order would have been filled at 115.80 just as readily as the others. The other illustration we looked at, the *limit order* (115.80 or better), stood no chance at all for stopping our friendly trader's fateful buy position in a falling dollar market.

So bottom line, of these four distinct orders, none really would have prevented or even limited the losses that awaited a bad strategic decision of being long in a bear market. What our friendly short-term trader needed was a defensive entry strategy for this market, given his buy position and knowing what we know now.

OCOs—A Real Help in Closing the Deal

There is a defensive order entry strategy traders can use, of course, that truly stands to maximize profits for them. I am talking about OCO, or one cancels other (also known as order cancels order).

With the market at 116.10 yen to the dollar on July 26, our friendly trader enters an OCO into his online trading platform. The OCO has two components, of course. And that permits a different entry strategy and, as we will see, a different exit strategy with a profitable outcome for our happy trader. With the OCO entry resource, our friendly trader does not have to commit to a buy position at 116; he can afford to let the market commit itself before he enters the market at all. In this case, he will enter a buy position if the market shows it is recovering or a sell position if the market confirms a falling price trend. The buy component of an OCO in this market is entered at 116.50.

Our trader also enters a sell order at 115.50 on the same ticket. With the dollar's market price levels already strongly in retreat, he wants to protect against what he perceives as a possible short-term trend to further lows, even in the face of four technical analysis indicators signaling the dollar will go higher. One order cancels the other. As we know, the market never actually touched 116.50, and when he is filled at 115.50 the next day, the buy order at 116.50 is canceled. Our happy trader, instead of buying into the market against the dollar's freefall, catches the market trend with a sell order and begins to accumulate profits instead of losses.

The real benefit of using the OCO entry strategy is that it enables a trader to use a defensive OCO entry strategy and then let the market turn him from a defensive trader to an offensive trader. The OCO ends up being an offensive entry strategy that puts our friendly trader on the side of the market price momentum whichever way it goes. This means, too, that he has not put himself into the position of committing to a single price direction, where if his perspective of market direction is wrong, he either eats losses from being in the market long, while the market falls, or he simply misses the move altogether. The OCO makes our friendly trader a player, and there is no more prescient observation in market lore than this one: You have to be in the markets to make money from them.

Q & A

Question: What is the single most important bit of advice you would give to help any trader close the deal and lock in profits from his trades?

Answer: The single piece of advice that comes first to mind is familiarize yourself with every conceivable incarnation of execution orders, some of which we discussed in this chapter. Even though you will not use most of them, I guarantee that the process of considering them will open up areas of knowledge that you had not previously been exposed to.

Using Technical Analysis

11

Advanced Use of Charts for Currency Trading

One of the most productive features of the online format and one that will continue to attract currency traders to it is its interactive character. We believe that many of the best uses of the Internet involve such interactive give-and-take. We want to borrow from that resource and discuss charts in the context of a question-and-answer format. We believe that the practical problems traders face and overcome in their day-to-day trading practices should be reflected here and shared in a way that will benefit us all, giving us that opportunity to provide practical solutions to the real problems that currency traders confront from time to time.

There is hardly a currency trader in the world who does not use or rely on charts to identify price trends or price levels in his trading practices. The fundamental trader who needs to know where the euro/yen has been trading as of a few days or a few weeks ago can glance at the chart and get his answer, precisely and immediately. The technician who trades intraday will use his charts to establish buy and sell signals and then make his entry and exit trades. So charting is one of those basic tools of currency trading that is quite literally indispensable. Like all such basic tools, various incarnations with specific applications will from time to time evolve and be invented. But one of the more interesting of those charting incarnations is actually an original creation of charting formats—the Point and Figure chart. Look at figure 11.1 and the Xs and Os of this chart. It will surprise you to learn that this format goes back to the late 1800s, a period in U.S. economic history I have

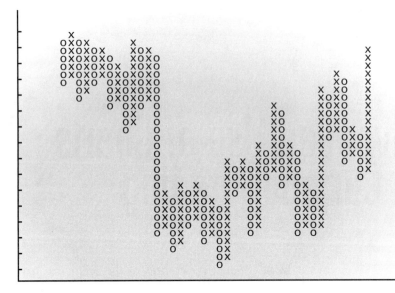

Figure 11.1   *A Point and Figure chart where a column might represent five days worth of trading or a few minutes.*

dubbed BIT, "Before Information Technology." It was also, interestingly enough, first used for intraday trading.

As equity prices came across the new herald of that era's version of high tech, the stock ticker, it was an easy task to register price movements up or down with pen and pad using Xs and Os. Later, after the crash in 1929, the Xs and Os "book" format picked up the name of Point and Figure, which it has kept ever since. Make no mistake about it, this dinosaur of stock chart formats makes a contemporary contribution to currency trading in the online era, and one that many—nay, most—traders are simply unfamiliar with. A trader seeking to be familiar with advanced applications of charting needs to be familiar with these price movement charts known as the Point and Figure. My advice is to get familiar with Point and Figure charts; you will like them. So let's look closely at this simple, but unusual, charting format and learn what it has to offer the online currency trader.

How Do the Point and Figure Charts Differ from the Conventional Chart Format?

Answer: The charts we have seen up until now, such as the bar, line, and candlestick, have a few simple things in common. They show the price, of course, plus the high, the low, and usually the closing and opening prices, too. They also provide a date and time frame that those prices traded in. In other words, if we want to know what the price of the USD/CHF was on July 13, 2000, we just pick up a chart from our online format and there it is: the open, high, low, and close. A chart's horizontal scale measures time. The other scale, the vertical, measures a currency's price value. If we are using an intraday application, we can see the ticks within a range for that day at specific times during the July 13th trading day, such as 2 P.M., G.M.T.

The basic Point and Figure charts are unique in one important respect. They are not constructed in relation to a market date and have no framework for the time of day. Neither do they display volume. A Point and Figure chart will not display what a currency's price was in relation to any particular time of the day or even its closing or opening value. Neither will it identify the high or low on any particular date. The X and O patterns do not show prices in relation to time. They show simply price movement. So the horizontal axis that serves as a time scale on conventional charting formats reflects nothing but price changes in a P & F chart. The vertical axes in bar charts measure price value, but on a P & F chart, the vertical scale measures price direction—that is, a currency's up or down movement, not its precise value. This pure price movement, independent of a time frame, does, and I may say surprisingly so, offer a resource to the arsenal of currency traders that few would expect.

What Do Those Xs and Os Mean?

Answer: Our glance at figure 11.1 showed a lot of Xs and Os that make up the Point and Figure format. A rising price is designated with the letter "X." Conversely, a falling price gets the letter "O." Each letter, X or O, fills a box in separate columns of your graph. An X is never in a column with Os, and vice versa. Simply put, a column of Xs reflects rising prices. A column of Os reflects falling prices. As prices change from rising to falling, columns appear on a chart to reflect these price movements.

What Does a Typical Point and Figure Chart Look Like?

Answer: We see columns of 10 to 20 Xs and Os. You will never see only two Os in this P & F chart. Why? Well, if the currency experienced a small decline of 20 pips, and each box represents 10 pips, the rule of P & F says that no O will be added to the chart, and no column change is permitted in the chart. In short, with a 20-pip change in prices, nothing is done. In this P & F format, the standard used is that it must take 30 pips of price change before a switch in columns is made, and then the three new boxes are filled with Xs or Os all at once. Another rule for P & F charts is that an "O" column starts one box below the highest "X." Both the three-box rule and the number of pips assigned to each box are, of course, flexible. Some traders use a four-box rule. Then, too, for example, some currency traders may assign 100 pips per box, such as for use in a long-term study by a fundamental trader. The flexibility of the P & F formats allows for these variations, which can serve specific situations.

Because a specific price value in pips is designated for each box, if the U.S. dollar/Swiss franc has an assignment of 10 pips per box, a box on your graph gets a new X every time the market gains 10 pips. That is why, although the vertical scale on a Point and Figure chart uses price numbers, the box increment of 10 pips (or more) does not present a precise scale of price movement, certainly not to the extent that a conventional chart does. If the market gains 65 more pips during the day, a total of six more Xs would be added, one at a time, to the graph, as a column is built reflecting an up price trend.

With a 65-pip price gain, only six Xs are added. The price increase would have to total 70 pips before a seventh box would be used. As far as the value assigned to each box is concerned, that can also be somewhat a function of whether you are trading intraday, short term, intermediate, or long term. An intraday trader would use a smaller number of pips per box. A long-term trader would select a higher number, such as 20 or even 50 pips per box.

Remember, however, experience has shown that the three-box (or higher) reversal rule is very effective in limiting the market price noise that could generate prolific column switches and general confusion.

So the P & F chart focuses on trends. I like to refer to it as a supply and demand chart. The Xs represent demand and the Os mean supply. The more Xs, then the more demand for the currency, and the higher the price. The more Os, the more supply and the lower the price. It is not a bad way to think of currency markets, and a quick glance at a P & F chart can provide this supply and demand snapshot of a currency for a particular moment. They are simple, easy to construct, and very accurate in terms of the information they communicate. The currency trader who takes the time to learn, construct, and use the Point and Figure charts is indeed placing himself in an advanced status among chart users, and he will benefit from that investment, I am confident.

How Can I Create a Point and Figure Chart on My PC?

Answer: A Point and Figure chart was originally constructed, as you might suspect, on simple graph paper, and anyone can still literally do it that way. On a PC, you just set up a spreadsheet and input your price data in a matter of only a few minutes. Start by placing a dot in one of the graph boxes at the left-hand side of your spreadsheet in the first empty column. Then place an X (prices up) in the box above the dot or an O (prices down) in the box below the dot, to reflect the first price movement on your chart.

I noted that I like to describe this format as supply and demand, where the Xs are demand (a rising price) and Os are supply (a falling price). I might just as easily describe it as accumulation and distribution. As Xs increase on a chart, you have a market that is accumulating the currency, and prices are rising. When Os predominate on a chart, you have distribution or selling of the currency. These are important concepts to keep track of in any currency market. The P & F chart is ideally suited to represent these big-picture concepts of supply and demand, or accumulation and distribution—much more so than conventional charting.

How Are Day-to-Day Price Changes Reflected in Point and Figure Charts?

Answer: Well, first, we have to re-visit the fascinating attribute in constructing these Point and Figure charts, which is that when you go about putting one together, you are not concerned about closing or opening prices, dates, and time of day. Near the center of the chart in figure 11.1, for instance, there are 23 Os marking a breakout to the downside for the USD/CHF. Let's account for these 23 Os in a hypothetical trading scenario. As we pick up the market price on this chart, the price of that currency may have fallen 120 pips on Monday, gained 20 pips Tuesday, fallen 30 pips Wednesday, up 10 pips Thursday, and down 80 pips Friday, and still show only one column of Os totaling a 230-pip drop over five days. That means one column, for five days, with no reference to opening or closing prices, and reflecting a sell off of 230 pips, with no highs or lows shown either.

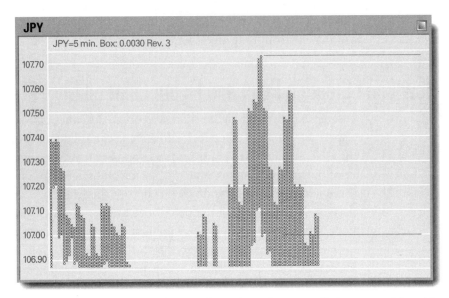

Figure 11.2 *Traders who study P&F charts will learn to identify "buy" or "sell" signals from charts like this one.*

Beginning with the next week of trading, the USD/CHF price may have gained 50 pips in morning trading, creating a line of 5 Xs, as you can see in figure 11.1, next to the long descending column of Os. Later that same day, the price dropped 70 pips, followed by a gain of 80 pips before closing that Monday. Those next three columns were generated in one day's trading: the five-X up moves, followed by the seven-O down moves and an eight-X gain. Remember the three-box rule that says in order to change columns from Xs to Os, the price must move a total of three boxes, or 30 pips; otherwise, no change is made in the chart columns. Gains or losses that exceed 30 pips are shown in distinct, adjacent columns, without respect to time of day or date. What this kind of format does is permit a focused, clear representation of *price movement,* independent of dates or time.

What Are the Buy and Sell Signals Like in a Point and Figure Chart?

Answer: This kind of charting produces advantages for a currency trader over the conventional line, bar, and candlestick charts. Buy and sell signals, as we will see, are much crisper. Entry and exit signals, as a result, are much more precise. Support and resistance levels are also much more discernible.

Look at figures 11.3 and 11.4, where the same currency move is tracked by both a line chart and a P & F. Notice that the line chart does not pick up the sideways movement clearly identified by the P & F format at points A and B. This kind of clarity from the P & F chart enables a trader to identify important sideways price movement, not always evident in other types of charts. Sideways movement in a 3 × 10 (3 box

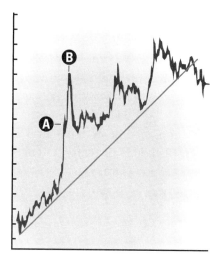

Figure 11.3 *A conventional line chart. Note it misses completely the support and resistance areas shown in points A and B.*

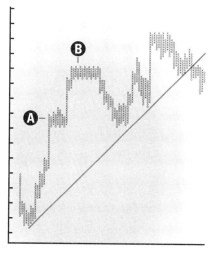

Figure 11.4 *A Point and Figure chart. It picks up the support and resistance pricing levels in these markets.*

reversal, 10-pip box) format P & F chart confirms a period of short-term and shallow price reversals.

This sideways price action in a market is also known as congestion. A congested price action often presages a breakout. It can also be useful in identifying support and resistance levels in prices. Point B was a resistance level in the EUR/CHF, not represented at all by the line chart in 11.3. Point A was a support level—again, missed entirely by the conventional chart.

Point B in fact turns out to be a basing price action prior to a downside breakout. With the Point and Figure charts, the currency trader will not only identify buy signals better, but target prices will be clearer, and they are so simple to read. Count the (maximum) number of Xs along a basing or a topping line. Multiply that by the box reversal number and stand that column count up (or down) to establish the target price of the subsequent breakout to the upside (or downside). For example, there were seven Xs along the horizontal topping line in figure 11.4. Using a three-box reversal, we count 70 pips, then times three, for 210 pips to the downside, and there you have the target price for taking profits in a breakout to the downside. The longer the consolidation pattern, the stronger the move.

What Does a Buy and Sell Signal Look Like on a Point and Figure Chart?

Answer: Table 11.1 is a very simple example of an incipient sell signal. I say incipient because, as it stands, the chart is not generating a signal at all, neither a buy nor a sell. But it will shortly. What is required for a sell is for prices to reach lower highs and lower lows through at least three adjacent columns. Note the column of Os on the left side of this chart. This chart has a 3 × 10 format, which means there is a 10-pip-per-box scale and a reversal requirement of 3 boxes. When another 10-pip drop in prices is registered, a fourth O will be added to the far right column. That next O will then establish the lower low required for a sell signal. (Note that the three Xs established a lower high.)

Turn next to table 11.2 to see a buy signal in a P & F chart. After the initial 130-pip fall in prices, the EUR/CHF makes an up reversal of 30 pips, followed by a 30-pip decline, followed immediately by a 40-pip rise in the EUR/CHF. Next the chart shows a 30-pip fall, followed again by another 30-pip increase. One more 30-pip decline is finally followed by a 50-pip increase in the eighth column, establishing a higher high by 20 pips. A buy

Table 11.1

O		
O	X	
O	X	O
O	X	O
O		O

Table 11.2

													X
												–	X
											–		X
										–			X
O									–				X
O								–					X
O							–						X
O						–					X		X
O					–				X		X	O	X
O				–					X	O	X	O	X
O			–				X		X	O	X	O	
O		–					X	O	X	O	X		
O	–		X		X		X	O	X	O	X		
O	X		X	O	X	O	X	O		O			
O	X	O	X	O	X	O	X						
O	X	O	X	O		O							
O		O											

signal is confirmed when both a higher low and higher high are printed on the chart, and, as you can see, the prices do eventually break the resistance trend line, represented by dashes along the top of the columns. A buy signal is strengthened when it is above the support line as shown in this chart.

You can customize from software programs that are available. For instance, you can specify a 2 × 6 format where each box represents two ticks, and a six-box reversal is used for establishing a new column. This 2 × 6 relationship permits the small two-pip price reference so that small intraday moves can be identified, while at the same time, a higher than usual six-box reversal formula is employed to filter the noise that would otherwise be generated from such a small two-pip-per-box price reference in a currency as volatile as the Japanese yen. So adaptability and clarity, again, are two premiums that contribute to the utility of the P & F currency charts.

Refer back to figure 11.1. This charting format is from a broker who allows a trader to draw lines into his chart for study. This chart reflects a sell signal and is known as the Blumanthal 20 box signal. If a move up in prices yields a printed chart of 20 Xs, the first (six-box) reversal is a sell signal. The top line was drawn to show a top after a 60-pip move up. The bottom line shows the depth of the following price decline, which was signaled by the 18-pip reversal on this chart.

In this column of 20 Xs, representing a 60-pip net gain, what we do not see are a series of small, 1- to 5-pip, shallow price-down reversals that occurred on the way up to this 60-pip price increase. That omission is an attribute of the Point and Figure format with a 3 × 6 reversal rule. A 3 pip/box with a 6-box rule is a filter that eliminates the shallow, unimportant price action that often confuses pricing patterns. Put another way, the shallow price reversals are trumped by the larger uptrend move in prices by the USD/JPY, not only on the chart but in the market itself. So the first 18-pip decline after a 60-pip increase is taken as a sell from the P & F chart. Look at the pricing patterns revealed by the P & F and how profitable this Blumanthal rule was intraday.

Is There an Advanced Charting System That Identifies Exit Points for Trades?

Answer: In chapter 10 we looked at entry trades and how critical they are for both maximizing profits and limiting losses. There is indeed a system created especially for identifying and then executing an exit trade. It is known as a Parabolic SAR, and it was created by J. Welles Wilder, the same man who created the very popular Relative Strength Index, or RSI.

SAR stands for Stop and Reversal, and this technical analysis study is one of the most reliable and productive formats that currency traders have for identifying exit points in their markets. It is also occasionally referred to as the Parabolic Time and Price System. Figure 11.5 shows a series of dots that look almost like a moving average, tracking the price movements of the yen futures in the summer of 2000. Notice a variation in this study, however, that you will not find in any other moving average lines. There are gaps in the line of dots periodically, which seem to correspond to price trend changes. These gaps in the SAR are indeed line transitions, which move from below the price trend to above it in a single day.

What is that all about? Well, two variables go to the heart of the currency trader's daily strategic dilemma. Number one is, "What is the price trend I need to identify in this market so that I can enter my trading position?" Once in a position, traders want to know how to protect profits by exiting their position with a gain, or, should the market reverse itself, they want to know when to exit their position with the smallest losses. Then dilemma number two is, "So where do I set a target or a stop to exit my position?" This SAR system addresses both. When prices are below the SAR line, traders should be short the market. When prices are above the

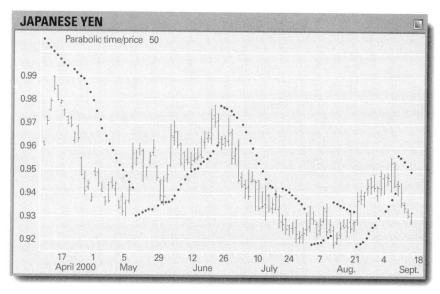

Figure 11.5 *The Parabolic Stop and Resistance chart. Notice every gap in the SAR lines correspond to a price trend change.*

SAR dotted line, traders should be long. A glance at figure 11.5 shows what a reliable signal the SAR is in that respect. Using that indicator alone, a trader can do very well in this market.

Currency traders by nature seem to be offensive-minded, and a few have even been described as aggressive. One of the other features of the Stop and Reverse system needs to be noted here for their benefit. Look at the price trend for the four weeks from the middle of April to the middle of May on the chart. Prices trended down from 0.9900 to 0.9300 in little over one month. The Stop and Reverse line, of course, followed that price trend religiously, and a trader who was short the yen would have profited nicely, as we can see. This particular trend line identifies one of the attributes of this system, and one that is consistent with established principles of good trading—namely, always adjust your stops in the direction of the trade. If you are long, adjust your stops higher. If you are short, adjust your stops to a lower price. In this way you are increasing your profits with every adjustment of your trailing stop. You are not letting the market steal your gains or surreptitiously maximize your losses. The Parabolic SAR is consistent with this fundamental trading principle and is a good match for an aggressive trader.

Look at the movement of the stop adjustments from May 3 to May 7 as prices reversed and moved higher, from the 0.9350 level to 0.9500. The stops for those dates continued falling lower, in the direction of the (short) trade, even as prices were going higher. Notice that when those stops moving lower and the prices moving higher converged, the short yen futures position was "stopped out" by the SAR on May 19. When a stop and reversal occurs, the line signal changes from a short to long immediately, or vice versa. So this explains why we see gaps in the SAR chart that do indeed correspond to trend price changes.

The single, important limitation of the SAR may be its performance in a choppy or sideways market, where trends cannot be established. In those markets, the SAR needs to be evaluated more closely. For instance, in the month of July 24 to August 24 on the chart, the yen futures market did trade in a sideways, choppy, and relatively shallow price range, moving from about 0.9200 on the low to only .9350 on the high. On July 24, the SAR was signaling a short position while prices based slightly below 0.9300. The market did trend marginally lower to 0.9200, before climbing again and being stopped out at 0.9300, making the trade only a break-even maneuver. The SAR then reversed and signaled a long position on August 4th, permitting an entry trade at about 0.9300. But by August 14th, the SAR had reversed again and exited the long position at about 0.9250, for a small loss. As Mr. Wilder says, the lesson of this example is that the SAR is best used *after* a trend is established. His book *New Concepts in Technical Trading Systems* describes the Parabolic SAR in great detail. My suggestion for intermediate- and long-term traders is to wait for a 100-basis point trend before entering a position with a stop based on the SAR levels.

The facility of using my 100-basis point trend rule for identifying buy or sell signals is illustrated in figure 11.8. This SAR chart shows up the use of the rule nicely in that yen move down, which began in mid-April, taking its futures price from 0.9900 to 0.9300 in a little more than one month. Our friendly trader waited for the first 100-basis point move before entering a trade at 0.9800, using the trailing stops of the SAR. By doing that, our trader accumulated profits in his short position from a down trend all the way to 0.9400. His exit eventually came on May 18 at 0.9400 with a 400-pip profit. Continuing with the 100-basis point trend parameter, our friendly trader spotted the next short signal at 0.9750, waited for a 100-basis points move before filling the short futures position at .9650 on July 5th, then followed the SAR stops once again, down to 0.9400, where he exited with a 250-pip profit.

Each discrete dot on the SAR chart represents the precise exit point for the currency position for that day. Again, if the prices are below the SAR line, the trader should be in a short position. As soon as the 100 bps trend is established, a trader should be in the market and place his exit stop. His exit stops continue moving lower, until the price level ultimately reverses and touches that day's exit point (stop). Notice that an exit trade automatically triggers a price trend reversal on the SAR format. Remember, when prices touched the buy stop exit price at 0.9400, on May 20, the SAR immediately signaled a reversal. I want to call your attention to the lone dot at the 0.9300 mark on July 20. That was the stop and reversal point for a down move from 0.9750 to 0.9400. The SAR immediately reversed again, back to another short signal, but our trader was unable to enter a new position under the 100-basis point trend rule.

Accumulation/Distribution Is a Chart Study Used for Stocks. Can It Be Used in Currency Markets?

Answer: Well, as you know, the AD chart is really an overbought/oversold oscillator, which some equity analysts do like to use as a part of their overall package of charting formats. I have looked at the AD for currencies and find that it is marginally useful, if at all. I would advise readers to look elsewhere for charting analysis in currencies. There is simply too much useful data around to waste resources on things like the AD, which simply do not produce what they need to, in order to justify the investment of time in them. But I believe that all traders need to come to their own evaluations, so let's look at what the Accumulation Distribution chart is all about.

Simply put, the AD chart measures the buying power (accumulation) and selling power (distribution) of the currency being studied. It is an oscillator that tries to identify overbought and oversold conditions in a currency market. It uses a 0 to 100 scale, with the 30 line on the low side and the 70 line on the high side being signal levels, much like the RSI, which J. Welles Wilder created.

Figure 11.6 shows an AD chart drawn over the yen futures. The Accumulation/Distribution line is constructed based on volume in relation to closing prices, and because it is an oscillator, there needs to be careful review of how to implement it with at-risk money in a volatile currency market like the yen futures.

The AD line will enter the overbought zone when a currency is being accumulated by the market. The mathematical formula takes a portion of each day's volume and adds or subtracts it from a cumulative total. If the closing price is near the day's high, volume is added to the cumulative total. If the closing price is nearer the low for the day, volume is subtracted from the cumulative total. In that way, the line moves higher or lower, indicating a buying or selling bias in the market. That is, the line traces a higher portion on the chart whenever the closing price nears the high for the day before. It traces a lower scale on the chart when closing prices near the day's low.

I recommend that currency traders consider implementing this analysis only under a divergence indicator. That means when the AD line is in the overbought area of the chart, and prices are falling, then consider such divergence to be an implied buy signal in favor of the AD signal. Similarly, if the AD line is in an oversold area of the chart, and prices are moving up, that is a divergence sell signal.

If we look for the July 12 area on the AD chart, we find a divergence of prices moving lower and away from a rising AD line during that week of July 10th to 17th. Unfortunately, if a trader had decided to go long based on this signal, he would have found prices continuing to fall from their closing level of 0.9335 on July 17th, all the way to 0.9200, as late as August 15th.

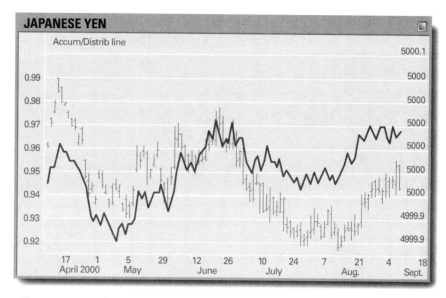

Figure 11.6   *The Accumulation/Distribution chart study is used widely in equity markets but has limited applicability to currency markets.*

Again, some traders may find a wrinkle in an application of the Accumulation/Distribution chart that I have not found, which may be of use to them as online currency traders. So I will follow my own advice and encourage traders to consider every new resource that may conceivably be helpful to them in maximizing profits in their online currency trading.

Is There a Technical Analysis Study That Professional Traders Seem to Use?

Answer: Well, the truth is that professional traders comprise, as do online traders such as ourselves, a diverse lot, and we find as many different trading systems and strategies among them as anywhere else. I can mention one interesting and little known system, however, that I know many futures floor traders pay attention to. It is called Pivot Point.

Figure 11.7 shows a JPY futures contract with a Pivot Point study overlay. This chart is used to generate support and resistance levels, which can then be used as part of an overall trading system involving other technical analysis contributors. So, like many charting tools, the Pivot Point should be seen as but a single component of a much larger strategy framework generated by many different formats. As you can

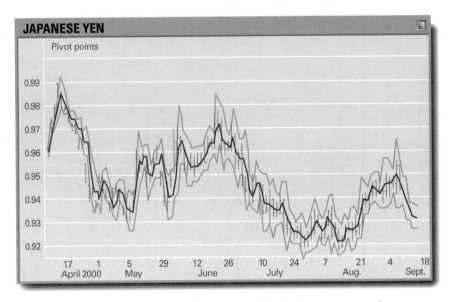

Figure 11.7   *The Pivot Point chart study identifies support and resistance levels based on the average of the previous session's high, low, and close.*

see, it has a support line, below the price level, and a resistance line, above the price level.

The formula is a straightforward mathematical average of the last session's high, low, and close. There is a method to calculate two distinct support and resistance levels. The first support and resistance price levels are shown on the chart in 11.7. Obviously, if the daily price range from the previous day was large, the support and resistance lines will increase in the chart analysis.

If the market price rallies above the pivot point and prices break the first resistance level, it is taken as a bullish signal. Conversely, if the price breaks below a support level, on a down move, that is read as a bearish sign of more falling prices.

It always seems to me that individual traders can find use for certain analyses that another trader finds of no value whatsoever. That is what makes markets, after all. Personally, I would like to suggest that readers look at as many technical studies as they can.

12

A Close Look at Technical Analysis for Forex Markets

Technical analysis for online forex traders is undeniably a state-of-the-art experience. Forex traders now have access to the most sophisticated software programs and online resources imaginable. They can produce formats and draw charts that incorporate anywhere from one to a dozen technical studies, almost instantaneously. They can test their systems on historical price data, going back decades, all with the flick of a key touch on their personal computer. Because many readers are discovering online currency markets for the first time, having either moved over from their trading experiences in stocks or by expanding their telephone-based currency trading formats into the online experience, in either case the online format can tend to obscure the historical roots of technical analysis, which, it is easy to forget, actually pre-date the IT revolution.

The premise of technical analysis, as applied to forex markets, is that future price movements in currencies can be predicted based on a currency's own record of past price relationships. Technical analysis studies apply these past price relationships in order to discern patterns of price behavior that will then be repeated at some point in the future. In the broadest sense, obviously that means future price levels are supposed to be identifiable in today's currency markets.

Looking back on the development of technical analysis, one can see that as price trends indeed did eventually come to be identified, it then made sense for traders to want to know when a market would be more likely to rise than fall, and vice versa. In other words, once the validity of trends had been established in the technical analysis environment (at least, in the sense that trends began to be accepted as fact), it was only a matter of time before the "genetic code," so to speak, of why trends develop, or why trends stop and reverse, would become the subject of study. So in these contemporary research technologies, technical analysis has actually evolved into a study seeking to identify a "genetic code" of currency markets.

Technicians believe that once this "code" is cracked, anticipating and profiting from markets will become a science and not an art. So technical analysts are, in that sense at least, researching price relationships in the same way that DNA science is researching the human genome and looking for the same type of breakthrough in their understanding of why markets act the way they do.

If forex trading analysts could find their financial markets' version of this "gene," which determines, for instance, why the euro/CHF currency price rises and then falls and *when* it will move up or down, then a trader will be able to enter his trade with a mathematically based, reasonable expectation and opportunity for profiting from that trade.

We want to take a brief journey, then, into the historical roots of our modern technical analysis studies, so that we can better master the IT resources of technical analysis. MACD, RSI, and the like are, at the end of the day, only tools for understanding and implementing *concepts* of price relationships and systems of trading strategies. In other words, we do not want to become so enamored and engulfed by these resources that we lose sight of the conceptual basis for making decisions with them. We want to use IT, with our PCs and their vast online capabilities, so that we can be more successful in our trades as a result of making the right decisions. We do not want to let the technical analyst's tools make our decisions for us.

It Bears Repeating

Technical analysis, no less than the medical or physical sciences, is founded on research that has come before, and we want to briefly review some of this basic science of technical analysis so that online traders are better prepared to use the online format like a surgical instrument and not as a substitute for the conceptual understanding of currency markets that makes the tools of IT useful and profitable.

The Great Pyramids and the Leaning Tower of Pisa

This review will take us back almost literally to the Great Pyramids of Egypt, for the conceptual discipline that underlies a large part of our contemporary technical analysis. Let us begin modestly, however, at the end of the 19th century, in 1897, with the discovery by Charles Dow that stock prices could be studied by recognizing their trends.

All stock traders have likely heard of, and perhaps even used at one point or another, what in some ways is the mother of all technical analysis—the Dow Theory. The Dow Theory asserts that, at any given time in the markets, three trends are at work. Dow labeled these as the Primary trends, which he likened to *tides;* Secondary or Intermediate trends he described as *waves;* and Minor trends Charles Dow thought of as *ripples.*

Technical analysis, like many a successful trader, posits that currency markets discount everything that is known about an underlying currency, so that a currency's price on a given date reflects fair market value. Dow developed two averages that still bear his name, with which he attempted to measure the broader market's valuation of stock prices. The Dow Jones Industrial Average and the Dow Jones Transportation Average are, of course, still followed today in the financial markets. Charles Dow originally studied these averages in order to assess business conditions, rather than stock prices, and he sought to use his averages to predict the changing character of the business environment. Subsequently, as we know, his Dow Theory was developed by others, who then applied it to market valuations and stock prices more specifically.

A Big-Picture Perspective of Markets

The Primary trend (tides) in the Dow Theory is a long-term (one year or more) price predisposition that is marked in a bull market by consistently higher highs and higher lows and in a bear market by lower highs and lower lows. So this identification of discernible price trends based on studies that were first made over 100 years ago really marked the beginning of modern technical analysis. This original breakthrough of Dow's—namely, that you could identify price trends through analysis—is today taken for granted, but it proved in fact to be the basis of much of today's technical analysis used in the forex currency markets. Higher highs and higher lows continue to mark the way many technical studies confirm their bullish trends.

Within each of the three trends that Charles Dow identified are three separate phases of price movement. In a bull market, Phase I is characterized through aggressive buying from a minority of traders. Phase II displays a gradual and spreading fundamental support for a bullish trend and is characterized by evidence of increased, market-wide buying. Phase III sees the relationships of a bull market in full blossom, as the majority of the market finally buys into a bullish perspective and solidifies the upward price trend.

Another feature of the Dow Theory that presages contemporary technical analysis is the requirement for this Dow trend or phase to have some confirmation from an independent source. A bullish trend in the Dow Industrials needs to be confirmed by a rising Dow Jones Transportation Average. Dow also used volume for a confirmation of a trend line.

So the 1897 development of Charles Dow's concept has really proved to be the foundation and beginning of modern technical analysis. Market trends, with phases within those trends, all reinforced by confirmation from one or more independent sources, are familiar to contemporary technical analysts today but were revolutionary at the time of Charles Dow.

The growth of this "trend and phase" perception of market prices eventually led to another theory, which is also used in forex trading today. Charles Dow's theory of tides, waves, and ripples provided a short "swim" through history that led to another wave theory. The Elliott Wave Theory, which discerns "waves" of price movements, is one we want to look at closely in this chapter. We are also going to review something called Fibonacci numbers, which play a role in identifying price trend retracements, as well as in setting targets for support and resistance levels in many modern technical analysis studies.

Fibonacci Numbers

In 12th-century Italy, in the little town famous for the Leaning Tower—Pisa—a mathematician named Leonardo Fibonacci formulated a value for relationships between numbers that is used quite widely in forex technical analysis today. The origin of Fibonacci's work was actually a rediscovery of the same principles that were used to build the Great

Table 12.1 *The Fibonacci Numbers*
0, 1, 1, 2, 3, 5, 8, 13, 21, 34, 55, 89, 144, 233, 377, 610, etc.

Pyramid in Gizeh, Egypt. Table 12.1 shows what the medieval Fibonacci numbers look like.

If you did not notice, I will point out for you that there are recurring ratios within this Fibonacci series of numbers. For instance, if you add any two numbers together, the following number is equal to their sum. So the numbers 2 and 3, if added together equal the number following 3, which is 5. The numbers 21 and 34 when added together total the next number, 55.

Every fourth Fibonacci number is divisible by 3. Every fifth number is divisible by 5. Every sixth number is divisible by 8. These divisors are themselves in the Fibonacci sequence (3, 5, and 8). Interesting, you say? Yes, but these ratio relationships will prove to actually have important applications in currency analysis. Finding a universal mathematical source for predicting market price relationships may, at first blush, seem sort of like pulling a rabbit out of a hat.

Pulling a Rabbit from a Hat

Fibonacci's skills were not so much those of a magician as they were the skills of a motivated scientific historian. It seems that Fibonacci's work led him into an ancient scholar's riddle that posed a question about how to mathematically account for succeeding generations of rabbits (of all things). Fibonacci tackled the riddle and laid out a set of numerical ratios, based on the ability of succeeding generations of rabbits to multiply. I kid you not!

It goes like this: He started with one pair of woodland rabbits, represented by the numbers 0, 1. He postulated that a newly born pair of rabbits, a male and a female, if turned loose into the woods, and being rabbits, would mate at the age of one month (that is normal for these woodland creatures). In Fibonacci's mathematically oriented world, the question occurred to him, "How many pairs of rabbits will there be in one year? In five years?" Don't ask me why he was thinking about these things; perhaps Pisa had a dull social life. Nevertheless, from the standpoint of a

21st-century currency trader, it is a good thing he posed that question. For in his answers (see figure 12.1) lay some of the technical analyses that you are using today in your forex trading.

Assume that it takes one month's gestation for a new pair of rabbits to be born. The Fibonacci sequence began then with 0, 1, for his first pair. At the end of the first month, the pair mated; however, we still have to wait one month for the happy event. So at the end of month one, there is still only one pair, (0, 1) one. The second number "one" in this series represents the same pair of rabbits after one month. We note this to make sure that we understand that we are learning about a time component to these Fibonacci ratios. Bear in mind that a new pair is expected at the end of the next month, month two.

At the end of two months the first new pair is born, making a total of two pairs (0, 1, 1) two, one new pair now added to the original.

At the end of three months the original pair produces yet another pair, and there are now three pairs (0, 1, 1, 2) three. The newborn pair from the second month is old enough to mate and, sure enough, is now awaiting the arrival of its offspring the following month.

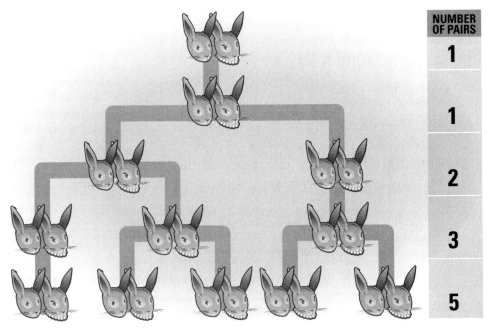

NUMBER OF PAIRS

1

1

2

3

5

Figure 12.1 *The Fibonacci numbers are represented by the single mathematical progression of a generation of rabbits.*

At the end of month four, the original pair continues in its productive ways and produces a new pair yet again, and the pair born two months earlier produces its first pair, creating a total of two new pairs for the growing woodland population, which now totals (0, 1, 1, 2, 3) five pairs.

So Fibonacci's listing of natural progression continues on, ad infinitum. This progression has been studied down through the ages since the 12th century and in due time was found to yield still other interesting applications that proved to have a use in today's modern technical analysis. For example, if you take any two adjacent values and divide each one by the sum of the two, you get a ratio of results that is constant. Take the numbers one and two. The sum of three divided by one is 33.3 percent. Let's follow this through in table 12.2.

The values in table 12.2 quickly converge to 38.2 percent and 61.8 percent. These two values, as it turns out, are basic numbers that identify retracement levels for support and resistance in currency market analysis. Measuring the percent retracement from a significant high or a significant low, based on those two values, is useful in establishing price targets and entry/exit signals for the technical analyst, especially in the Elliott Wave system.

Look at figure 12.2, which draws in the Fibonacci retracement targets for the British pound. In this case, the Fibonacci retracement values are shown as horizontal lines, but they can be displayed as arcs, fans, or vertical time lines as well. When the price touches each line in a downtrend retracement, you can expect to find support at that level.

Table 12.2

The First Number Divided by the Sum	The Second Number Divided by the Sum
1/3 = 33.3 percent	2/3 = 66 percent
2/5 = 40 percent	3/5 = 60 percent
3/8 = 37.5 percent	5/8 = 62.5 percent
5/13 = 38.5 percent	8/13 = 61.5 percent
8/21 = 38.1 percent	13/21 = 61.9 percent
13/34 = 38.2 percent	21/34 = 61.8 percent

Figure 12.2 *The horizontal lines are drawn at the Fibonacci retracement values.*

There is also a little used and, frankly, not very productive application of Fibonacci values called time zones. A time zone Fibonacci chart will show the time zone ratios drawn according to the Fibonacci format, starting from a pivot point, which is merely a significant price level indicating either a high or low price event that is then used as a starting point from which lines are drawn vertically according to a scale format using the Fibonacci values—that is, at 1 day, 3 days, 5 days, 8 days, and so on. Of course, they can be drawn on an hourly, weekly, or even yearly basis as well. On those dates, delineated by the time zone lines, significant highs or lows are expected. As the chart prices approach each vertical line, significant changes in the price action are expected to occur. Many analysts use this time application of Fibonacci numbers in combination with other signals.

There are some other interesting ratios developed by Fibonacci in table 12.3.

Progress in Technical Analysis

The work of the medieval Italian (Fibonacci) and the 19th-century American journalist (Charles Dow), in retrospect, seems to have coalesced into

Table 12.3 *Fibonacci Ratios*

0, 1, 1, 2, 3, 5, 8, 13, 21, 34, 53, 87, 144, etc.

Any number is 0.618 times the following number. Hence, 21 is 0.618 times the number 34. And 144 is 0.618 times 233.

$8 \times 0.618 = 3$	$13 \times 0.618 = 8$	$21 \times 0.618 = 13$	$34 \times 0.618 = 21$
$55 \times 0.618 = 34$	$89 \times 0.618 = 55$	$144 \times 0.618 = 89$	$233 \times 0.618 = 144$

Any number (in the Fibonnaci chain) is 1.618 times as great as the number before it. Hence, the number 34 is 1.618 times the number 21. And 144 is 1.618 times 89.

$1.618 \times 5 = 8$	$1.618 \times 8 = 13$	$1.618 \times 13 = 21$	$1.618 \times 21 = 34$
$1.618 \times 34 = 55$	$1.618 \times 55 = 89$	$1.618 \times 89 = 144$	$1.618 \times 144 = 233$

The reciprocal of 0.618 = 1.618. Hence, 1/0.618 =1.618.

A first number divided by its succeeding number is 0.618. Hence, 13 divided by 21 is 0.618.

$3/8 = 0.618$	$8/13 = 0.618$	$13/21 = 0.618$	$21/34 = 0.618$
$34/55 = 0.618$	$55/89 = 0.618$	$89/144 = 0.618$	$144/233 = 0.618$

the most comprehensive technical analysis system ever produced—the Elliott Wave Theory. The tide, wave, and ripple projections of market analysis produced by Charles Dow in 1897 morphed sometime during the next 40 years into wave patterns in an entirely different conceptual format produced by Ralph Elliott. Elliott was a 20th-century American accountant who, though he studied and admired Charles Dow, believed he could take Dow's theory a step further and improve on it. Indeed, there is an important difference between the two theories. For all its per-spicacity, the Dow Theory is, at base, a trend-following system. One can use it to identify trends *after* they are formed. In the case of Elliott's system, predictive qualities of technical analysis were introduced for the first time into market analysis, and the effort to crack the financial markets' "genetic code" of price movement took a giant leap forward.

Figure 12.3 shows what an Elliott Wave analysis looks like in the pattern chart. As you can see, in an advancing market, the basic cycle consists of eight waves. Five of the waves mark a price advance trend,

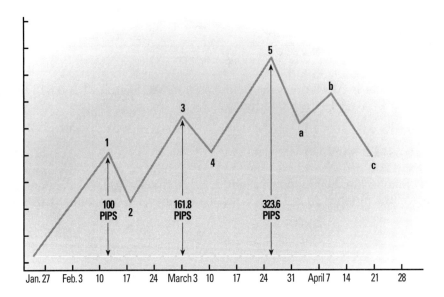

Figure 12.3 *The ratio relationship between Fibonacci numbers expressed as price values in this chart pattern.*

and the three following waves are part of a price trend correction. Those eight waves are the basic outline of the cycle on which the Elliott Wave Theory rests.

The Elliott Wave Theory

Ralph Elliott believed that Dow's concept of three trends, which, as we have said, were not originally supposed to discern price movements in markets so much as they were supposed to be broad indicators of the business environment, needed elaboration and could, with some re-working, find an application in market price analysis.

That is what Elliott created in the 1930s. He found prices to be not only cyclic but identifiable as patterns—also, more specifically, wave-like patterns that repeat themselves over and over again, from the smallest intraday scale, which he dubbed the sub-minuet and lowest degree cycle (on an hourly basis), to the grandest time scale, which covers price movements of up to 200 years, in what he called the Grand Supercycle. Regardless of the time frame, the basic cycle of price movements was the same—five waves in a major trend move, and three waves in a counter-trend direction.

So Elliott's revolutionary analysis asserts that market prices move in a five-wave pattern in the direction of the trend, followed by a three-wave pattern moving opposite the trend. The value of that, for forex traders, is the knowledge that all it takes to predict price levels is to identify where prices are in an Elliott Wave's current cycle. Simply put, which waves are prices riding at any given moment?

Look at figure 12.3 again; we find five numbered waves and three lettered waves. Waves 1, 3, and 5 are up moves, known in the Elliott Wave vernacular as "impulsive" waves, while waves 2 and 4 are short-term "corrective" price waves. The five numbered waves identify the predominant trend. But assume that wave 5 is to be followed by waves A, B, and C, which, in a bull market, are part of a shallow trend correction and which by their nature will offset only a fraction of the gains made in the first five-wave trend move.

The Fibonacci Influence

I said that the Elliott Wave system would incorporate the work of Leonardo Fibonacci into it. Can you guess where the Fibonacci influence is? You guessed it—well, at least part of it. The three-, five-, and

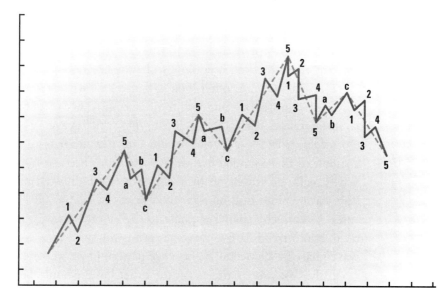

Figure 12.4 *The dotted line is a higher degree wave superimposed over the wave referenced in figure 12.3.*

eight-wave cycles are, of course, Fibonacci ratios. But there is more. The distance that the price peak of wave 3 reaches from the bottom of wave 1 is a ratio from Fibonacci's work. Also, the retracements of waves 2 and 4 reflect Fibonacci numbers. Fibonacci is indeed woven throughout the Elliott Wave system and is in many respects really its foundation.

Obviously, while the zigzags of the chart in figure 12.3 look something like many price charts, they do not seem to reflect every conceivable chart pattern. Elliott hypothesized that individual waves within a cycle will extend into mini-cycles, a subset if you will, of additional groups of eight waves. Figure 12.4 shows such a subgrouping.

The dotted line in figure 12.4 is the basic wave line of the same market shown previously in figure 12.3 but superimposed to show the subsets of extended waves within the basic wave cycle. Elliott identified a potential for nine different "degrees" of waves, where a new degree was defined in every subset of waves such as shown in figure 12.4. Such wave extensions can be developed so that their total wave count is a Fibonacci number, such as 34 or 144. Again, wave numbers 1, 3, and 5 are always the impulsive waves of Elliott's model, regardless of their incarnation in lower or higher degree cycles, while waves A through C are corrective.

We want to take a look at Elliott's use of Fibonacci ratios a little bit more, because with them, forex traders can set retracement and entry/exit targets for their own currency trading strategies. There can be both higher and lower "degrees" of waves in a particular cycle. What that means is that a five-wave price move could be part of a higher-degree numbered wave in a bull market. It could also be the lettered wave phase of a bear market price move. Another look at figure 12.4 will show two versions of a five-wave move, one in a bull trend and the other in a corrective trend. So in the Elliott Wave format, identifying which wave a price movement represents provides a critical insight into near-term price direction. For example, if the extended five-wave pattern our friendly trader has identified is really an extension of a higher-degree numbered impulsive wave (say wave 5) in a bull market, then prices will be headed lower as they enter the corrective, lettered phase of the Elliott Wave Cycle. Why? Well, recall that a trending five-wave pattern is followed by a corrective three-wave phase in the overall eight-wave pattern of a complete cycle.

If the five-wave pattern, on the other hand, should be an extension of one of the waves in the lettered phase (say, in wave C) of a bear market move, then prices may have more higher moves still.

Refer back to figure 12.3 for a moment, to see the simplest Elliott Wave price formation. There are a number of features to the construction of these price waves that, once identified, can anticipate future price levels based on Fibonacci ratios.

If we want to know where price wave 3 will peak, we use a Fibonacci ratio based on y/x = 1.618. These ratios are shown in figure 12.5. Elliott believed that there was a definite relationship, or ratio, between one wave's height as compared to another in any given cycle. So to set a price target for the peak of wave 3 (before we know prices will get there), let's take the length of wave 1 in price units, say 100 pips, and multiply that by 1.618, then add the total to the bottom of wave 1. So 1.618 × 100 pips yields 161.8 pips, which, when added to the bottom of wave 1, sets the peak of wave 3 and a price target in a bullish price environment of 161.8 pips.

If our friendly trader wants to know the price peak level in wave 5, he can turn to the Fibonacci ratios and multiply the known length of wave 1 by (2 × 1.618), which equals 3.236. With wave 1's price length known to be 100 pips, 3.236 × 100 pips yields 323.6 pips, which is added to the bottom of wave 1. We want to note that the bottom of wave 1 is also the start of this bullish trend cycle.

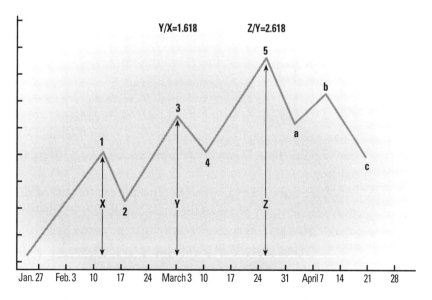

Figure 12.5 *The ratio used in Elliott Wave analysis. Fibonacci ratios between waves will yield price targets.*

Retracements similarly are identifiable in advance of market price action. The retracement of wave 2 from the peak at wave 1 is in the ratio of 0.618. A retracement of a longer wave, like wave 3 or 5 will be in the ratios of 1.618 or 2.618. So our friendly trader will look for support at those price ratios, all convertible from the Fibonacci numbers to market price values.

In the Elliott Wave scheme of things, each wave has distinctive characteristics that help a trader to make its identification. For example, we described how to determine whether a particular price wave is part of the 5th wave in a bull move, such as in figure 12.4, or whether it could be wave C in a corrective move on the end of a cycle. This is the difficult, but important, part of learning the Elliott Wave system: identifying waves correctly. An abundance of software providers will offer analysis and identification of Elliott Waves for forex traders. Their computer resources simplify and make clear any market's status in the Elliott Wave Cycle.

There are general definitions to follow that will help make the wave distinctions necessary for using Elliott Waves in forex markets easier.

Wave 1 can be identified by confirming it as a move coming out of the sideways price travel, typical of a basing or topping pattern. Wave 1s are typically shorter than the other impulsive waves in a cycle.

Wave 2 is, of course, a corrective price move and can retrace up to about two-thirds of the price moves in wave 1.

Wave 3 is expected to be longer than the first wave, of course. If wave 3 extends, then the two adjacent waves will stay simple (not extended).

Wave 4 is the second and final corrective price move in a bull trend and is not expected to fall below the peak of wave 1. If you find that what you thought to be a 3 wave does fall below wave 1's peak, then you should think about re-defining your wave pattern analysis in that market.

Wave 5 for forex markets is typically the longest of the three impulsive waves. In this phase of the cycle, oscillators will begin to show price weakness, signaling a retracement into the corrective phase of an Elliott Wave Cycle. These next three corrective waves, lettered A, B, and C, have characteristics as well.

Wave A shows increased volume as prices fall.

Wave B is a simple price bounce, but it gives traders a second chance to exit their long positions with a worthwhile profit.

Wave C must fall below the trough of wave A, and its price target on the downside can be established with a Fibonacci ratio. How? Multiply the price length of wave A by 0.618 and subtract the total from the top of the A wave. For instance, if the price decline in wave A was 50 pips, $0.618 \times 50 = 31$ pips. That sets a price retracement for wave C at 81 pips (50 + 31) from the start of the corrective phase, which was also the peak of wave 5. Elliott Wave analysis provides many traders with the edge they need to keep ahead of the curve in the fast-paced currency markets. Especially in the hyperbaric environment of technical analysis, it provides a framework for looking at where prices stand in a longer-term perspective. That is something even day traders can factor into their trading strategies to help them maximize profits.

Q & A

Question: What is the most important contribution that the Elliott Wave Theory makes for the currency trader who may not accept the whole theory?

Answer: That will, of course, be a subjective answer. Others will have their own ideas. I believe that the Elliott Wave system attempts to implement short-term trading strategies by keeping in mind big-picture dynamics that all technical analysts agree influence price movements in the currency markets. In my opinion, that kind of perspective needs to be in every trader's strategy arsenal.

13

A Close Look at Technical Analysis for Futures Markets

The exchange futures market offers an abundance of opportunities for the currency trader that are unique but that, at the same time, parallel the spot forex trading environment. Exchange futures parallel forex, of course, because every third month, at contract expiration, spot and forex prices converge. Also, no matter what time frame your trades are placed in, be you a day trader or a long-term position trader, you can make, dollar for dollar, the same profits out of the same position in futures as you do in forex.

Exchange futures markets do have their own unique aspects, of course, not shared by forex. For one thing, there exists a vibrant options market that is based on the underlying futures contract value. Using options, trades can be created that totally offset your risk in a futures position. For example, our friendly trader may initiate a long position in the USD/CHF. He can then immediately buy an option on the USD/CHF contract in the form of a deep, in-the-money put, whose Delta is 90. If the market crashes, his long put gains 90 percent of the amount of his long futures position's loss. He could—if he chooses, of course—create 100 percent security by selling two calls, each with a 50 Delta, so that a virtually equal and balanced offset occurs. So in this instance, if market prices fall, his calls gain an amount essentially equal to the loss from the long futures contract. Should the market rise, creating a profit in his futures contract, then his two short calls will, of course, essentially offset those gains.

Why would a trader do that? We will go into that in our next chapter on options. But we want to make the point now, that futures traders need to keep in mind the option "option," in their trading perspectives. As we have said before, minimizing losses is a big part of maximizing profits. Now let's move to some important technical analysis studies that are touted as working really well for futures markets.

In chapter 7, we looked closely at the Relative Strength Index as one example of an oscillator that does in fact do well in forex markets. So, yes, oscillators work just as well, and some may say even better, in exchange futures markets, and we want to describe a few momentum studies, in the form of oscillators, that futures traders will want to consider and maybe use in their own strategies.

The RSI oscillator uses 0 to 100, with the 70 and 30 lines as reference marks used to signal overbought and oversold price conditions. Occasionally, zero lines are also used in other oscillator applications, with moves above or below zero signaling a buy or sell implication.

Recall that an oscillator is a moving average that references price momentum and is typically expressed as a line plotted along the bottom of a chart with a range of values to indicate price direction. Momentum itself, of course, can on occasion be a trend-predictive chart study. The formula for momentum is $M = V - Vx$, where M is momentum, V is price levels today, and Vx is price levels x days ago. As you can see, the formula for the momentum indicator places a premium on recent prices. For instance, a currency whose price has just climbed to the mid-point area of its recent range may have a momentum value that is quite high due to that recent rise. That high momentum value will signal a trend rise in prices for the near term. So a currency may only be moving from a lower range to the mean of its mid-range and still exhibit a high momentum value, which is therefore one implication of further price increases. So having the momentum indicator at a trader's disposal incorporates a predictive component into his trading arsenal.

In its simplest terms, an oscillator compares today's closing price with the closing price a certain number of days prior to today. If this day's closing price is higher than, say, 14 days ago, then a positive value is generated. When prices are lower than they were 14 days ago, a lower value is generated. Although oscillators reflect price momentum, they are not very useful for existing momentum or clearly trending markets. They are more useful in sideways-moving markets, when traders need a signal for a price breakout due to imminent, momentum-induced price trend changes.

We want to note a few useful, general principles for applying oscillators in exchange futures markets. As we said, oscillators are all about momentum, so values in the top or bottom ranges imply price trend changes, due to overbought or oversold price conditions. In the case of a zero line application, ranges above or below zero generate those signals.

As a rule of thumb, then, oscillators are used most effectively when:

1. An extreme reading is presented.
2. The oscillator value suddenly goes to the opposite of price direction, creating a divergence.
3. The oscillator value crosses a signal line, implying a change in direction of price trends.

A Look at the Volume Oscillator

One of the purposes of this book is to evaluate trading systems and information based on the real world of trading. We are not here to produce an academic or theoretical treatise on how a Volume Oscillator, for instance, is supposed to work. We want traders to be realistically prepared to maximize profits and not have to confront theories with real-world circumstances that all of a sudden do not fit those theories, especially while using their at-risk money. We will start this chapter with a look at a technical analysis study called the Volume Oscillator. It is one of those studies that traders find promoted for our use in futures trading as a good currency price trend indicator but is also one that, as we will see, does not meet our "reality test" for applicability in currency futures trading.

The premise for using the Volume Oscillator is that increasing trader participation in an environment of rising prices should define a bullish trend. Conversely, more trading volume in a falling price environment should define a bearish trend. The theory also states that a decrease in trader participation in a falling price environment is actually bullish, because traders are not reinforcing the decline in prices. Simple enough. It is certainly hard to argue with the theory, at least in its general terms. But let's see where it falls down in our practicality test for currency futures trading.

Volume analysis posits that when you measure the buying and selling pressure of a market in terms of volume, then coordinate that with price movements, you will be able to identify trends in those prices. But as we will see, in practice, the Volume Oscillator runs into problems essentially due to the nature of exchange currency markets. Let's look at the Volume Oscillator as applied to currency futures and in the process deposit two important assets into our bank of understanding of currency trading and technical analysis.

The first asset we are going to derive from an evaluation of this study is to understand that we need to institutionalize into our strategy framework a simple principle: Discard unproductive charting formats as quickly as you can. The second asset we will acquire as traders from this evaluation of the Volume Oscillator is that the process of evaluation itself is an important and beneficial one, even if the outcome is to discard completely "this idea" or "that format."

What Is the Volume Oscillator?

The Volume Oscillator uses the difference between two moving averages of trade volume, one short term, the other somewhat slower, and together they identify whether the overall market price trend is decreasing or increasing. The formula is Volume Oscillator = fast exponential average volume – slow exponential average volume ($\times$ 100)/ slow exponential average volume.

As a charting study (see figure 13.1), if the oscillator line moves above zero, that indicates the short-term moving average has risen above its longer-term moving average, and so, ipso facto, the near-term volume trend is up. The question then becomes this: If we know the near-term volume trend is rising, compared to the long-term average, where does that get us?

Well, the proponents of the analysis assert that a rising volume of trades will indicate that the present price trend will continue, regardless of whether it is bullish or bearish. They also believe that when prices are rising along with volume, then the Volume Oscillator has in fact confirmed a bullish trend. A falling volume of trades in a falling price environment, perhaps counterintuitively, similarly means that, because traders are leaving a falling market, prices will return to a bullish trend in the near term. In other words, if the Volume Oscillator is below zero and the price trend heading lower is receiving no reinforcement from trading volume, prices will turn higher shortly. So the oscillator is used

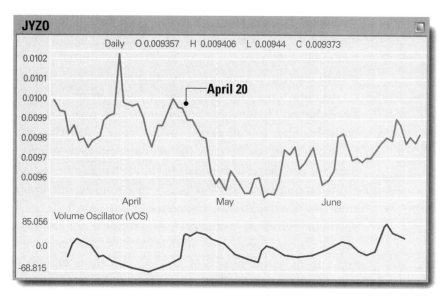

Figure 13.1 *This graph plots the Volume Oscillator beneath the yen. Note the late-March action where the VO signals declining volume in the face of a record bullish price breakout.*

in combination with prices, and a conclusion is reached about price trends.

That is where a breakdown in the applicability of the Volume Oscillator for currency markets occurs. Referring to figure 13.1, we see the Volume Oscillator falls below zero after the price trend begins rising on March 15. Thus by March 20, the Volume Oscillator signals a declining volume in a rising price market, which generates an implied bearish trend. In other words, it signals a short position. Unfortunately the market price rises and stays above its March 15 level for five weeks. The Volume Oscillator was recording declining volume in a rising-price environment, meaning that the Volume Oscillator simply missed a historic high in the USD/JPY.

So the Volume Oscillator, in my opinion, is one technical analysis study that does not work consistently enough for currency traders to rely on it in their strategy decisions.

Here is a second defect the volume study has with currency markets in general. Currency futures valuation will typically move substantively on thin volume trading days just as shown in the chart. The number of currency futures contracts extant in the Chicago Mercantile Exchange or the MidAmerican Exchange contract months on any given day are a minuscule fraction of the forex contracts traded worldwide. So volume is, in exchange futures environs, comparatively speaking, very light anyway. In addition, half a dozen separate contracts can be traded on any given currency, each with its own distinct and separate valuation, but, nevertheless, all are based on the same forex spot market price. The September, October, November, December, and March contracts all trade their own price values simultaneously, but they are all priced off the same underlying currency. So the futures markets are by their nature, comparatively at least, thinly traded markets, and that is indeed part of the exchange futures environment.

Referring back to figure 13.1 to complete our evaluation of this study, we see the Volume Oscillator around April 20 briefly move back above the zero line, just as prices are topping out and turning lower by over 400 ticks, a bearish trend that will continue for the balance of April and into the entire month of May. Here a rising volume (note the Volume Oscillator on April 20) is supporting the price decrease on April 20 (increasing volume should reinforce an existing price trend), implying correctly a strong price reversal, which actually does happen.

The Volume Oscillator subsequently meanders above and below zero for the next two months, not really providing any guidance for the bullish retracement that takes the yen from 0.9550 to 0.9850.

This illustration is representative of the misapplicability of the Volume Oscillator to currency futures markets. A 50-50 success ratio is essentially not a help to currency traders in the real world. To miss a historical high bull price trend so badly and then fail to adjust to another retracement really defines a technical indicator that currency traders are best off to ignore. Currency traders, being a hopeful bunch, are going to be pleased, however, by our next review of several more studies.

Price Oscillator

There is a Price Oscillator that, while measuring a different feature of futures markets, is very similar to the Volume Oscillator and produces a much more salutary result for currency traders. The Price Oscillator takes the numerical difference between two moving averages of a currency contract's price and displays their difference as an oscillator line. The value ranges can be either in percentages or points.

The format for the Price Oscillator actually very closely resembles the MACD, another good technical analysis study for currencies. The ambitions for the Price Oscillator are more modest than for the MACD, though, as its objective is merely to imply whether an existing trend will continue. In simple terms, a positive value in the oscillator line means the trend will continue, while a negative value implies a diminishment of the existing trend.

When the short-term moving average—for instance, a 12-day—rises above the slower moving average, say, the 26-day, the oscillator line will rise into the positive area, indicating pricing pressures that will confirm a bullish trend. Conversely, if the fast-moving average crosses below the 26-day moving average, the oscillator lines falls into negative territory and that implies a reduction in pricing pressure supporting the currency trend, signaling an end to the rising prices trend.

Figure 13.2 shows the Price Oscillator plotted against the yen futures. One can see that at the end of April, the Price Oscillator crosses below the zero line and moves into negative territory, anticipating the yen crash from its historic highs of earlier in the month. Notice, too, that unlike the Volume Oscillator, the Price Oscillator correctly signals a bullish retracement starting in June, as the line moves into positive territory at that time.

These two oscillators, Volume and Price, really confirm the need for traders to evaluate carefully and in real-time currency futures environments

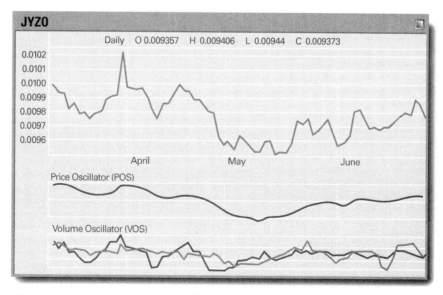

Figure 13.2 *The Price Oscillator study is an excellent predictive analysis for exchange futures currencies.*

the effectiveness of each and every technical analysis study available to them in their trading. Even though the Price Oscillator is a trend-following study, it is one of the more effective tools a technical analyst can use to anticipate price trend changes.

De-Trending Price Oscillator

One of the marvels of the high-tech age is that someone, somewhere is always coming up with a new wrinkle that adds a new dimension, however minor, that can prove useful to an online currency trader somewhere in the world. The Price De-Trender is one such wrinkle, minor to be sure but still an example of how being on the lookout for continuously improving one's use of technical analysis studies is sort of like the story of the little ant, taking one grain of sand at a time out of the earth until he successfully excavates a foundation for his underlying structure. In the meanwhile, because it is underground and structural rather than "superficial," no one guesses how well it is really serving him.

Somewhere along the line, someone saw a need for de-trending the Price Oscillator, basically because the longer trend cycles that oscillators use are actually made up of shorter-term components. The intent of the De-Trender is actually to purge out of the study long-term cycle information that has been input into the oscillator line. In fact, software programs are available that enable a trader to exclude all price cycle data longer than a specific duration from the Price Oscillator analysis of your markets.

For instance, since short-term price moves are always part of a longer-term cycle, they can be exposed, isolated, or highlighted by de-trending or purging the longer-term data from the study. What happens is that we find that the resulting oscillator provides a clearer short-term price pattern. Well, since it is obviously the short-term move a trader needs to be alert to, in order to initiate his trades in response to what markets are doing in real terms, some find the Price Oscillator De-Trender useful.

Bottom line is this: You can use the Price Oscillator chart study to generate signals based on the difference in moving averages that exclude those longer-term trends, leaving only price data of a shorter duration, such as less than 20 days. You punch in the data that you want to have de-trended out of your Price Oscillator analysis, and, voila, you get an oscillator line that is highly sensitive to short-term price movers and signals. Efforts to improve various oscillators are ceaseless, as you can see, and that is no more evident than in the next technical analysis study we will look at, "The Ultimate Oscillator," created by storied futures trader Larry Williams.

The Ultimate Oscillator

The "De-Trended" oscillator could really just as easily have been named the "De-Smoothed" oscillator. For the elimination of the longer cycle from one of the moving average inputs into the oscillator purges one of the smoothing benefits from having two moving averages. That is, smoothing an oscillator line comes from the addition of longer-term data, which moderates the noise of rapidly changing price data and seeks to avoid the fits and spurts of market price action from your signal generator.

So having considered de-trending one oscillator, now let us look at a different kind of oscillator that "adds" trend data and see what the ultimate smoothed trend indicator, Williams's Ultimate Oscillator, will do for currency traders. Williams's format captures three period cycles into one oscillator line value. He uses a short-, intermediate-, and long-term market cycle input in the form of weighted moving averages. The three oscillators are typically 7, 14, and 28 days ago. The resulting line moves between 0 percent and 100 percent.

The Williams Ultimate Oscillator needs to be used with close attention paid to its rules, if traders are to maximize its benefits. Let's look at an overview of how the Ultimate Oscillator should be interpreted and then go into some of the minutia of its applications, which can get very intricate.

Like other oscillators, divergence is one of the key applications for this study. A glance at figure 13.3 shows such a divergence for the yen futures during the month of May. As the yen price plunges over 700 ticks, from 1.0200 to 0.9500, and the market proceeds to make a series of lower lows around May 7 to 15, the oscillator rises first slightly, then more prominently.

We clearly have a divergence here, but what is the rule for trade signals from the Ultimate Oscillator? Well, has the oscillator been below 30? Here, the answer is yes. Does the oscillator then rise above its prior low made during this divergence? Once again, the answer is yes. Third question, the lower lows in the market are not supported by lower lows in oscillator values, right? Answer? Right. Then all three conditions have been met for a reinforcement of a bullish divergence signal. The Ultimate Oscillator gets even more specific, however. It will tell the trader his

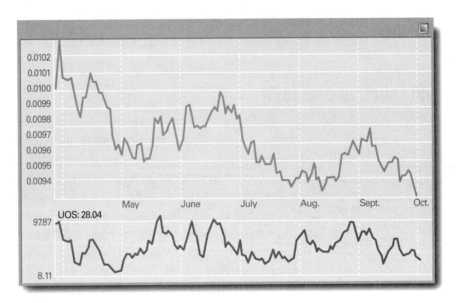

Figure 13.3 *Larry Williams's Ultimate Oscillator study. Note the bullish divergence in May.*

entry point. Here the entry point signal occurs precisely as the Ultimate Oscillator surpasses its previous high, in this case, at 0.9500—a buy.

There is what I call a subset of signal rules that backs up the first-tier set of rules for this technical analysis study. The rule says "sell" if the oscillator has been over 50 and there is a negative divergence, which is where the price rises, while the oscillator value decreases. A careful review of the chart in figure 13.3 shows that the yen makes a series of higher highs back above 0.9700 on May 20, while the oscillator values plunge from near 100 percent on May 20 to below 50 percent on May 30, as the market plunges. Table 13.1 shows the overview and subset of rules for trade generation from the Ultimate Oscillator.

Stochastics

Stock traders moving over into currency futures markets will very likely be familiar with, and perhaps even have used at one time or another, one of the most universally popular technical analysis studies in any financial market environment, the Stochastic indicators. George Lane, back in the 1960s, developed the system for trend-reversal signaling, and by the 1980s currency futures traders were among the many who began to

Table 13.1

Tier I Rule for Ultimate Oscillator Signal Generation—Bullish

Bullish divergence (buy)—currency price makes lower low, while the UO fails to match market with its own lower low.

1st Rule for Signal Generation (Enter a Long Position).   Buy on bullish divergence where the value of the oscillator falls below 30, as prices increase.

2nd Rule for Signal Generation.   When currency prices make lower lows but are not supported by the Ultimate Oscillator's lower low, then a buy signal is generated, provided the oscillator falls below 30 "during" the divergence, and the oscillator then rises past the high it made during the divergence.

3rd Rule for Signal Generation (Exit Point from Long Position).   The ensuing bullish trend can be supplanted, if the Ultimate Oscillator exceeds 70.

4th Rule for Signal Generation.   The ensuing bullish price rise can also be supplanted, if the Ultimate Oscillator runs over 50 and then dips below 45.

Tier I Rule for Ultimate Oscillator Signal Generation—Bearish

Bearish divergence (sell)—currency price makes a higher high, but the UO fails to match it with its own higher high.

1st Rule for Signal Generation (Enter a Short Position).   After prices reach a higher high, and while the Ultimate Oscillator fails to reach its higher high, then a sell signal is generated, so long as the Oscillator exceeds 50 during the bearish divergence.

2nd Rule for Signal Generation.   A short position is confirmed if the Oscillator falls below the lowest point it reached during this divergence.

3rd Rule for Signal Generation (Exit a Long Position).   The ensuing bearish trend can be supplanted, if the value of the Ultimate Oscillator exceeds 65.

4th Rule for Signal Generation.   The bearish trend can also be displaced if the value of the Ultimate Oscillator dips below 30.

adopt it as their own. As we said, since stock traders use Stochastics prolifically, we want to review what Stochastics is all about in application to the exchange futures market, and for those currency traders unfamiliar with George Lane's format, let's introduce it to them as well.

In our review of technical analysis thus far, we have looked at many formats, most of them bringing clear benefits to an online currency trader. None of them, however, really stand out as "the" signal marker that a currency trader will embrace and look upon as his single anchor for currency futures strategies, to the exclusion of all others. Put another way, we have found many studies that are very useful, but none that seem to dominate the field in terms of applicability to currency markets. Stochastics, based on its popularity, is certainly one of those analyses that has found a spot right up there at the top of most lists for first choice among chart studies.

Take a look at figure 13.4 to see what a Stochastics chart looks like. As you can see, it has two lines and, like all the others in this chapter, is an oscillator. That means, as usual, that our friend divergence plays a large part in the interpretation of the data generated in this format. Also, you can see that Stochastics has a range of values from 0 percent to 100 percent, typical of so many of the oscillator-based studies available for futures traders.

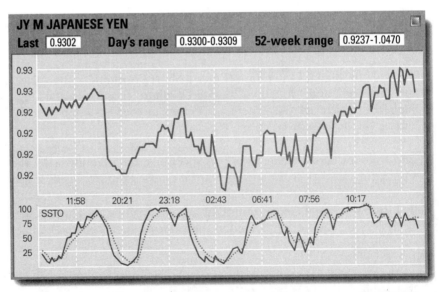

Figure 13.4 *The slow Stochastics analysis plotted beneath a yen futures chart comparing %K and %D.*

Reaching a Comfort Level with Stochastics

By now, everyone should be comfortable with the drill for following and using oscillator-based technical analysis studies. They are, on one level at least, all alike. Of course, number one, look for a divergence between prices and the signal lines, for implications of price retracement. Number two, look for the lines' entry into extreme ranges as a sign of overbought or oversold conditions. Number three, there are two lines that are used in the Stochastics format. Look, therefore, at the relationship between those two lines, where the faster line either crosses above or below the slower line, signaling either buying or selling opportunities.

Your comfort level with oscillator analysis is an important intangible for successfully integrating it into your trading strategy. Confidence in understanding the numbers behind a study facilitates reviewing complicated-looking charts, full of zigzags, dotted lines, and so forth. Traders achieving this kind of comfort level can glance at a chart; see the mish-mash of lines, bars, and so forth; and understand cognitively, and simply, what the study is saying, again, all at a glance.

What Stochastics Is All About

Well, what is a Stochastics? What is it all about, and what value does it have for online currency futures traders? The Stochastic Oscillator measures the position of a currency price in relation to its own recent trading range. To start our journey toward ultimately achieving the comfort level we all would like for a Stochastics chart, simply draw a line across a chart at the low point of a futures contract's price during the past 14 days. That line represents the low range of prices for a Stochastics chart study through that day. Next, draw a second line across the chart at a point equal to the highest price the futures contract has closed at in those past two weeks, and that line will represent the high range for the Stochastic format. Now then, to identify the oscillator's value on this day within its 14-day range, it is a simple matter to express the market price as a Stochastics percentage. Zero percent is the equivalent of the low of the range, and 100 percent is equal to the high of the last two weeks.

This exercise allows us to show the Stochastics study to be very simple and make it very comfortable for new users. Suppose that the low price during the past two weeks was 0.9500 on the Japanese yen futures

---

Table 13.2

$$\frac{\text{Today's close} - \text{low price in period } n}{\text{High price in period n} - \text{low price in period } n} \times 100$$

Or, substituting the values in the explanation above:

$$\text{(Fast Stoch.)} = \text{Raw K} = \frac{0.9600 - 0.9500}{0.9700 - 0.9500} \times 100$$

Or:

$$\frac{0.100}{0.200} \times 100 = 50\%$$

As you can see, the Raw K study produces a ratio of the difference in today's closing price with the lowest price in the past two weeks.

---

contract, while its two-week high price was 0.9700. A 50 percent Stochastic value would derive from a price of 0.9600. Simple enough! If the closing price this day was 0.9700, that would generate a 100 percent reading. A closing price of 0.9500 would produce a 0 percent Stochastic level.

Table 13.2 above describes the way the formula looks and works. The premise of the Stochastics analysis is that prices tend to close near the high end of their recent range whenever they are in an upward trend. Conversely, a bearish-trending market finds prices tending to close at the lower end of their recent range.

If George Lane's theory is right, then a downward-trending market would generate a downward-sloping oscillator line that, as it gets toward the low end of its 14-day range—say, around 20 to 30 percent—will, like all good oscillators, signal an oversold condition, and a "buy." We can understand the merit of such an "oversold" condition, as prices will ultimately begin to close *above* their lows for the day, signaling a pending price trend reversal, and that will be shown by the oscillator, with the Fast % K line beginning to cross above the % D line and reflecting the move up in closing prices. Glance at figure 13.4 to see what this scenario looks like on a Stochastics chart. This is a tick chart that finds the yen futures contract at a low at this point in the day, at about 5 A.M. Notice the heavy % K (fast) line just crossing above the % D line in an oversold range. Many traders feel that this feature of the study, which catches a price trend maturing, before an actual price reversal, makes George Lane's Stochastics analysis one of their most important tools for price evaluation.

Call up a Raw K Stochastic study from one of the many online charts available. Note that this signal is highly sensitive. We can see that the line is highly sensitive to price changes, and most traders will prefer a "slowed" Stochastic version, to avoid this kind of volatility from its use. The slowed Stochastics version mathematically uses three-day exponential smoothing factors to get a less volatile reading from the study. Some Stochastics provide a Raw K line overlaid on the prices in the chart body proper, which tend to make this chart somewhat too confused to read readily. A better format for Stochastics is the use of the two line signals plotted along the bottom of the chart. A smoothing is expressed in table 13.3.

Because we know the mathematical formulas for calculating the Stochastic, we can see that another premise of this study posits that price trends have a limit somewhere around 14 days, to a greater or lesser degree, at which time they can be expected to correct. We should interpret the framework for a Stochastic study along these lines: During any 14-day period, if closing prices rise above the 80 percent level of their past two-week range, that would signal an overbought condition. If prices, however, were to continue to rise (and close at their daily highs) for, let's say, another 14 days, then those traders who took the 80 percent value as a signal to short the market would still be waiting for a market decline long after the sell signal was generated.

Suppose that closing prices continue to rise a full 28 days beyond the initial 14-day period. Well, you can see that the general premise for the

---

Table 13.3

Slowed % K = 2/3 previous (raw) % K = 1/3 Raw Stochastic Value.

Slowed % D = 2/3 previous % D = 1/3 new % K

% K is the slowing of the Raw K data. % D is a slowing of the % K or, in other words, a double slowing of the Raw K numbers.

The Slow Stochastics (figure 13.4) shows the slower % K and % D values.

Stochastics is that 14 days (assuming you set the range to 14 days) is on average the length of a mature price trend, after which a correction is expected. The study, like all studies, can be adjusted by your software program to extend or reduce the default period, if you so choose. As in a few other technical analysis formats, very serious, intelligent traders began to experiment and, after using the analysis, came up with improvements, refinements, and new interpretations for its applicability to their own markets.

Interpreting the Stochastics

Identifying market retracements as they transition from one trend to the other is, of course, at the heart of profitable trading in currency futures markets—or any other market, for that matter. The Stochastics' contribution to identifying these transitions accounts for its popularity across so many markets. Stock traders, commodity traders, even bond traders use this study and for good reason.

The relative position of a currency's close to its 14-day range is, as we have said, at the heart of the analysis. The belief is that as a declining market gets close to the end of its current run, closing prices will shift from the lower end of their daily ranges toward the upper end, even though closing prices themselves may not have yet turned higher, on a day-to-day basis.

The % K oscillator line then will cross above the % D line and begin to move higher in advance of the price increase. Many traders will wait for this % K line crossing and upturn, although many others will simply use an 80 percent sector encroachment as a straight overbought signal. The 20 percent sector represents a straight oversold signal. The combination of the two—that is, a fast line crossing the slow line *and* entry into an extreme of the range—is obviously a stronger signal.

Remember, software programs permit traders to adjust their 14-day period to 9 days, or 20 days, or any other number they choose. The parameters that traders select, needless to say, affect the performance of the study, and, as we have indicated, it never hurts for a trader to experiment (without at-risk money, of course) and evaluate every study for applicability to his own individual market and trading style.

George Lane originally thought of divergence as the only useful signal generated by Stochastics and said so for many years. Lane thought that divergence between price and his % D line had to occur first, and then a crossing of the % K and % D lines, or an entry into an extreme top or bottom range could serve as a reinforcement for the diverging signal. Now it is generally accepted that although divergence in all oscillator-based studies is an important signal generator, it by no means needs to be the only one.

Generally speaking, today, while divergence is the most accepted indicator of a price change, the line crossings or a move into an overbought/oversold area on the chart are used quite often in various markets, often even without divergence.

Q & A

Question: Can you elaborate on the buy and sell signals that the two Stochastics lines offer a currency futures trader?

Answer: You bet I can. There are nine rules to keep in mind when using Stochastics.

1. Occasionally the % D line will lead the % K line in a change of direction. When that happens in combination with either divergence or a move into the overbought/oversold zones of their range, then a longer-term price retracement is implied.

2. When the % K line leads and crosses the % D line first, and then the % K line gives a head fake back toward the % D line, so long as % K does not intersect a second time but resumes its direction away from the slower line, that is taken as a confirmation of the original crossing signal.

3. Look for a scenario where both lines flatten out, as a precursor to a new, impending price retracement, very similar to a consolidation before a price breakout.

4. Use the % D line in confirming a divergence.

5. A bearish divergence signal is generated when the % D line is over 70 and the line creates two consecutive lower peaks, while prices continue moving higher.

6. Look for % K line crossing the slower % D line *after* the D line has changed direction. This crossing should take place to the right of any peak or trough in the slower D line.

7. If the % D line is in the extreme (20 percent or 80 percent) of its range, and prices make a move to retrace, if the % D line makes another move back toward the extreme of its range, then take that as an entry point in support of the *price retracement.*

8. Buy when either line falls below 20 and then rises above 20.

9. Sell when either line rises above 80 and then dips below 80.

CHAPTER

14

A Close Look at Technical Analysis for Currency Options

Readers will know by now that we believe currency exchange options are the most under-used and under-appreciated resource an online currency trader has at his disposal. So many traders, some unfamiliar with options, have been exposed to a lot of ink from assorted pundits who seem unequivocally arrayed against the idea of options. Their criticisms are employed to the effect that options represent a risky trading instrument, with seemingly unlimited loss potential, especially in currency markets. Their arguments are replete with horror stories of traders who have lost fortunes or were wiped out while holding option positions.

Forex OTC Options

Forex options are known as OTC, or over-the-counter options, and they are typically utilized by large corporate and institutional hedgers and traders. In forex, options positions that are used by large institutions to actually take physical delivery of cash now account for nearly 50 percent of the OTC trades, whereas the figure is likely less than 10 percent in exchange-traded options. Retail trading of forex options is quite minuscule. By retail is meant small, individual traders with accounts under $1 million. So we have chosen to highlight the exchange-traded format because of the many advantages it has, but also because of some of the deficiencies we do find in OTC options.

The absence of structure for the OTC option is one of the concerns we have insofar as small corporate and retail traders are concerned. For instance, with regard to issues of contract size and terms, these are often subject to negotiation between dealers and traders. Then, too, the credit risk is borne by the traders themselves, as opposed to an exchange clearinghouse format, which effectively eliminates credit concerns among the counterparties to trades. Liquidity and access to price information are also not as favorable in the forex OTC environment. So on balance, there are major comparative benefits for option traders who use the exchanges, and we encourage the exchange format. Also within the greater options-trading environment, we have taken note of the fact that the forex component has been the focus of some of the most flamboyant excesses in options. The recent collapse of one of London's oldest investment institutions comes to mind.

Here in the United States, stock option traders have a sort of dual relationship with their exchanges because such a large portion of the options bought or sold on the Dow and Nasdaq exchanges are employed as vehicles to actually acquire or sell share positions in the market, not unlike the larger hedge traders in forex. But at the same time, many other users of stock options also trade without any intention of actually converting their option for the underlying stock. These option traders look upon the option vehicle solely as a trading instrument. From their perspective, options are traded for their own value and appreciation, and their premiums' movement is what generates profits. This category of "option traders" never at any point considers exercising an option in order to acquire stock shares.

Balancing the Option Risk with Reward

For exchange currency traders, the vast majority see options as opportunities to create profits, through their role as a trading instrument, and not as a way to convert an option to a underlying currency contract. Like always, options have to be understood as involving substantial risk, every bit as much as trading forex or currency futures contracts do. But having said that, and understanding that currency markets by their nature involve risk, we want to understand more reasonably and in a more balanced way the role options can play as a risk-limiting and profit-maximizing vehicle. We hope that all traders take a look at the exchange environment and find ways to incorporate options into their own personal trading strategies. We want familiarity with exchange options to give rise to a more realistic perspective of their risk/reward profiles.

For instance, any *purchaser* of an exchange option is assuming a risk limited in amount to the premium he pays. A trader who purchases a call on a yen futures contract for a premium of 2.00 pays $2,500 for the right, but not the obligation, to purchase a futures contract on the yen at the strike price he chose when purchasing the option. He cannot lose more than that premium cost for his contract. So the risk is defined and limited up front.

That brings us to another benefit the exchange option provides for a currency trader, which, though generally known, deserves to be restated. Dollar for dollar, a currency option generates more profit, with *less* risk, than an outright currency futures contract.

Why? Well, let's say that on this day, the margin for a futures contract on the yen is $5,000. If the yen gains 100 ticks, the gain would be $1,250 on a long contract for our friendly futures trader. That is a risk capital ratio of $5,000/$1,250, or 400 percent.

For comparison in terms of risk and reward, let's say that another, number 2, friendly trader, chooses to purchase two in-the-money calls, each of which has a Delta value of 90. As the market gains 100 ticks, his call premium gains 90 percent of $1,250 or $1,125/call, for a total profit of $2,250. Each call's premium was 2.00 or $2,500 per call, for a total cost of $5,000, the same charge our futures contract trader had debited to his account for a single futures contract. So our friendly trader number 2 who opted to purchase these two options then had the same amount of capital at risk, $5,000, but profited by a factor of nearly two, compared to our friendly futures trader number 1, for a capital risk ratio of $5,000/$2,250, or only 222 percent, about half the 400 percent risk/reward ratio as the outright futures contract purchaser.

In addition, the option purchaser has limited risk—the amount of his premiums—whereas the futures contract purchaser has virtually unlimited theoretical risk, since the maximum losses could follow his contract down to zero. By comparison, then, the options trader has less risk, more profit, and a better risk/reward percentage for the same dollar investment as compared to a futures contract. It would be hard to make the case that an option in this instance was anything less than a risk-minimizing vehicle generating greater profit potential. In other words, the exchange currency option can be a great trading resource!

Remember, the option holder (purchaser) carries no obligation to purchase the underlying futures contract. Then, too, if the market falls, he could have a stop loss in place to limit any potential premium losses, further minimizing potential losses on his option. A purchased option gives him the right, *but not the obligation,* to buy a futures contract. Notice that in the previous example, the friendly option trader did not have to exercise his option in order to realize his profit-with-limited-risk benefit. The premium on his call gained 90 ticks at $12.50/tick. He off-set and liquidated his option at the higher premium price without exercising it into a futures position. So he traded his option position the same way a futures trader buys and sells his contracts, or an equity investor buys and sells his shares of stocks.

Now is a good time to remind traders that, unlike the equity or OTC forex markets, virtually all exchange currency options expire without being exercised. They are indeed bought and sold as trading instruments and are not considered by most exchange traders as "options to purchase" in the strictest sense of the term.

Just as currency traders, as a rule, do not intend to exercise their options into a futures position when they acquire or sell options, the counterparties to these option purchases, the option writers, depend on an option expiring unexercised and out-of-the-money to make their profit. When that happens, the option seller can keep the premiums he receives from the buyer, which is his sole profit.

Selling Options

Option writing has perhaps the worst reputation as a trading vehicle of any currency market resource one can think of. How many times have you heard the warning, "Stay away from those naked options"? Plenty, I would guess. But let's look at the option-selling concept and then deal with it in the real currency-trading world, so that we can use it cautiously when necessary, and prudently always, but opportunistically when the profit potential arises.

Unlike the call purchaser, who has no obligation to purchase an underlying futures contract, the option seller, or writer, as he is known, does in fact have an obligation to sell an underlying futures contract if his counterparty, the purchaser of his option, elects to use the rights he purchased and exercise his option. So in this relationship between an option purchaser and an option writer, the purchaser is the one with both limited liability and a real "option" to exercise or not. The choice is entirely his, and that is a benefit he received by paying a premium to the option writer.

Option Seller—More Risk?

So right off the bat, it would seem that the option seller, with his unlimited potential risk and his contractual obligation to deliver a futures contract (in the case of a call) upon exercise by the purchaser, is at a major disadvantage. His unlimited risk potential seems hardly fairly balanced by a profit potential that is limited, in that the "only" profit he can realize is the amount of the premium received for the option he has sold. So let's return to the previous example of our friendly trader number 2, but instead look at his trade from the standpoint of friendly trader number 3, an option seller, who receives $5,000 for his two in-the-money calls.

He is looking for the futures price to fall below the strike price of his sold option, in order to protect his short position as an option seller in this market. If the market rises against his position, he faces unlimited losses. Also, if the market falls but does not close below the strike price on his short call position, he loses every tick above the strike price the futures market remains at expiration, or at the time the call is liquidated by the purchaser. So it would seem that the naked option seller (naked, referring to the fact that he does not own a futures contract to deliver if called upon to, should his option be exercised) has not only unlimited risks but a preponderance of market probabilities stacked against him. Is that really true? Well, let's see if it is.

Limiting "Short" Option Losses

As a call seller, when the premiums rise, he is out money since he would have to buy the two calls back that he sold at a higher price. Or, he could have to buy two futures contracts at the higher prices if "called" by the option purchaser. But if our friendly trader number 3, who has sold two market options (in this case calls), sees the market heading higher, of course he can immediately offset his position and limit his losses, at any time. Conversely, suppose the market gives back some of its gains near the contract's expiration date and heads below the strike price. Well, the seller is home free, since if the contract is not exercised by the purchaser while the strike price was in-the-money, and the market stays below the call's strike price at expiration, it will have no intrinsic value, and at expiration, of course, no time value. It in fact would expire worthless, and the seller would bank his full $2,500 premium.

So if you intend to hold a short option to expiration, yes, there is the risk of losses if the option is in-the-money. And yes, the loss would increase the higher the futures market takes the underlying prices. But because most option sellers are prepared to buy back their options before expiration, an option writer can liquidate his position at a predetermined stop loss point, just as a trader would with any tradable asset. Then, too, if the market should go down 100 ticks, and our friendly trader number 3, who has sold two calls with 90 Deltas, discovers that the premiums on his short positions have lost 90 ticks, he could buy back those options in an offsetting trade and take those profits long before expiration. So, exchange option sellers view their role as traders and can profit as easily as any other trader holding a futures contract, a forex contract, or a share of stock. Exchange currency option traders, it turns out, have an abundance of resources that limit risk and maximize profits, so let's find out what they are.

In chapter 9, we looked at a bull call spread (see table 14.1 following) and noted that the loss risks from such a position in options were limited to the difference in premiums, regardless of how great the futures price moves against the position are. That is an important loss-minimizing feature to note when thinking about option spreads.

Figure 14.1 is a graph from a software program that uses the standard technical format for graphing options. This unique chart format resource is one option that traders should study and familiarize themselves with. For one thing, it identifies maximum loss potentials on a given spread, the maximum profit available from the spread for any given futures price level, and many other bits of information useful in a fast-paced market environment.

As you can see, the bull call spread will generate losses if prices fall from their current 0.9350 level. Note, though, how losses reach a maximum level and then flatten out, regardless of how far futures prices drop against the bull spread. This loss-minimizing feature of option spreads is well represented in this graph. The software program also

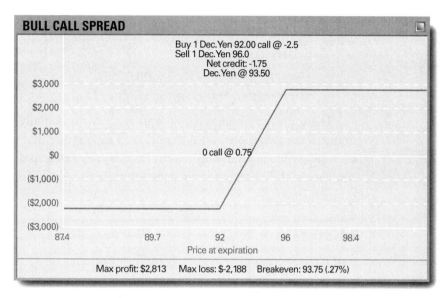

Figure 14.1   *A bull call spread. Note the abundance of information available through this format.*

identifies the break-even price level of 0.9375 for the spread, just slightly above current market prices. And, as you can see (because this is a bull spread), as prices rise, profits rise all the way up to the 0.9600 level, where they level off at $2,813 maximum gains for this option-spread position. You can also figure the cost to your account, in this case, 1.75 in premium value, or $2,187.50.

The bull call spread shown in table 14.1 is known as a debit spread. That means that the position represents a net debit or cost to the trader's account. Another feature of this bull call spread is that it is vertical, which means that the spread's strike prices ascend: One is always higher than the other. You can construct an option spread where the strike prices are equal, such as in table 14.2, and these are called horizontal spreads.

Table 14.1   *Underlying Futures Price at 0.9350*

Beginning Account Balance	$50,000.00
Buy December 92 call at 2.50	Account debit (–$3,125.00)
Sell December 96 call at 0.75	Account credit +$937.50
New Account Balance	$47,812.50

Table 14.2   *Underlying Futures Price at 0.9350*

Buy December 93 call	Buy December 93 put
	(Straddle)

There are an abundance of option spreads, actually upward of a hundred combinations, all different, and each structured so as to minimize risk while maximizing profits. Each is suited to a specific price environment in the underlying currency futures market. Table 14.3 lists over 60 such strategies.

Table 14.3

Call Back Spreads	Long Iron Condor
Call Ratio Spreads	Long Call Condor
Long Put Spread	Long Gut Iron Condor
Long Straddle	Long Call Christmas Tree
Long Strangle	Short Iron Albatross
Long Butterfly Call	Short Gut Iron Albatross
Long Butterfly Put	Short Gut Iron Butterfly
Long Combo	Long Put Synthetic
Short Fence (up)	Long Call Semi-Futures (up)
Short Fence (down)	Long Call Semi-Futures (down)
Short Put	Long Call Synthetic
Short Call	Long Put Semi-Futures (up)
Put Backspread	Long Put Semi-Futures (down)
Put Ratio Spread	Short Put Albatross
Long Gut Strangle	Short Put Christmas Tree
Long Call	Short Put Spread (up)
Short Call Albatross	Short Put Spread (down)
Short Call Butterfly	Short Semi-Futures (up)
Short Call Synthetic	Short Semi-Futures (down)
Short Strangle	Short Straddle

Short Condor Call	Long Semi-Futures (down)
Short Condor Gut Iron	Short Gut Strangle
Short Condor Put	Long Call Spread (down)
Short Condor Iron	Long Condor Put
Long Call Albatross	Long Call Spread (up)
Long Iron Albatross	Long Call Spread (down)
Long Gut Iron Albatross	Short Call Semi-Futures (down)
Short Combo	Short Call Semi-Futures Synthetic
Long Underlying	Long Butterfly Iron
Long Fence (up)	Long Albatross Put
Long Fence (down)	Long Butterfly Gut Iron
Long Semi-Futures (up)	Short Call Semi-Futures (down)

Bear Call Spreads

But now on to the bear call spread. This spread (shown in table 14.4) is vertical, but it turns out in this case to be a "credit" spread. A credit spread means the option leg that is sold takes in more for our friendly trader's account than his purchased call leg spends, and, as a result, the position produces a net credit to his account. Here, using an option spread to take a bearish position in the exchange futures market will at the same time greatly reduce risk for our friendly trader.

His short call, because it is in-the-money, has more value. He is buying a 96 call that has a higher strike price, which is out-of-the-money and less valuable. Table 14.4 shows the premiums and net credit of this position. This spread position will gain if the underlying futures price falls. So our friendly trader has invested in an option spread that gains as the futures market declines, hence, a "bear spread."

Summary of Features, Bear Spread

As you can see in table 14.4, the strike prices are vertical while the spread generates a credit to our friendly trader's account. It is bearish,

Table 14.4   *Underlying Futures Market at 0.9400*

Sold December 92 call at 2.50	$3,125	Balance to start	$50,000
Bought December 96 call at 1.50	$1,875	Credit from spread	$ 1,250
Difference (credit to account)	$1,250	New balance	$51,250

since its value as a spread will rise as the market falls. Our friendly trader is expecting the market to fall. But let's see what happens if the market price goes up, and then evaluate how well an option spread can minimize losses when the market goes against it.

Minimizing Losses

Say the market opens at 0.9400 and closes at 0.9500 in one day. The call premiums will each, of course, increase in value. The shorted, in-the-money call (strike price 92) has a handsome Delta of 80, while the long, out-of-the-money call has a lower Delta of 40. The 92 call gets an 80-tick increase from the futures move up, and so it has acquired a new premium value of 3.30. The 96 out-of-the-money call has a Delta of 40, which gives it a 40-tick increase, so its premium value is 1.90. Table 14.5 summarizes the day's action and its effect on the spread and the trader's account.

Let's say that the next day the prices continue going higher—say, to a total of 300 ticks—here is what the bear call spread will look like (table 14.6). Remember now, this option spread is designed to make money in a

Table 14.5   *Underlying Futures Price Opens at 0.9400 and Closes at 0.9500*

Sold December 92 call at 2.50	Now 3.30 ($4,125)	Today's loss ($4,125 − $3,125) = $1,000
Bought December 96 call at 1.50	Now 1.90 ($2,375)	Today's gain ($2,375 − $1,875) = $500
Reduction in account balance after one day	$500	

Table 14.6   *Underlying Futures Now at 0.9700*

Sold December 92 call at 2.50	Now 5.20 ($6,500)	Today's loss ($6,500 − $3,125) = $3,375
Bought December 96 call at 1.50	Now 3.10 ($3,875)	Today's gain ($3,875 − $1,875) = $2,000
Reduction in account balance after second day	$1,375	

falling market. But the market continues going higher. Also, remember that a loss on the first day's price action from a short "futures contract" trade would have been $1,250. The loss from the bear option spread by comparison was $500, or only 40 percent as great in the same market.

Because the 96 call was originally out-of-the-money, and the exchange futures market increase drove it in-the-money, its Delta has now increased from an original 40 value to its new value of 60. The second day's 200-tick increase in the futures price results, therefore, in a 120-tick pop for the premium. The 96 out-of-the-money call now has a premium value of 3.10. Notice that on the first day, the premium went up 40 ticks on a 100-tick increase in the futures price. But now on the second day, with its higher Delta, a day's 200-tick increase in the underlying futures market produces a larger "ratio" increase—not 80 ticks, but 120 ticks—in the premium value of this option. The call option's premium on this second day gained value at a 50 percent greater rate than in the first day's price action.

The 92 call started in-the-money but has now moved deeper in-the-money, and so its premium is now also increasing at a higher rate due to its new, higher Delta value of 95. That values the premium now at 5.20. Because our friendly trader was long on this option, this rise in the premium value of the 92 call represents the profit portion of this spread. That profit is eroded because of the gain in the short 96 call's premium, which our friendly trader has to now buy back at its higher premium value.

So, remember, in a 300-tick price up-move against the bearish spread, the losses were limited to $1,375. A short futures contract, by comparison, would have lost 300 ticks at $12.50/tick or $3,750, with additional, potentially unlimited losses in the event that the market had continued to rise. So an option spread, we can definitively conclude, does indeed *minimize losses.*

We should also keep in mind that if the market fell in support of our bearish option spread position, as soon as the spread gains reached the $1,250 level, our friendly trader would have liquidated his spread and banked his profits. Why? Well, the graph in figure 14.1 shows that there would be no advantage in waiting for the market to continue its bearish move, since the most profits available from the spread were $1,250. Also, liquidating the position preempts a possible market retracement, and the resulting diminishment of some of the gains made by the spread in a falling price environment.

Using Option Spreads to Maximize Profits

Because option valuations are based on contract futures prices, an options trader has to follow both markets in order to maximize his profit opportunities. But more opportunities are available for option spread traders. In figure 14.2, we see a 15-minute chart of a yen futures contract. On this day, our friendly trader is wearing an intraday trader's hat. On October 12, he initiates a bear spread position with the market opening at approximately 0.9400 on the Merc. He watches the futures price decline nearly 65 ticks in just one hour, in support of his bearish options spread position. His online data provider, as is rather typical for the options market, shows no trades printed for either of his options, the 92 and 96 calls, three hours into the trading day. Our friendly trader has no idea then of his spread's valuation. For an option trader, premium value uncertainty can be costly. Option traders quickly learn that confirming current premium values on particular options is not always that easy. In our friendly trader's case, however, his online broker does provide a phone help desk, and he calls in to get the quoted bids and asks on both call positions directly from the pits of the Chicago Mercantile Exchange. Almost immediately, he gets his quotes. The 92 call has a spread of 1.95 bid and 2.00 ask. Checking his records, he sees that he sold the 92 call for 2.50 in premiums. He can now buy it back at 2.00, a 50-tick profit. So he does.

Next, he reviews the bid/ask on his 96 call, and that spread is bid 1.20 and 1.25 ask. He bought the 96 call for 1.50, so he faces a 30-tick loss, should he elect to sell the option at the bid price. Seeing that he will net a 20-tick premiums profit on balance from the 65-tick price action this morning, he decides to offset both legs of his spread and bank his

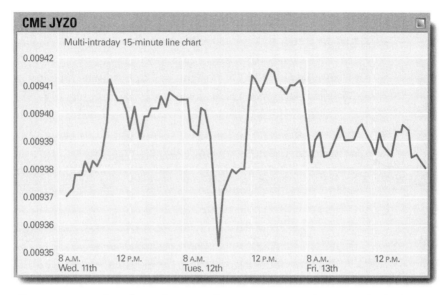

CME JYZO

Multi-intraday 15-minute line chart

0.00942
0.00941
0.00940
0.00939
0.00938
0.00937
0.00936
0.00935

8 A.M.   12 P.M.   8 A.M.   12 P.M.   8 A.M.   12 P.M.
Wed. 11th   Tues. 12th   Fri. 13th

Figure 14.2 *The chart for October 12. Notice the 65-tick decline at about 10 A.M. Stops on spread positions lock in gains and limit losses.*

profit. He enters two market orders through his online trading platform, gets a confirmation, and is ready for his next trade.

"Stopping" Even More Option Losses

Using options, as we have seen, positively restricts losses in exchange for limiting gains. In the volatile currency markets, that is not such a bad trade-off, especially for those of us who want to protect our resources with conservative investment strategies. This may be a surprise to many of you who have never thought of currency option trading as "loss-minimizing" or conservative. And there are, of course, many more ways to maximize profits, limit losses, and increase gains by using options.

Let's follow a bear spread in table 14.7 and suppose that our friendly trader had used market order stops and limits to further modify the risk/reward probabilities in his favor.

Table 14.7 *Underlying Futures Price at 0.9400*

Sold December 92 call at 2.50	Buy stop at 2.75
Bought December 96 call at 1.50	Sell stop at 1.30

Let's say that with a short 92 call that was instantly filled at 2.50, our friendly trader then placed a buy stop above the premium price. Remember, buy contingent orders above currency market prices must use a stop. So he places a buy stop at 2.75 on this call option, which he just sold earlier for 2.50. This stop restricts his losses to 25 basis points of premium value.

Next, he looks at his long 96 call, which was filled at 1.50. He elects to enter an online sell stop for it at a premium value of 1.30. Here, as well, a sell order below the market must be a stop format. Sell limit orders below market are not accepted. So this stop will restrict his losses to 20 bps on the premium value.

Now let's watch again figure 14.2, as the market plunges approximately 65 ticks at 10 A.M. in support of the bearish spread position our friendly trader has put in place for this market.

In terms of these stop orders, the first thing we notice is that the 92 short call goes on to book its gains; the stop loss will not come into play on it. The long call, however, has been stopped out at the 1.30 premium level. As the market fell, both call premiums dropped, and instead of falling all the way to 1.20 on the price move, as would be the case had the option been left with no protective stops, the premium value instead was filled by our friendly trader's sell stop order at 1.30, saving him 10 ticks, or $125, on this trade.

Of course, there are an abundance of applications for order entry or exit strategies, with stop orders, limit orders, order cancel orders, and so on. All of them should be evaluated for use with options, in order to further minimize your losses and maximize profits. We encourage all traders to develop fully their familiarity and comfort level with options, always with the caveat that currency trading involves risk and options improperly employed can *add* risk, rather than minimize it, so be careful!

The Long and Short of Strangles

One of the most popular option spread strategies is known as a "strangle." Besides being popular, this option strategy, for our purposes, is

Table 14.8 *Underlying Futures Price Now at 0.9335*

Sold December 92 call at 2.50	Now 2.10	Profit $500
Bought December 96 call at 1.50	Now 1.30 (stopped)	Loss $250

both interesting and informative, especially for online currency traders now considering options for the first time in the exchange futures markets. There is, as one might imagine, a long strangle and then there is a short strangle. The long strangle is a position that is constructed by purchasing a call and a put. Nothing much unusual about that. A long position always seems to involve a purchase. What is interesting is that the long, or purchased, strangle is used for an entirely different purpose than its cousin, the short strangle.

In the case of a purchased call and put in a strangle format, the trader expects a volatile market and wants to take a position in that market without having to know which way prices will break: higher or lower?

So, what is a strangle? Well, our friendly trader buys a call, out-of-the-money, and then a put, also out-of-the-money. Table 14.9 shows a typical long strangle. Once again, the futures price is at 0.9400. Notice that each option is out-of-the-money. A long strangle would be a purchased call at a strike price of 96 and a purchased put at 92; the two options selected are as equidistant from the market price as possible. Either way the market breaks, the supporting option gains value, and a profit for the trader. The other option loses value, with the maximum loss from this option equal to the premium paid for it. The use of stops is important to minimize the losses from the non-supporting option (meaning the one that loses value from the market price action).

The short strangle is used much more than the long version. In the more common short strangle incarnation, a out-of-the-money call and put are each sold as equidistant as possible from the current market price. Unlike the long strangle, the trader who uses a short strangle expects the market to be relatively stable, for the duration of the option contracts. Look at table 14.10, which shows a short strangle.

One of the instructive distinctions between the two is how the profits are made. In the case of a short strangle, if the market trades in a range between 0.9000 and 0.9800 for the duration of the contract, the trader keeps both

Table 14.9 *Underlying Futures at 0.9400*

Bought December 92 put at 1.45	$1,812.50
Bought December 96 call at 1.75	$2,187.50

Table 14.10   *Underlying Futures at 0.9400*

Sold December 98 call at 1.15	$1,437.50
Sold December 90 put at 0.85	$1,062.50

Table 14.11

Calendar Spread (Underlying Futures at 0.9500)
Sell November 95 call at 3.50
Buy January 95 call at 6.00

Ratio Call (Underlying Futures at 0.9500)
Buy 5 November 95 calls
Sell 10 November 100 calls

Butterfly (Underlying Futures at 0.9500)
Buy 1 November 90 call at 6.50
Sell 2 November 100 calls at 7.00
Buy 1 November 110 call at 2.00

premiums collected as his profit. If the market should trade briefly at, say, the 0.9810 level but retrace back below 0.9800 at expiration, then so long as the short call was not exercised, our friendly trader keeps both premiums. So there is considerable flexibility in this strategy; however, it must be employed within a trading range defined by the strike prices selected.

We will close this chapter on options with a few more examples from the list of 60-plus option strategies in table 14.4 (see table 14.11). Each is suited to a particular price environment, and each applies to a specific price expectation.

These, as with all option spreads, should be used with appropriate stop, limit, or other order restrictions.

Q & A

Question: Are there some general impressions you can share that will help traders incorporate options into their own personal trading strategies?

Answer: Yes, I want to list 10 rules, some that we have already discussed and a few that come from my personal experience in trading options.

1. Remember that when you purchase any exchange option, the most you can lose is the price you pay, which is to say, the premium.

2. Also, remember that purchasing an option exempts you from a margin requirement, insofar as the option itself is concerned.

3. If you elect to sell (or write) an option, the premium you receive is the most profit that you can realize from that option position.

4. Writing an option requires a margin debit against your account and will vary depending on the spread it is part of and the strike price.

5. Writing an option opens you up to a theoretically unlimited risk. So use it in a spread and/or with stops to limit your trading losses in unexpected market environments.

6. Options will lose the time value component of their premiums more rapidly as the contract expiration date approaches.

7. Liquidity may become an issue with options.

8. If the underlying futures are in a low-volatility environment, options may become slightly undervalued, offering buying opportunities.

9. Conversely, if the underlying futures contact is experiencing a high-volatility environment, option premiums may be overpriced and could offer a selling opportunity.

10. The vast majority of options expire worthless, so pay attention to expiration dates and liquidation plans in your trading strategies.

15

Integrating Fundamental Analysis with Technical Analysis

It is our intention in this chapter to promote a big-picture perspective of online currency trading in a way that integrates fundamental analysis with technical analysis. Indeed, we feel that the two are not just compatible, but that both are in fact vitally necessary ingredients for that final recipe that can produce a feast of successful trading strategies in our currency markets. We want traders to have a conceptual notion of the strengths and limitations of each. In currency markets, it is quite clear that fundamental forces determine currency prices. For starters, interest rate differentials are an accepted component of what drives capital flow from one currency to another. Selling a currency and buying a second lowers demand for currency number 1 and increases demand for currency number 2. Supply and demand rule, and no more so than in the currency forex and exchange markets.

It is the premise of this book that currency prices in the real world react to and are moved by a mix of factors, and not all of them fundamental. The mix is so varied, in fact, that it is imperative we take a practical approach to trading strategies. We need to incorporate elements from both technical and fundamental sources in order to be consistently successful and profitable.

In the real world of trading currencies, we see technical analysts' trading strategies foiled by, for example, the September 2000 coordinated intervention by the world's major central banks on behalf of the euro (and the European Central Bank), in their efforts to support a sagging new unified currency (see figure 15.1). Central bank intervention is something that

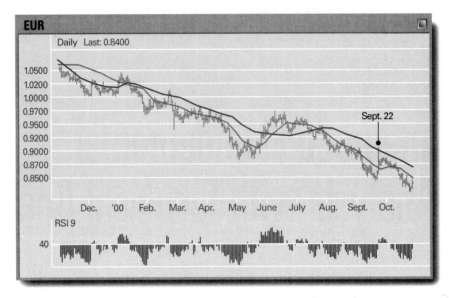

Figure 15.1 *Note the September 22, 2000, spike in the EUR/USD. On that date, the ECB led a coalition of other world central banks, including the United States Federal Reserve, the BoJ, and the Bank of England, among others, to buy euros. Notice the large move the currency made in response.*

fundamental traders take notice of and react to in their trading strategy framework but that technical analysts' studies do not recognize.

But technical analysis can point to *its* real-world impact on currency valuations and forecasts. In Japan, for instance, we see domestic exporters using substantial dollar accounts from their U.S.-based sales revenues, ready for repatriation into yen at explicit technical resistance levels for the USD/JPY. When their trades are executed, you can see their technical analysis–inspired trading actions reflected in the higher prices that support the yen. So technical analysis is a factor in currency markets, but so are fundamental forces. This division between fundamental traders and technicians revolves to a great extent around price forecasting, although price valuation distinctions are involved as well.

Remember the Stock Market?

There is hardly a currency trader one can meet who did not begin with an interest, as well as a participation, in the stock market. Chances are, today's average online currency trader very likely began his investment career experiences by studying some company's sales revenues, earnings per share, profits, sector growth, or similar data that we would think of today as an exercise in fundamental analysis. In financial markets, traders will find value in one asset, which in comparison to another seems less attractive, and so a trade is inspired. In many respects, it is just that simple. So that is what the fundamental trader likes to focus on, since an accumulation of these "value-based" trading decisions, market-wide, by thousands of investors will ultimately be reflected in prices.

In order to better introduce the fundamentalist's framework for trading currencies, we want to first go back and briefly revisit those halcyon days we spent as neophyte investors in stocks. We will in the process undertake to do an updated, more contemporary review of fundamental analysis as it is used in stock market applications. Then we will transition into a conceptual integration of fundamental analysis with the kind of technical studies we have already looked at in earlier chapters for currency market applications.

Fundamental Versus Technical?

From the very top level of institutional traders in our financial markets, all the way down to the smallest retail trader, a division—one might even call it a chasm—is evident. It suggests to us that in financial markets, there is a broad opinion that these two methods of price forecasting (and price valuation)—at least in the minds of many experienced and knowledgeable traders—are competitive and even in many respects mutually exclusive.

For example, Louis Rukeyser has a long-running television program, *Wall Street Week*, that features interviews with the top money managers from Wall Street and all around the globe. Rukeyser's *Wall Street Week* has a "technical market index" that features what Rukeyser euphemistically and somewhat playfully refers to as "elves": a panel of 10 technical analysts who try to forecast the Dow Jones stock market average 90 days out, using only their personal technical analysis strategies. The index looks at the mix of various forecasting models from each of the technicians and arrives at a consensus forecast of the Dow Jones price levels three months hence.

In reporting their week-by week-performance, Rukeyser barely disguises his sly skepticism, perhaps even a subtle disdain for technical analysis, in that he never seems to miss an opportunity to poke fun at the technicians. At the same time, he enthusiastically supports the fundamental analysis framework in both the market as a whole and for its use with individual stock selections in particular.

Famed market investor Warren Buffet is considered a practitioner of fundamental analysis, and he has many well-respected colleagues throughout the stock market environment who follow his style. As in any instance in which two sides exhibit passionate feelings on a subject, an abundance of different opinions will surface that describe this relationship between fundamental and technical analysis for valuing stock prices.

William O'Neil (chairman, *Investors' Business Daily*) says of these two contrasting trading disciplines, "From my experience, it's not an 'either-or' question. Rather than limiting yourself, you should consider both fundamental information about the internal strength of the company and the technical side of how a stock is actually performing in the market place." O'Neil says one way that he combines the two is by simply reading the volume charts on a stock he may be interested in. "Volume, or the number of shares a stock trades either per day or per week, is one of your big keys to interpreting supply and demand correctly. It's important to know if your stock is going up or down in price on greater, or less-than-normal volume. (Why?) This can be a signal that big institutions may be buying or selling your stock, which will impact the price either positively or negatively. Some time in the future, this critical data might save your neck."

Of all the various perspectives that try to describe the relationship between the fundamental trader and the technician, the one that I prefer, and one that is so very simple as well, can be summed up in these three little words: cause and effect.

Describing Some Differences

A fundamental trader studies and then implements his trading strategies based on those factors that "cause" stock prices to move higher or lower. He wants to establish, to his own satisfaction, a fair value for the price of a stock, and once that has been done, he can then compare it to the market price and make a determination as to whether this or that stock is overvalued, undervalued, or fairly valued at its current market price. One can see, then, that this fundamental framework becomes a forecasting tool as well.

A fundamental trader knows obviously that if he can establish the intrinsic value for an AOL share of stock, say, on the NASDAQ exchange, then it stands to reason that he will maximize his profit opportunities by making use of that knowledge. In other words, the fundamental trader expects that those AOL share prices will inevitably reach their "fair value." If fair value is above the current price, he will buy the stock, fully expecting the current price to rise and reach the fair value level identified in his study. If current prices exceed fair value, he can short it.

The technical analyst disagrees profoundly with this approach. The technician believes that fair value's price discovery comes directly from the efficiency of the marketplace. That is to say, the market price in itself is the only "true value" for any asset, be it stock share, bond, or currency. Since today's market price reflects all contemporaneously known information about the asset, that asset's price therefore reflects, as accurately as is humanly possible, fair value. For the technician, markets are used for just such asset valuation. For the fundamental trader, price discovery will be found in the intrinsic value of the underlying asset.

So there is indeed an apparent, diametrically opposed framework between how a fundamental trader sees price values and how a technician determines his valuations. They may in fact both get to the same, precise valuation levels on any given day for that AOL stock, despite the fact that their paths converged after starting from opposite points of the compass.

For our purposes, "we cannot get from here to there" without considering the pros and cons of each side. We want to explore both sides of some of the arguments in favor of each, since it will help us to evaluate the contributions they both have to offer. In the process we can reach the level of balance and knowledge that is needed to successfully trade in the online currency markets.

So, as you already might suspect, we are going to advocate that currency traders take the best elements from both frameworks and incorporate whatever each can contribute to their own personal judgment of what constitutes "fair market value" in a currency. One trader may choose elements from each that are completely different from another trader's mix of strategies, and that is all right. Trading for now remains an art, not a science, and that goes for both fundamental trading as well as technical analysis. Also, remember this: If all traders used the same exact strategies, it would be impossible to make markets. Everyone would try to be on the same side of a trade.

Fundamental Traders

We want to begin to resolve some of the differences between these two valuation/forecasting formats by reemphasizing probably the most important distinction between them: Technicians are not concerned with intrinsic value. However, as far as the fundamental trader is concerned, intrinsic value is a requirement that he needs to discern and identify through a process that has come to be known as "fundamental analysis." Fundamental traders live and die on the conviction that an asset, be it stock, bond, or currency, has its own intrinsic value. Since we are briefly referencing this part of our review in terms of stock valuations, let's look at the following table 15.1, which lists some of the fundamental factors that stock traders use for their determination of intrinsic shareholder value.

The Debate Goes on

A fallout has resulted from the debate between technicians and fundamental traders, which has unexpectedly crept into the larger financial world and taken center stage. There we find a schism in the United States appearing over the issue of the so-called "New Economy." Specifically,

Table 15.1

Today's Volume High, Low (Price)	Price/Sales
Last Tick	Quarterly Earnings (this)
52-Week High and Low	Quarterly Earnings (last)
PE Ratio	PE Ratio
Earnings/Share	Share Target Price
Dividend/Share Yield	Whisper Number
Estimated Growth Rate	Price/Book Value
Market Cap	Percent Owned by Institutions
Percent Owned by Insiders	Next Year's Earnings Estimate
Book Value	Year Ago Earnings
Revenue/Share	

the question being kicked around in financial markets all over the globe is, "Are the elevated stock price valuations in the United States representative of a new framework for valuing assets? Are the United States' historically high P/E ratios valid? Are they permanent and a result of the higher productivity that has been a companion of the Information Age technology revolution in America?" People ask, "Is the historic, nearly two-decade-long bull run in the U.S. stock market a confirmation of these higher stock valuations? Or are the U.S. markets, as the Federal Reserve chairman wondered aloud, way back in December 1996, an irrationally exuberant environment that has the profile of an asset bubble? Are the U.S. stock markets in fact in an asset bubble? A bubble environment that will inevitably burst like other asset bubbles have in the past?"

This New Economy debate in the United States has, in many respects, come to represent a point of departure of sorts for the two sides involved: fundamental traders versus technicians. In a big-picture sense, on the one side of the question are what might be termed the New Economy fundamentalists. They believe that the unprecedented, historic burst of growth in U.S. worker productivity that the United States experienced during the latter half of the 1990s has in fact driven asset valuations to higher levels and that these do represent fundamentally fair value. For them, the United States' high level of stock valuations is explained by the nation's higher productivity numbers.

Advocates for the New Economy at the same time argue that two, up until now generally accepted, economic indicators favored by technicians have been largely discredited by the value-based New Economy experiences of the late 1990s in the United States. The argument goes that now, in the face of the fundamental revaluation of assets occurring in America, these two relics from the past should be discarded.

What are these technician-friendly studies? One such old standard is NAIRU (non-accelerating inflation rate of unemployment), which fixes a theoretical limit on economic growth (generally in the 2 to 3 percent range), which, when exceeded, will generate higher unemployment.

Then, too, the Phillips Curve is another economic indicator that seemed to some to be technical in its character, and it has been roundly discredited by the New Economy growth numbers. The Phillips Curve prescribes that if unemployment falls below the 5 to $5\frac{1}{2}$ percent range, inflation will rear its feared and ugly head. The fundamental side responded with its claims that both of these "technical indicators," which do not support the new paradigm economy, were flawed, and a few of them scheduled regular burials for NAIRU and Phillips Curve analysis on more than one occasion, as U.S. economic growth proceeded to print out historic gains that consistently exceeded 4 percent for the last half of the 1990s, while inflation remained at surprisingly low levels. During this time, unemployment, too, fell below 4 percent, without generating inflation.

Whether these two studies actually are in fact technical analyses in their nature can be debated. But as far as the value trader is concerned, these studies are recalcitrant ideas that are the kind of misapplication of technical analysis that obstructed the New Economy juggernaut. The value trader feels that because certain opponents of the New Economy oftentimes defended these "old economy" theories, it offered an excellent vehicle for New Economy partisans to trounce upon the technical analysis fraternity. It was no surprise that many, Louis Rukeyser included, were early and unqualified proponents of the New Economy framework and at the same time pooh-poohed those who were encouraging the Federal Reserve to raise interest rates based on NAIRU and Phillips Curve models, in order to preempt an anticipated high-inflation level that supposedly lay just around the corner during the latter half of the 1990s in the United States. So the schism in the financial world over fundamental versus technical analysis is alive and well and being fueled by contemporary issues. Be that as it may, this competition of ideas is good for the trading world. Out of these debates will emerge a new and clearer understanding of how underlying assets are valued by markets, and that knowledge will engender successful trading.

We find that in the case of a stock price, the fundamental approach wants to determine "why" the share price is valued where it is. There is a value-based reason or explanation for everything in the fundamental trader's world. Learning those reasons opens up a whole new environment of opportunities for him, since considerable potential benefit awaits a fundamental analysis practitioner if he can get a handle on the structural forces that drive prices.

It is as if a research chemist has two options. He can understand and discover the formula by which a chemical reaction takes place, such as the one that permits aspirin to relieve a headache, for example. Or, he can focus on a regimen of technical analysis, where he would project what various combinations of chemicals should do, based on their past record in other situations that have led to beneficial results in pain relief, and use that kind of deductive model as a framework for his strategic studies.

From the fundamentalist's point of view, there is no choice. He wants to unlock the dynamic that causes and explains price valuation. The technician, on the other hand, could care less. He believes that whatever the causes for price valuation may be, they will be reflected in the stock or currency prices in the marketplace, and a future share price value can be forecast by using one or more of the various technical models that are in essence *deductive* like the chemists'. Once a trend is in place, the technician could care less what caused it.

Underlying the macro-analysis of fundamental studies in currency applications are a few basic theories that derive from supply and demand. Here they are.

Purchasing Power Parity Theory

Purchasing Power Parity is a theory from fundamental analysis positing that currency exchange rates will stabilize based on relative prices (purchasing power parity) between two countries. We can use as an example the relative prices for the same basket of goods produced in two respective countries. Let's say that a week's worth of food costs $100 in the United States. In Euroland (we will call Euroland a country, for our purposes), the same food basket for a week costs 125 euros (100/125 = 0.80). That means, according to the PPP Theory, one euro should be worth 80 U.S. cents. Why? Well, because that exchange rate would represent purchasing power parity between the two currencies. In fundamental analysis, then, this theory would define *fair value* as the exchange rate that achieves purchasing power parity between two currencies. Fundamental traders are supposed to use this analysis to target or forecast currency prices.

A number of marginal issues, however, make the PPP impractical in the real world, either as a way to establish currency valuations, such as in the euro/USD example we just stated, or in forecasting currency rates on any level.

The 30-percent decline in the euro/USD, beginning with its introduction in January 1999, through October 2000, is an excellent case in point. On that issue, for instance, a clear consensus has emerged that there were indeed fundamental reasons for the euro's decline during its inaugural two years' introduction into currency markets, but those elements do not support the PPP theory.

For example, capital flow out of Euroland, especially Germany, was immense and strong, not unlike the way a magnet seeks iron, as investors sought the enhanced returns available in the United States. It is, of course, an incontrovertible fact that capital flow impacts exchange rates.

Also, the performance of the U.S. stock market attracted what are known as "portfolio flows." These are distinct from, and in addition to capital flow driven by mergers and acquisitions, or interest rate differentials, and these portfolio investments streaming out of Euroland and into the United States were one more contributor to the skyrocketing American dollar valuations. A lot of euros were being sold for dollars, as U.S. bonds and stock account holders listed new, foreign ownership addresses.

Then, too, although Germany led Euroland with some important domestic structural reforms in this period, especially in the tax area, the euro-zone was still left with far more to do in its domestic pension and business regulation reforms, where many problems remain. As a consequence, Euroland seemed comparatively unattractive as a destination for the surging global capital investment flow available from a growing world economic environment. Euro-zone returns on capital investments remained weak in comparison with many other financial markets, especially the United States. The euro-zone was created, of course, in order to build a marketplace where its members could trade with each other and would not have to be sending their capital wealth and resources overseas. But their common market thesis is being trumped by the larger global economic environment, which is draining their capital investment resources and in the process leaving the euro under pressure.

One of the prerequisites for membership was a low inflation rate (2 percent maximum). As a result, euro-zone interest rates overall tended to be lower as compared to those in the United States. So with interest rate differentials also favoring the U.S. markets, investment capital found one more reason to want out of Euroland, and much of it made a beeline into other countries, especially the United States.

On balance, then, the PPP theory is an extremely oversimplified view of exchange rate valuations. Frankly, because it is so narrow and incomplete, it is just not reliable in the real trading world as a currency valuation theory.

One positive judgment that can be made about the Purchasing Power Parity study is how inflation differentials between currencies are routinely arbitraged through the exchange rate mechanism, along the lines of this theory. Because inflation erodes purchasing power, the costs for holding one currency versus another are in fact offset through the market's exchange rate price mechanism. So, as in the case of so many generalist theories for currency valuations and forecasting, there is always some benefit to be gleaned from them; you just have to scrutinize each theory carefully and closely enough to find out what the benefits are.

Trade Deficit Theory

The Trade Deficit Theory asserts what in today's world seems a rather odd-sounding proposition: that a *fairly valued* currency exchange rate will seek a level that tends toward balanced trading accounts. As a result, the Trade Deficit Theory postulates that if a nation's international trading account goes into a deficit, it will, of course, experience a draining of its currency reserves away from its borders. When those (let's say) U.S. dollars are sold for assorted domestic national currencies, the dollar's international value is reduced, thanks to basic laws of supply and demand. So the flow of capital out of a country will then in turn tend to depreciate the value of that currency. Hence, a country with a large trade deficit is supposed to have a weak currency.

According to this fundamental analysis theory, because the now depreciating currency is making U.S. exports cheaper, while its imports are becoming more dear, the result will be an increase in exports and a reduction in imports, thereby bringing the U.S. trade account deficit nearer a balance through the exchange rate mechanism.

The United States has, as we know, racked up increasing record (4.3 percent GDP) trade deficits throughout the '90s. As a result of these trade deficits, it is quite true that, as of the year 2000, approximately two-thirds of all U.S. dollars in circulation were held offshore, in foreign bank accounts. This outflow of capital did not, however, depreciate the value of the dollar, as the trade balance theory expected.

Just as with the PPP analysis, in the real world an abundance of extraneous factors come into play that simply destroys the Trade Deficit Theory. For instance, although the United States was printing ever-larger record trade and current account deficit numbers throughout its economic expansion during the 1990s, the dollar's global value was gaining strength, not only against the euro, but against virtually all the other world currencies as well (see figure 15.2). Also, strong Nasdaq and Dow Jones markets combined with the record productivity created by the United States' aggressive implementation of high-tech capital expenditures, and U.S. productivity gains surged year after year. These higher stock valuations and higher U.S. worker productivity attracted investors, who exploited asset appreciation from stocks and capital appreciation from the purchase of U.S. businesses.

Then, too, as we have noted, interest rates were higher in the United States than in most other countries. Japan, for instance, had a ZIRP, or zero interest rate policy, during that period (while U.S. Federal Funds rates varied from 4 percent to nearly 7 percent in the last half of the decade of the '90s). So once again, capital flow trumps Trade Deficit Theories, like the one just described, with the same dispatch that it brushed off the Purchasing Power Parity Theory.

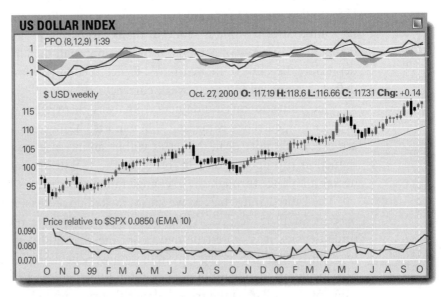

Figure 15.2 *This is the U.S. dollar index, a valuation chart for the U.S. dollar against major world currencies. Notice that beginning with the date of the inauguration of the euro (January 1, 1999), the dollar gained steadily.*

Interest Rate Parity Theory

The Interest Rate Parity Theory, like the other fundamental theories we have reviewed, is, similarly, sadly out of date, but it, too, can be useful to reference, since it reinforces the importance of testing valuation and forecasting theories against the real world and then adapting or discarding those theories that will not pass muster.

The theory states that if one country's interest rates are higher than another's, then there will be a corresponding currency exchange rate disparity. According to the theory, the currency with the lower rate will be undervalued and will start to appreciate versus the higher rate currency. In this case, if euro-zone interest rates are lower than U.S. rates (which they were in the 1990s), then the euro is supposed to gain strength against the dollar. Since we know that did not happen, we can conclude that this theory is simply a victim of the computer-driven, instant capital flow of today's floating exchange rate global environment. Currencies today, as we have seen, will flow to the country with the greatest total return on foreign investment. Interest rate differentials have been trumped by currency flows that are now growth driven.

So just as the technician-friendly Phillips Curve and NAIRU models have been called into question by the New Economy advocates, so, too, our evolving financial markets have made obsolete many of the theories involved in fundamental analysis. The big-picture lesson from this is that for both fundamental and technical analysis, no single approach can be expected to perform consistently or without modification from time to time and from market to market. Which leads us to the inevitable conclusion that in the real world of currency trading, both formats have something to contribute to every currency trader's arsenal of trading strategies, and a truly successful trading strategy needs to incorporate many different elements from varying sources.

Q & A

Question: What is your bottom-line advice for successfully integrating fundamental and technical analysis?

Answer: Well, first of all, I have to be a realist and acknowledge that there are strong advocates for both frameworks of trading strategies in the currency markets. My advice to dyed-in-the-wool fundamentalists, and dyed-in-the-wool technicians, is to open up your conceptual framework to take notice of the other side of the subject. One way to convince traders on each side of the debate to do this is by focusing on a simple example in a distinct major market move of how one could have helped the other. Look at the record of the USD/JPY and the BoJ interventions and how the market wins on every occasion. During the 12 months ending in April 2000, the BoJ intervened a dozen times to weaken its own currency, and during that time the yen *gained* from 130 to 105 yen. Table 15.2 records six of those attempts at controlling markets just during the summer of 1999, in which the BoJ spent over $30 billion for naught. Both sides of the debate missed opportunities in the summer of 1999 as the yen appreciated against the U.S. dollar, even as the BoJ intervened to weaken its currency.

Technicians who were not alert to the consistent signals of imminent BoJ interventions were simply left out of the loop on these major market-moving events during this period. For fundamental traders, a trend was entrenched in the USD/JPY during this period that heaven and earth could not prevent, so the trend-studying technical analysis side had its turn, but neither side seemed to have the whole picture that successful trading strives for.

So, you asked for my bottom-line judgment about how to integrate fundamental with technical analysis? All traders should adopt a conceptual framework that is grounded on this idea: *Markets rule, technical analysis guides.*

Table 15.2 *Record of BoJ Interventions to Weaken Its Currency in 1999*

June 10	dollar/yen	117.70 to 119.20	$1 billion
June 14	dollar/yen	118.10 to 120.90	$10 billion
June 18	euro/yen	122.80 to 125.80	$6 billion
June 21	dollar/yen	120.80 to 122.50	$8 billion
July 5	dollar/yen	121.00 to 122.50	$5 billion
July 15	dollar/yen	120.30 to 121.00	$1 billion

Over the past 30 years the yen has appreciated 200 percent versus the U.S. dollar.

Navigating a Course to Maximize Profits

CHAPTER

16

Some Rules of Trading and Order Entry

Imagine our friendly online trader in his chair, focusing on the console-monitor of his PC, reviewing the data referencing his trading positions. Occasionally, he inputs data to change his positions, as he moves closer to his intended destination—the profit target he has set for today's trading. He might, for a brief instant, appear to an observer like an apparition of a pilot at the controls of an Airbus jetliner, focused on his flight plan: inputting data through his console, changing course occasionally, reacting to the flight conditions he encounters, all interpreted through the framework of his flight plan. Actually, there are more similarities than mere appearances between an online currency trader and a pilot.

The pilot of an airplane is in an environment of managed risk. That is, he would, needless to say, be a lot safer on a couch in his living room than he is at 30,000 feet in a pressurized cabin flying 500 mph. This risk by the pilot, of course, is an assumed risk on his part. A risk that is assumed, one might add, not only willingly but expectantly. The pilot anticipates a benefit from his participation in this assumed risk. His reward, at least on one level, is that he expects to deliver scores of passengers to their destinations much faster than they could otherwise arrive by using any other mode of transport.

The online currency trader is in a very similar position to our airplane pilot. A currency trader assumes a risk in order to achieve *his* goal (financial gain), in a manner that he believes will lead to a maximum gain as compared to any other form of investment vehicle available to him.

The successful Airbus pilot implements skills from his cockpit seat that he could only have dreamed about as a novice flyer. The same is true for the online currency trader. The seat in front of a PC monitor that the online trader occupies is a sort of cockpit from which he also maneuvers in ways that seemed improbable to him when he dreamed about making his first trade.

Cockpit Skills

So there is a lot of personal development waiting out there for currency traders to take advantage of. The one thing standing between them and their personal goals of financial wealth is skills development.

The pilot has an abundance of many and varied resources that he calls on during the course of his flight: mathematics, engineering, navigation, and so many others. One of those resources is what I might term "cockpit" skills. Knowing how to maneuver and engage the various systems that make the plane's flight successful is a key part of the overall success of this pilot and his flight plan.

For the currency trader, too, there is a comparable skill requirement that is not too far removed from the pilot's cockpit skills, and this involves knowing the trading rules of his environment. For the trader, no less than a pilot, it is an important skills-development process to be able to sit in front of his computer terminal and perform at a high skill level that leads him to his ultimate destination, profits.

For currency traders, being facile in these "cockpit" skills means knowing how to execute trades. Another element is having in place, as part of your flight plan, the proper stop or limit orders that can be called on in an emergency situation, in order to protect your basic position. Becoming skilled in such areas as rules of trading and order entry contributes to the level of "cockpit" skills currency traders need so they can navigate through their own, sometimes difficult, airspace.

A Trader's "Flight Plan"

When a pilot encounters bad weather, he has to rely on his instrument training for a very human sort of reason. His natural sense of orientation is unreliable, and also inadequate, in an environment where he may be traveling through the sky at great speed, at high altitudes, with low visibility, and amid risk-heightened circumstances. In fact, the pilot's console instruments are what will permit him to achieve his big-picture objective of a safe landing and, most important, a route blueprinted from his flight plan.

The online currency trader can experience an environment where he, too, can find that his natural sense of orientation has become inadequate and unreliable for the circumstances he faces. For example, in a market where our friendly trader has a long position exposing $50,000 at risk, let's say the market falls rapidly and unexpectedly. Our friendly trader will need to have training and a frame of reference to work from that are not too dissimilar from a pilot's flight plan and instrument training. A trader's framework should enable him to react at his maximum skill level and to his greatest effect as he passes through difficult environments and on to a "safe landing."

In thinking about and even writing about currency trading, we naturally tend toward the abstract a little too much and away from the reality of those circumstances that define and limit the situations traders actually navigate in. For instance, no trader is ever able to sit in front of his PC terminal all day long, every day, week in and week out. So we can all relate to the trader who returns from a dentist's appointment or the store and checks his trade position status, only to discover the market has turned unexpectedly, all of a sudden and in the wrong way. He indeed is losing money, the way a pilot loses altitude, and that was not in his plan. In those circumstances, errors and misjudgments become not just possible but predictable, unless he has a framework (or flight plan) to anticipate and deal with such situations.

The emotional temptations that arise will inevitably produce the wrong decision and can obstruct the safe-landing outcome we all seek. Night-experienced pilots will tell you that the absence of a horizon is so disorienting that they have no choice but to rely on their cockpit instrumentation to stay on course. Watching a skilled pilot deal with the myriad of challenges that accompany his risk-laden environment points out very convincingly how preparation and skills can see you through any environmental risk, successfully.

In our previous chapters, we followed our friendly trader as he employed both fundamental and technical analysis with a number of different trades and in the context of different market environments. We have also discussed various aspects of his trading framework as we went along. Now let's flesh out some more of our friendly trader's basic trading framework, since that is where his "rules of trading" flow from. His framework will also dictate how his trader's "cockpit skills" will be employed. In other words, it lays out his "flight plan."

As we have seen, our friendly trader follows a single currency, the USD/JPY. He trades the pair in both the forex and futures/options markets. This issue of what market to involve yourself in is an important component of every trader's framework. How many currencies will you trade in and in how many markets? Put another way, what is the niche that you want to carve out for yourself? The answer will differ from one trader to the next, and that is fine. However, we would like to suggest a general principle that a trader should factor into his decision on this subject.

It is very difficult to coordinate your at-risk money in more than one currency and especially if you trade both forex and futures/options. That is not to say it is impossible. And that is not to say you cannot switch in and out from one currency to another, or from one market to another, if that is your preference. But simultaneous currency positions, in, for example, the EUR/USD and the USD/CHF, and in both the forex and exchange futures markets, require a level of experience and expertise that is best left to the very top traders, who could be described as "long in the tooth."

There are exceptions to every rule, and our proposed rule is not carved in granite. Multinational corporations may be in the position of having no choice but to hedge in multiple currencies. But for these hedgers who hold positions in multiple markets, it is likely to be somewhat more manageable, since they are not in and out of the markets as traders are.

Then, too, a trader may be in one currency and, although he is comfortable and doing well with it, he finds he wants to experiment in another currency market that he is familiar with. So long as he uses an appropriate stop loss and other reasonable precautions in his strategic plan, he can do that successfully.

Risk Capital

It is an oft-repeated caveat that one should only trade with capital that one can afford to lose. That is what is meant by risk capital, of course, and it is an important component of the framework a successful trader develops.

Once your pool of risk capital is quantified, it is your next requirement to establish what share of it you will put into any given trade or position. Here, a lot of varying theories are propounded. One often-heard axiom is that you should only put 10 percent of your risk capital into any one trade. I disagree with such rigid formulas.

It is quite reasonable that a trader with $100,000 to trade may initiate a position that, with his broker's margin requirement, may debit up to half of that against his account balance. Assuming he has limited his losses in an option spread position, or with stop losses, that is perfectly all right. Here is what I mean.

Our friendly trader has wired $100,000 into his online broker's office, opening an account with a new online broker for the first time. He is trading forex and he has adopted a strategy that uses tight stop losses in his 10-contract position. Table 16.1 reviews his first trading experience.

Note that his broker's margin requirements consumed a debit of 40 percent against his account balance when initiating this position. His

Table 16.1

USD/JPY market opens at 107.66.

Today's market forecast is short USD/JPY.

Sell 10 ($100,000) lots ATM.

Margin is 4 percent or $4,000/lot. Total margin = $40,000.

Fill comes in at 107.56.

Trader enters buy stop loss at 107.86.

Trader enters buy limit gain at 106.86.

Market rises, moving against trader's position; market now at 107.80.

Trader leaves stops in place.

Market rises through stop loss; market now at 108.01.

Trader's buy stop loss triggered and filled at 107.86.

Gross loss from trade = 30 pips/lot at $12.50/pip or $375 each lot.

Total losses from trade = $375 × 10 or $3,750.

$3,750 loss from an account balance of $100,000 represents something less than 4 percent loss from his margined account debit. This was not an unreasonable position to take. So, hard-and-fast rules on how much of your account to put at risk in any given trade are of limited value. What we recommend as a rule is that a trader identify, as a percentage of his account balance, the permissible losses that he wants to absorb from any given position and govern his at-risk money according to that formula. Generally, a 4 percent loss from your account balance is a reasonable position to put at risk in a single trade. So if a trader can put in stop losses that limit potential downside risk to about 4 percent of his account balance, even though margin requirements or risk of the position, especially in the case of options, may total up to half of his account balance, he is using a reasonable framework for day-to-day trading.

Our friendly trader has established three facets of his overall trading framework that we want to highlight. He had a trade "on" recently where he believed that the USD/JPY would appreciate strongly, and so he had then taken a bull position in that market. Three days later the market was languishing, trading in the narrowest of ranges, and his long forex position was going nowhere. He referenced, in a very indirect and even somewhat intangible way, a few touch points that he calls upon for dealing with these situations, and we want to highlight them here.

First, his perspective of this market as a bull market was not panning out. In fact, by day number three, he became convinced that this market was nondescript and could now go either way. He was in doubt, and so he marked one point in his mental checklist in favor of "closing out." When in doubt, close it out!

Second, he had lost his conviction and confidence that he still knew in a basic sense why he was still in this market. So there was strike two against continuing his position.

Third, he found himself *guessing* where and when the next breakout would go and at what time.

With that, he went to his online console and closed out his bullish forex position, taking a loss of $3,750 as it turned out.

In the life of every trader, these three "flight conditions" will occur more often than we would like to admit. Things seem to "pile on" and simply get the best of us. Markets rule, after all, and good traders have to be prepared to throw in the towel, so they can live to fly another day.

The market will, on many occasions, greet the online currency trader with the realization that not only was his assessment of market direction wrong, but he really has lost his bearings totally and is left without a conviction about where the market is going, except that he knows it is not doing anything that he can understand. In those instances, a trader has to call up from his framework a very simple response—when in doubt, close it out.

Here is a list of the components of our friendly trader's framework that we have looked at so far.

1. Establish a niche in currency trading that focuses your attention and risk capital to one currency.
2. Identify a maximum level of margin-denoted risk capital you will accept as a percentage of your account balance.
3. Create a "permissible loss" total as a percentage of your account balance.
4. Do not trade after realizing the market has told you that you have misjudged it.
5. Do not try to speculate on market tops or bottoms. If you do not feel confident about a market's trading characteristics, be prepared to exit.
6. When in doubt, close it out!

Fear and Greed; The Market Rules; No Margin Calls

Our friendly trader has often exhibited certain characteristics of his trading style that we would do well to emulate. For one thing, he does not let the traditional companions of every market, fear and greed, get a leverage into his framework or "cockpit skills." In other words, if he is ahead of the market in a position, he understands that the market will inevitably turn and begin to eat into those gains. He is quick to take profits. He is not looking for excuses to milk a little more out of winning positions.

On the losing end of trades, which in most cases is the majority for almost all traders, he does not marry his position. In other words, he is willing to accept the fact that he was wrong. He does not expect the market to learn from *him*. He exits early, and he resolves to learn from the market's price action. He believes in the principle that the markets rule.

When it comes to market tops or bottoms, he looks for thinning volume to reinforce the notion that a turn may be eminent. He does not expect the market to blow past every top and through every bottom. He knows the market is more likely to break trend, especially on declining volume, than it is to make new highs or lows.

One other intangible that our friendly trader incorporates into his trading framework: If he ever gets a margin call due to losses, he has predetermined to exit his trade and not meet the call for additional margin from his broker. A wise idea.

Currency Exchange "Flight Plans"

It has been our clear and express intention to portray the online currency exchanges as "trader friendly," and we certainly believe they are that. In our next chapter we will examine the leverage an ordinary retail trader can exert in a dispute with his broker, an exchange clearing member, or even the exchange itself.

The National Futures Association, in coordination with the Commodities Futures Trading Commission, has established a format for arbitrating and mediating claims against exchange members that do not have to rise to the standard of a violation of law. An assertion of *unfair treatment* from a trader against any member of the exchange can be enough to trigger an arbitration hearing.

We believe that by knowing the rules by which the game is played, a trader places himself at a distinct and meaningful advantage not only in comparison to the exchange, which creates the market trading environment he hopes to profit from, but as compared to the other traders he is actually competing against.

Globex2

The electronic currency exchange format at the Chicago Mercantile Exchange, as we know, is called Globex2. Over a dozen currencies trade electronically in that format. They are listed in table 16.2. Table 16.3 gives the specifications on these futures contracts.

Fills from Globex2's electronic trading are faster, and they eliminate totally the inconsistencies that are always a component of pit trading. The floor traders, and brokers trading for their own accounts, will occasionally withhold bids and asks based on their own discretion and trading circumstances. That is part of the open outcry trading environment. So, daytime pit trading will be slower and somewhat less consistent than

Table 16.2

Australian dollar	South African rand
Euro FX	Canadian dollar
New Zealand dollar	Mexican peso
Brazilian real	Swiss franc
French franc	Deutschemark
Russian ruble	E-Mini yen
British pound	E-Mini euro FX
Japanese yen	

Table 16.3

Currency	Contract Size	Electronic Trading Hours	Tick Value	Margin
AUD	100,000 Aus.	2:30 P.M. to 7:05 A.M.	$10.00	$1,000
BRL	100,000 real	2:30 P.M. to 7:05 A.M.	$10.00	$2,800
GBP	62,500 sterling	2:30 P.M. to 7:05 A.M.	$12.50	$1,000
CAD	100,000 Can.	2:30 P.M. to 7:05 A.M.	$10.00	$1,000
DEM	125,000 DM	2:30 P.M. to 7:05 A.M.	$12.50	$1,000
Euro FX	125,000 Euros	2:30 P.M. to 7:05 A.M.	$12.50	$3,200
FRF	500,000 francs	2:30 P.M. to 7:05 A.M.	$ 5.00	$1,300
JPY	12,500,000 yen	2:30 P.M. to 7:05 A.M.	$12.50	$3,000
MXP	500,000 pesos	2:30 P.M. to 7:05 A.M.	$12.50	$2,500
NZD	100,000 NZ dollar	2:30 P.M. to 7:05 A.M.	$10.00	$1,500
RUR	500,000 rubles	2:30 P.M. to 7:05 A.M.	$ 5.00	$3,000
CHF	125,000 S franc	2:30 P.M. to 7:05 A.M.	$12.50	$2,500
E-Mini yen	6,250,000 yen	2:30 P.M. to 7:05 A.M.	$ 6.25	$1,500
E-Mini Euro		2:30 P.M. to 7:05 A.M.	$ 6.25	$1,600

the electronically filled orders. Currently, the currencies that are traded on an electronic, 24-hour basis at the CME are the E-Mini yen and E-Mini Euro FX.

That means there are, in a sense, two markets at the Merc. There is the open outcry futures trading in the pits that takes place during the day between 7:20 A.M. and 2 P.M. That session will trade both futures and options contracts. Then, at 2:30, the Globex2 electronic session opens, with futures contracts trading electronically, until the next morning at 7:05. Options contracts are presently only liquid enough for trading in the day session, open outcry format at the CME.

If your online broker has the software capability to interface with the full range of Globex2 order formats, you can execute the order entries shown in table 16.4 electronically on the Globex2.

When placing orders online, you will have to follow the format, of course, set up by your online broker. It is important that you go over, orally, every abbreviation or initial used by your online broker in his trading platform. Do not assume, for instance, that OCO orders are available online, even when they are listed in the format and even if they are confirmed by a trade confirmation screen on your PC. The fine print of your broker relationship contract may reference that contingency orders are subject to change and must be confirmed by the broker prior to entry.

Also, confirm the broker's interpretation and meaning of well-known, common trading terms. For instance, does your online trading broker's trading system presume that a buy stop order will only be

Table 16.4

Market	Market on Open
Limit	Market on Close
Stop	Limit on Open
Stop Loss	Limit on Close
Stop Limit*	Stop on Open
Market if Touched	Stop Loss Close

*Stop limit orders are triggered by filled trades on Globex2, not by a best bid/offer, which is the protocol in the pits.

accepted when the stop price is above the market price? Have your broker confirm whether your sell stop order is only accepted by his system when the stop price is below the market price. Does your buy limit order have to be below market prices? Does your online platform accept a sell limit order only when the limit price is above the market? Believe me, even on the exchange, which has its own published rules on order entry, futures brokers apply individual interpretations to each order application. Make sure your broker and you are on the same page of the CME rule book. Let's look at what one broker's online order entry system requires in the way of order entry (table 16.5). This may not be the system of rules of your own online trading system. So check it out!

When you speak to the broker to clarify an order entry from your online platform, make sure you listen to *his* vernacular. As an example, suppose you have entered a limit order to buy 10 December futures contracts on the yen at 0.9480 or better. The system is not accepting your order, and you phone your broker to clear this buy order, before the market has passed your price target. He says, "I have your online order as, 'Buy 10 Japanese yen December contracts at 80 or better to open.'" Understand and accept his use of these terms. Typically, brokers will use a shorthand to refer to various parts of your order. In this instance, the broker refers to price targets by using only the last two digits. He also uses the term *open*, not to mean the market's opening but to confirm that you want to open a new position. Other brokers may not say "open" unless it refers to a trade to be executed at the market's opening trade. So learn your broker's language and use it precisely as he uses it.

Table 16.5 *Order Entry Rules by Our Broker*

Market price at 0.9500

Buy stop to enter/exit market 0.9520 (the buy stop price must be above market)

Sell stop to enter/exit market 0.9480 (the sell stop price must be below market)

Buy limit to enter/exit market 0.9480 (the buy limit price must be below market)

Sell limit to enter/exit market 0.9520 (the sell limit price must be above market)

Do not get into the habit of trying to make him accept your terms. The same is true for other aspects of online order communication.

Let's say you have entered a bull call option spread into your online format but want to add a contingency not available online. You call your broker on the phone and request a contingency addendum to the online option spread order you are about to enter. He asks for the order verbally, since your order has not been entered electronically as of yet. You will use the same vernacular you have heard him use. Thus, "I have a bull spread to open. Buy five December 93 calls for 3 and a quarter or better. Sell five December 95 calls for 1 and three-quarters with a one-quarter discretion." Our friendly trader has adopted his broker's vernacular precisely. He is asking his broker to enter the following online order with discretion:

Buy 5 December 93 call options at 3.25 (or better).

Sell 5 December 95 call options at 1.75 (or better).

The broker has received an order to open a new position by filling a bull call spread with the following discretion in his order execution. He must fill the two legs of this option spread at a total debit of no more than 1.50 to our friendly trader's account, with a variation of one-quarter point on either leg. That means our trader may receive the following fill, and it would be within the order parameters he just gave his broker:

Buy 5 December 93 calls at 3.25 or better (filled at 3.10).

Sell 5 December 95 calls at 1.75 or better (filled at 1.90).

As you can see, the fills each came in at different values than the order noted, but within the one-quarter point discretion allowed. The total debit of 1.20 points was better than the trader's entry numbers of 1.50, so the broker was able to fill the trader's order 0.30 ticks below his stated maximum debit on this fill. Not all online brokers, of course, will entertain discretionary contingencies to online trading.

Access to Institutional Market Data

Stock traders want to know about and factor into their trading frameworks the market price influence that money managers or other large institutional traders introduce into their equity markets. They know that if an institution with deep pockets buys into a stock, the volume and price will be moving higher. Conversely, if an institutional money manager pulls out of a stock, that price will be pressured lower. The stock that has no institutional attention or interest can languish at lower price levels indefinitely. A number of online resources have developed for stock traders to use that will help them keep track of money flow from these institutional investment houses.

In the world of personal online access to information, the currency trader, too, has resources available to him that are expanding each and every day, as much or more than the equity markets have experienced.

Commitment of Traders Report

Futures traders have a resource available to them from the CFTC that performs the same function for currency markets as is available for the stock markets. In the exchange futures and options worlds, there are big institutional traders whose positions move currency prices. The information collected by the Commodities Futures Trading Commission delineates these large institutional positions in a report that will "net out" the number of contracts the big traders have committed to on a day-by-day basis. These net long and net short position totals are available to the retail and smaller institutional trader from his online resource, the PC.

The CFTC requires exchange clearing merchants to list those trades involving major currencies that total 400 contracts or more on any given day. For minor currencies, the threshold is 100 contracts traded. These are known as the "reportable" trades, available in the Commitment of Traders weekly report. Any currency market that has 20 or more such traders is included in the CFTC report. Exchange clearing members are also required to classify those traders who take large positions as either hedge traders or speculators. So all of this information collected by the CFTC is kept current up to the preceding Tuesday of each week and is published every Friday on the Internet.

As a result, on Friday, online currency traders have information available for them that identifies what positions the large institutions have taken as late as Tuesday of that same week. That is an important resource, and traders should access this data and learn how to interpret and incorporate it into their trading "flight plans."

The Commitment of Traders report includes a calculation of open interest. Open interest, of course, is the total of the long and short contracts that have not as yet been offset. There will always be an equal balance of long and short positions. Why? Well, obviously for the buyer of a futures contract, there has to be someone who takes the short position of the trade.

The CFTC report does not leave out small-trade activity. But because small traders' positions are not required to be listed and recorded by clearing members of the exchange, their count is arrived at by adding together the Large Commercial (hedge) positions and the Large Speculators' positions, and that total is then subtracted from the total open interest number. So the three categories included in the COT report include all traders. In the currency world, an open interest value of 1000 means that there are 1,000 long contracts and 1,000 short contracts as of a specific date in a given currency.

That being the case, it might seem at first blush, then, that the data would be a wash or simply a lot of numbers that add up to an equal balance and of little value to a currency trader. Well, that would be wrong, and here is why.

Large Commercial (hedge) traders are those likely to hold a cash receivable or other cash asset whose value they want to protect against a market's exchange rate devaluation. If prices are slowly rising from a given level and these hedge traders want to protect their cash assets against lower prices, they will be selling more futures positions than buying. In that case, in a declining market the CFTC Commitment of Traders report will show, let's say, 30,000 long positions and 50,000 short positions. The Large Commercial position in the COT report will be net short – 20,000.

Traders are interested in knowing the status of the Large Commercial trader category because by comparing through graphs, the historical levels of the hedged Large Commercial trader category, an assessment can be made as to whether currency markets are overbought or oversold.

As we know, overbought and oversold conditions can be used to anticipate a market trend reversal. Should prices continue to trend higher over a given period, there will continue to be additional hedge-short selling. If prices reverse and trend lower, hedge traders will cease selling contracts and begin buying futures contracts to take advantage of the falling market price levels. So the net position of hedge traders will begin to reflect the opposite side of the falling general valuation of the markets. The COT might report a summary for that week of 42,000 long and 38,000 short or a net long of +4,000.

Institutional money managers that provide liquidity to the futures markets through arbitrage tend to be mostly large commercial banks and are also included in this category of Large Commercial traders alongside the hedge traders. In their case, if they have built a large net short position, it is because the market has trended higher, forcing them to accumulate more short positions as a result of their arbitrage strategies.

So the Large Commercial traders, be they hedge trader or arbitrageur, are selling as the market takes prices higher, or buying as the market takes prices lower. By graphing weekly net short and net long positions against historical highs and lows, traders can evaluate overbought and oversold market conditions and use those numbers to anticipate a trend breakout.

Online market services provide both graphing and signal generating studies based on the weekly COT reports. Figure 16.1 shows one such graph. We can tell you that it is a widely accepted judgment among currency traders, that Large Commercial traders listed in the report tend to be right in terms of market direction more than any other category of traders listed by the CFTC. This category is reputed to be right 67 percent of the time where there has been a trend-reversal signal generated.

The second category of large traders required to report to the CFTC is the group known as Large Speculators. The majority in this category seems to be made up of a group of Commodity Pool operators, who by their nature like to be trend-following traders—the exact opposite of the Large Commercial traders, who either hedge or arbitrage against the trend. So the Large Speculators take the opposite side of the trade from the Large Commercial group.

When the net position of the Large Commercial group begins to approach historic levels on either the long or the short side, chances increase that the Large Speculators group will change course and begin to follow the Large Commercial traders when market prices do change direction. When that happens, the market gains maximum leverage in favor of one price direction.

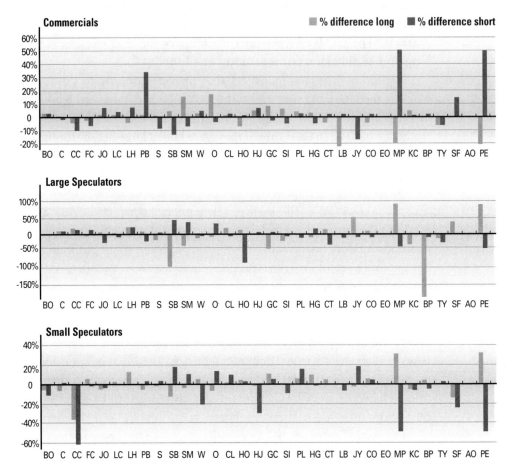

Figure 16.1   *The three graphs from the Commitment of Traders report reflects the following: Commercials are short the yen; Large Speculators are just barely short the yen; small retail traders are long the yen.*

Q & A

Question: What is the most effective use of the COT reports that I will now access from their Web site, *www.CFTC.gov?*

Answer: Knowing that two large blocks of institutional traders may be on one side of a market trend can give the retail trader an insight into the certainty and sustainability of a given market's momentum that cannot be equaled by any combination of technical studies.

CHAPTER

17

Watchword—Be Careful!

The competition in today's online currency trading environment is fierce. It is keen not only for traders but for brokers as well. For many brokers, trying to win customers for their firms consumes much of their interest and, on occasion, their time. All traders have, from time to time, run into a broker who "promises the sky" to them. We may hear brokers' assurances that certain types of orders are accepted by their firm, only to find out later that this is not the case. Other brokers may promise that Greek option values like Delta and Theta are available to their firms' clients; yet we may realize, only after opening an account, that the broker makes the calculations "in his head." There are a myriad of disappointments and downright, if minor, deceptions that virtually every trader has heard of or experienced for himself along the way. So, knowing how to head off these "disappointments" in advance will be based largely on a trader's own experiences and his knowledge of the business.

There is, however, an after-the-fact venue available to currency traders that few know about in as much detail as they should, and we will remedy that ignorance later in this chapter. Knowing what resources are available to deal with errors or even the occasional mischief on the part of that small fraction of currency dealers or brokers who bend the rules, helps a currency trader to more correctly frame the trading environment he is exposed to and, one might even say, the currency environment he is at risk in.

Keeping All Lines of Communication Open

Currency traders place substantial sums of their money in jeopardy by trading forex or exchange futures contracts. The one error that can be most painful to them, and potentially the most expensive, is an error either by the trader himself or by his online broker that results in account losses. We should not forget that even when trading online, communication has to exist between the trader and someone at the broker's office to address issues that normally come up in everyone's trading experience.

For instance, because online traders rely on the Internet, there is always a possibility that Internet server problems will prevent them from accessing their account and placing a trade at the time they absolutely counted on for a trade execution. So having a phone line of communication and a fee arrangement that enables a trader to switch to a broker-assisted relationship when necessary is an important backstop to have in place at the start of an online relationship with a broker, and *before* a problem surfaces.

Then, too, online broker execution systems themselves have the potential to create errors. For instance, the margin charged to your account may be badly overstated, limiting your ability to place the quantity of trades you need. Or it may be understated, causing you to get a corrective margin call unexpectedly. If margin issues occur, your broker should make good on an adjustment to your tradable account balance.

Worse than margin issues, your stop or limit order may on occasion simply be missed in an online order execution. That requires a degree of personal responsibility that can test some brokers' professional standards, depending on the circumstances and your losses involved. Other errors of various kinds will manifest themselves in ways and at times that are completely unpredictable, and always, it seems, at the worst possible times. We have to be alert for ways not only to catch these mistakes but to quickly communicate and resolve them with our brokers.

Dealing with Errors

One online trader entered a market entry limit order to buy five EUR/USD forex contracts at 0.8500 with the market trading at 0.8550. His order came back filled at 0.8550. In a situation like that, a trader asks himself first, "Did I enter the order wrong?" In this case, our trader can confirm whether it was he who erred or not, because he makes screen prints and saves his order entries at the time he enters them from his trading platform, keeping a record of them until they are not only confirmed but filled and subsequently closed out. Remember, when you press the "enter" key on your online platform, *your* record disappears, and what you then have to rely on are your broker's records.

Procedures like this, where an online trader takes care to print out and save his orders from the trading platform's Web screen, and then also keeps his end-of-day closing account statements, are two useful safeguards we recommend that all traders use. A paper trail is sometimes the only thing that stands between you and substantial unearned losses due to system or broker error.

In the previous instance, our friendly trader was on the phone immediately, calling his broker, and was able to get the erroneous fill removed from his account. Usually, in such cases, the broker will admit his error, but one cannot always depend on someone else fixing *his* mistakes when it is *your* money at risk. Be watchful!

Another potential slipup is to have the wrong (existing) position liquidated on an exit order. Let's say that a trader-acquaintance of ours has accumulated a long forex position of five contracts on the EUR/USD. He purchased one contract each day for one week, as the market steadily moved higher. Now on Monday of the new week, he enters an exit sell order for three EUR/USD contracts, in order to offset and take some profits from the position, even as the market is still trending up. The very next day, as he accesses his account statement on the Web screen, he finds that the broker sold three contracts all right, but they were the wrong three. His broker, of course, should sell the first three contacts purchased, following the first-in, first-out rule. Look at tables 17.1 and 17.2 and note the cost from this broker's error.

Because the broker should have liquidated the three earlier trades (those placed first), instead of the three latest trades, our friendly trader suffered a substantial loss from this broker error. Table 17.1 shows what account summary our trader discovered on the day following his order to liquidate three positions.

After reviewing his account statement summary, our friendly trader got on the phone immediately and, in calling the error to his broker's attention, demanded an adjustment to his account summary's balance so

Table 17.1

Trade No. 1	9/23/00	Bought 1 EUR/USD contract	Filled at 108.55
Trade No. 2	9/24/00	Bought 1 EUR/USD contract	Filled at 108.99
Trade No. 3	9/25/00	Bought 1 EUR/USD contract	Filled at 109.55
Trade No. 4	9/26/00	Bought 1 EUR/USD contract	Filled at 110.11
Trade No. 5	9/27/00	Bought 1 EUR/USD contract	Filled at 110.50
	9/30/00	Sell Order 3 EUR/USD contracts	Filled at 110.75

His Account Summary Statement on 10/1/00 Reads:

Trade No. 5	9/27/00	Bought 1 EUR/USD	Filled at 110.50	Sold at 110.75	Profit: 25 pips
Trade No. 4	9/26/00	Bought 1 EUR/USD	Filled at 110.11	Sold at 110.75	Profit: 64 pips
Trade No. 3	9/25/00	Bought 1 EUR/USD	Filled at 109.55	Sold at 110.75	Profit: 120 pips

Total Gain: 209 pips

209 pips showed a gross profit on these transactions of $2,612.50.

it would reflect the correct liquidation values from his position. The broker, of course, saw the error and made the adjustment to his client's account that same day. This was a systems error by the broker's online trading format, and he made the necessary corrections immediately.

Regulated Forex (by the Futures Commission?)

One of the image problems that the broader forex industry has suffered from has been a perception generated by the occasional bad press story that highlights the mischief that will occur among a small minority of

Table 17.2

Trade No. 1	9/23/00	Bought 1 EUR/USD	Filled at 108.55	Sold at 110.75	Profit: 220 pips
Trade No. 2	9/24/00	Bought 1 EUR/USD	Filled at 108.99	Sold at 110.75	Profit: 176 pips
Trade No. 3	9/25/00	Bought 1 EUR/USD	Filled at 109.55	Sold at 110.75	Profit: 120 pips

Total Gain: 516 pips

516 pips showed a gross profit on these transactions of $6,450.

This system error cost our friendly trader $6,450 – $2,612.50 = $3,837.50.

forex brokers or dealers. Now, because for the first time a U.S.-based forex dealer has applied to and been accepted for membership in the National Futures Association and has also registered with the Commodities Futures Trading Commission, these stories may become a thing of the past.

This forex dealer was the first, in what is hoped will be a new trend that sees all U.S. forex dealers registering with the CFTC. In addition, of course, in order to be "regulated," forex dealers will also need to affiliate with the National Futures Association. There is a possibility that your U.S.-based forex dealer may be considering registration and affiliation with the NFA. You should ask him if he has joined yet. Futures traders already benefit from the considerable protections that this NFA self-regulatory body offers them.

Because this industry's self-regulatory body is so respected, we want to spend a little time explaining how futures traders and, as we have said, those customers of forex dealers who affiliate with the NFA, can protect themselves against errors or even mischief from brokers in the currency markets. I dare say, few traders, however, are as yet familiar with the extent and breadth of protections available to them through this venue. So, because these safeguards now reach into the forex trading world, as well as into futures and options exchange trading, we want to explore this institutional "hazard insurance" that is out there for traders to take advantage of.

As you recall from chapter 4, virtually anybody associated with exchange futures trading, on nearly all levels, must register and submit to supervision and accreditation by the CFTC and the NFA. Associated persons, introducing brokers, floor traders, floor brokers, futures clearing members, and others *must* join the NFA.

Joining the NFA is not like joining a fraternity. It has legal and binding restrictions through its dispute settlement processes, with penalties that can result in fines or expulsion from the industry for any members involved in the currency trade who are judged guilty of violating rules and practices laid down by the NFA. A broker or floor trader, for instance, who does not pay a fine imposed as a result of a complaint filed against him could be expelled from the futures industry for not obeying these NFA orders resulting from arbitration. So now let's look at a futures trader who goes through an arbitration process with the NFA, as she files a complaint based on an alleged error by the broker's handling of her account in a trade dispute.

On November 4, our friendly trader enters an online order to buy 5 December yen futures contracts at the market. She gets a fill at 0.9233. The next morning her online account balance summary correctly shows the position as an open trade. Three days later, she enters an order to liquidate those five long December yen contracts, which she sells and obtains a fill at 0.9586. Her profit on this trade is $4,412.50 per contract or $22,062.50 for all five contracts. Upon examining her broker's account statement for November 8 (the day after her position was closed), she finds no record of the trade made on November 4, which was the opening trade in her long position on the yen futures contract. Her broker's records instead show her now holding five short December yen contracts in an up-trending market, gathering losses, and on top of that, she is out her profit of over $20,000.

Here is where the NFA can enter the picture to provide the "hazard insurance" we talked about and protect her trading profits. Let's follow the claims against her broker and, in the process, use her experience to illustrate the benefits traders have available to them in any disputed issue with an NFA-regulated forex or futures broker.

Our friendly trader has saved her screen printouts from each trade entry dealing with this issue and has faxed them to her broker. Her broker, however, still refuses to credit her account for the profit she was due from this position, and he subsequently closes out her account. She believes that her broker somehow failed to enter the November 4th orders listed on her own personal account summary records, which bought the five yen contracts. Although he disputes her records, he agrees to reinstate her principal to the level it was before the trade in question by canceling the debits resulting from the five remaining and disputed short contracts that were accumulating losses in her account.

She faces a decision now on whether to hire an attorney and file a lawsuit to try and recover her unrealized profits. Considering the costs for attorneys and the time delay in backlogged civil court cases, this is an extremely unsatisfying remedy for her. So there she stands, with a loss of over $20,000 and no apparent good options? Well, she actually has one ace-in-the-hole, the National Futures Association, which she will now turn to for help. Here is her experience.

She files what is called a Demand for Arbitration, which, as the name implies, is a mandatory procedure that her NFA-membered broker cannot ignore. Her claim will be for $66,187.50, treble the amount of her broker's trading error, based on a state statute permitting treble damage claims in the state courts. Notice that the NFA's arbitration procedures permit a state's statute to be used in its guidelines for basing treble damage claims.

She will also request that the NFA order her broker to compensate her for any and all attorney's fees (if any) that she might possibly incur as the procedure moves forward. It is useful to note that a claim under the NFA protocol does not require attorneys, and typically, attorneys are not needed, but if a trader prevails and has required some legal advice or assistance, then she can ask her NFA panel to order the broker to compensate her for those attorney fees. (There is a very small fee for the NFA's arbitration service itself.)

Next, she has to make a choice between two dispute resolution formats available through the National Futures Association. The first is mediation. As we know, mediation is a dispute resolution process that tries to arrange an agreement that the two parties themselves come to. Upon reflection, she decides that since a resolution through mediation cannot actually impose a resolution to the dispute between the two parties but rather tries to get movement toward middle ground by each side, letting them come to their own agreement, she feels that she would be at a great disadvantage with her broker, since he has shown a distinct unwillingness to compromise.

In arbitration, a panel listens to evidence and then arrives at a judgment that both parties *must* accept. They each stipulate such acceptance as a condition for membership (on the part of the broker) and as a complainant (on the part of the trader). For NFA member and customer alike, this judgment, then, will be final and binding on both. Once a broker is found at fault, he has virtually no legal appeal in the courts, and if a claim against a broker is found to be justified, he must pay the award cited or face a penalty, including expulsion from the futures (or forex) industry. In addition, the winning trader (complainant), by contrast, *can* seek court action to compel payment from her broker by using the state's courts. If you are beginning to get a picture of a trader-friendly arbitration process, then you are getting the true picture of this NFA arbitration format.

Delays in the Process

Upon filing her claim on November 14, she will be given until January 13 to make a detailed discovery request for documents from the broker. That means she will require that her broker turn over his internal office documents relating to her account and her trading history with the firm. There are, it turns out, tapes of phone conversations made between the broker and herself that she wants to present to the panel. If the broker does not fully and promptly respond to her request for all documents, she can ask the NFA to compel the broker to comply, which the NFA will do on her behalf, including by subpoena.

The NFA arbitration procedure will hold a discovery conference between the two parties, as a way to emphasize the panel's interest in an expedient disclosure and exchange of documents for the arbitration proceeding. If the broker still refuses to comply with the request by our friendly trader, the NFA's arbitration panel can default the basic complaint in her favor and order the broker to pay the full amount of the claim. So our friendly trader can receive the full amount of her claim summarily, as ordered by the NFA, due to uncooperative conduct that is in violation of NFA rules. Also, the broker would face subsequent, additional disciplinary action from the NFA's Business Conduct Committee.

Her broker, as by now could be expected, in response to her document requests, asks the panel to dismiss his client's complaint, but the arbitration panel turns him down. He then objects to her request for documentation to help prove her claim, and the panel, after considering his objection, nevertheless rules in our trader's favor. A trader has the right to ask for a preliminary hearing for the purpose of imposing sanctions against the broker for refusing to be forthcoming on the office documentation detailing our friendly trader's account traffic.

The panel had ordered the broker to provide the trader with all requested documents 30 days before the hearing date. The panel reminds the broker that if he fails to meet this deadline, he will be subject to sanctions from the NFA.

Eventually, the broker finds that he has been put in the position of having no choice but to produce the asked-for documentation and he reluctantly does so. When the documentation is finally forthcoming, our friendly trader is able to finish preparing her case.

NFA Arbitration Is Independent of State Courts but Supportive of State Law

Although she researched the state statutes and found that she could request treble damages based on the state law, she does not have to prove a violation of any state law to prevail in the NFA procedure and collect her treble damages. Also, a complaint would be heard by the NFA even if it did not involve any loss from her account. All she needs to establish for the three-member panel is that she incurred any sort of loss through broker error or mischief and prove that she should be compensated for it.

It is worth repeating that claims such as the one our friendly trader is initiating need not be a violation of law whatsoever and that this arbitration procedure mandates broker and all other NFA member participation once they are named by the complainant. Essentially, a trader can bring a complaint against virtually anyone in the futures industry, in which any form of unfairness can be alleged that led to a cost of some kind to the complainant.

A Flexible Procedure

For example, a broker may have made misstatements as to services available from his firm, in an effort to persuade a trader to open an account with him. Our friendly trader could assign a compensation value to such misfortune and complain to the arbitration panel for reimbursement. So we see that this program is a very broad and trader-friendly format that traders should be prepared to use whenever necessary.

By now, a few weeks have passed and the panel is set to schedule a hearing site; absent an unusual reason to justify his nonattendance, the broker is notified he must appear. Our friendly trader has selected the city where she lives as the site for the arbitration case to be heard, and a hearing date has been set.

Our friendly trader is very busy exercising all the rights she is granted by the NFA, and she now makes a decision as to who will sit on the NFA arbitration panel hearing her case. Will it be other brokers, or should it be nonmembers of the futures industry? Our friendly trader also exercises her rights by asking the NFA to review the three prospective members of the hearing panel themselves, to affirm that they have no relationship with her broker and no real or apparent conflict of interest in this case, which is in fact done by the NFA. Our trader ultimately decides on an all NFA member panel. As we said, she also had the option of having nonmembers, as well. The choice was hers. Three impartial NFA members and trading professionals are eventually seated as arbitrators for her case.

NFA statistics show that nearly half of all arbitration cases are resolved before the panel convenes its first meeting. Our friendly trader has made repeated efforts to reach such a conclusion with her broker but to no avail. He has been uncooperative, as we have seen, and this case will need to go to arbitration for its conclusion.

Point–Counterpoint

As the hearing date approaches, things start happening quickly. Our friendly trader has a witness for her case—her accountant, who has kept her records of trading transactions and profits/losses—but he will be unable to be in the city where the hearing is to take place on the scheduled date. At the trader's request, the panel agrees to hear his testimony by speakerphone.

The broker once again, it seems, takes the initiative and presents a motion to dismiss the case against our friendly trader, but the panel refuses to agree to the dismissal and reaffirms the original hearing date. Our trader, meanwhile, has a business date that conflicts with the scheduled hearing date, so she asked for a continuance, which is granted by the panel. Although continuances carry a $250 fee, the fee is waived by the panel, as it decides that her business appointment conflict was unforeseeable and unavoidable on her part.

Her broker next asks the panel to convene for a summary hearing. This is where the two parties to an arbitration proceeding present their arguments only in writing, and the panel enters a judgment based solely on written information. There would be no oral testimony or personal appearances. Our friendly trader does not agree for two reasons: First, the amount is over $10,000, and she knows that the panel typically prefers personal presentations on such larger amounts; and, second, she asks the panel to consider her belief that it is important for her to present her arguments to the panel in person in order to be effective. Once again, the NFA panel rejects the broker-respondent's motion for a summary decision.

Our friendly trader has also subsequently requested information from the broker's immediate supervisor, who refuses to comply. It seems that the telephone tapes of phone conversations between the trader and broker, as well as internal office memos relating to her account, are in the possession of the supervisor, so the broker avoided having to present these documents in his discovery packet. Under the arbitration rules, a subpoena is ordered by the NFA for the tapes that were made of all phone conversations between the customer and her broker, as well as internal notes from the firm's office dealing with her account. The subpoena is served, and our friendly trader finally gets to hear those phone tapes, which, as it turns out, will seal her case against this resolution-resistant broker.

The broker reacts by requesting information from the trader, as to her past trading accounts with other brokerage houses, and so forth. The panel reviews this request but, in the end, refuses to order her to produce that information, concluding that it does not bear on the issues in this case.

Our friendly trader, upon reviewing the additional information from the broker's supervisor, amends her claim for damages to include the supervisor in the amount of $10,000. The panel accepts the amended complaint, and her claim now totals $76,187.50

On the re-scheduled hearing date, the National Futures Association arbitration panel finally convenes for two-and-a-half days, hearing all the evidence from both the broker and his customer, our friendly trader. After the panel concludes its hearing, it takes nearly three months to issue its verdict—a cash award on behalf of the claimant for the full amount of her claim, $76,187.50. Her now-defeated broker tries to appeal the decision through the state's courts and is rebuffed. The courts will typically not review arbitration awards from the NFA.

The broker is advised by the NFA that he has to pay the award within 30 days or face suspension of membership and, in effect, expulsion from futures trading in the United States. In addition, the courts will enforce the award on behalf of the trader, if she has to take the judgment of the NFA to a state court against her broker. Case closed.

We would like all traders to visit the *www.nfa.org* Web site, acquaint themselves with the resources available from this excellent regulatory group, and support it in their trading relationships.

Q & A

Question: What do you see as the primary contribution that the NFA arbitration processes offer the online currency trader?

Answer: Needless to say, the resources that the NFA brings to a trader's relationship with his broker, and indeed with the entire futures (and potentially, forex) markets, are a key benefit for the online currency trader. They open up an understanding by the dealers and brokers that the playing field will be level.

18

Case Histories of 10 Forex Trades

There is no better way to explain and illustrate the advantages and benefits of the online resource for currency traders than to use it as part of our format in these next two chapters. We will reference charts and other information for the reader to access through the online resources of *www.theFinancials.com*. Our readers have their own special reservation for a unique access to the varied resources at theFinancials.com Web site. Go to *http://book.theFinancials.com/interactive/* right now for a quick look at what this online feature can offer you.

The best traders tell us that their greatest asset as currency traders is their experience. So we want to emphasize, over and over again, the value of trade simulation and experimentation in executing your trading strategies *before* you trade with at-risk money. You can access free simulated forex trading on theFinancials.com Web site, so plan to take advantage of this resource.

We intend to follow our own advice and tie together many of the components of currency trading that we have talked about up until now by using case histories of 10 forex trades here in this chapter to reinforce the value of real-world trading experiences without risk. We want to examine closely how online currency trading is actually implemented through the applications of stop, limit, and other orders in a realistic trading environment. The fundamental trader will show us how to trade intraday using fundamental analysis, and we cannot forget, of course, that risk management of our account, when markets do not go as we planned or would like them to go, is essential to bottom-line profits for the online currency environment. Put another way, we will make a substantial effort to institutionalize into your trading frameworks the idea that minimizing losses must always be on your radar screen and will in fact lead the way to maximum profits from your online currency trading experiences.

Painting the Big Picture

We all know that an unpredictable percentage of the trades we make will turn out to be money losers. We can hope that the ratio of winning trades to losing trades will break slightly to the majority in favor of winning trades. That hope helps keep the currency trader going. But the realist's rule of thumb I like to use is two winning trades for every three losers. Using this rule of "down-to-earth" expectations, if you exit winning trades with the same dollar figure as you exit your losing trades, obviously, with a 2:3 winning-to-losing trade ratio, your account will be drawn down in no time at all. So that should be a rather transparent tip-off that you need to factor another dimension into your trading game plan.

Simply put, you must lose less per trade than you gain. Minimize losses! These two ratios should be the foundation of any trading strategy, and they work equally well for technical or fundamental analysis. Again, one is the ratio of winning trades to losing trades, and the other is dollar profits to dollar losses. These are the important brushstrokes that an online currency artisan needs to employ in painting a big-picture trading outline for himself.

That second ratio I referenced is the ratio of real profits to real losses in your personal trading account. In fact, these ratios are in reality two different sides of the same coin. As a way to make that point, we want to suggest that you should use a strategic trading framework that employs stops and limits on both sides of your initial fill. That means a targeted loss and a targeted gain for each trade should be established in your own mind *before* a trade is executed. Go to *http://book.theFinancials.com/interactive/chap18.html* for charts illustrating the use of targeted gains and losses.

For example, let's suppose our friendly trader plans to use stops to initiate a trade that will set up a profit target of 70 pips and, on the down side, will limit his losses to 30 pips. This creates a rather reasonable profit-to-loss ratio of 70:30. So if a trader's framework or strategy has a ratio of 2:3, winning to losing trades, that could translate into 140-

pips profit for every 90 pips in losses—two wins (70 pips) to every three losses (30 pips). After allowing for slippage, our friendly trader would find that he has created a strategic framework that can produce a realistic but nice profit. Again, notice that both of these ratios need to work together and complement each other to establish a maximum gain and a maximum loss in your strategic plans. Notice also that the loss has to be much smaller than the gain. Minimize those losses!

Maximize Profits, Minimize Losses

You can be flexible in setting these ratios, but be careful not to get carried away. A few traders have been known to implement rather unreasonable profit/loss ratios. For instance, one trader's favorite ratio was 100:10, where the profit target was 100 pips and the stop loss would be 10 pips below his fill price. As I trust we all know, that would surely result in getting stopped out with such frequency that first, the probability of ever achieving a 100-pip profit target is severely diminished; second, that strategy could never expect to achieve a 2:3 winning to losing trade ratio. It would more likely be around 1:12, one winning trade for every twelve 10-pip losses. That produces an unacceptable 100-pip profit to a 120-pip loss expectation.

So coordinating these two ratios is a very important aspect of constructing a personal trading strategy. As you can see, by controlling these ratios, you really can minimize losses and maximize profits. Look at these ratios carefully when evaluating your trading strategies, and plan on using stops and limits with all your fill orders. Once your winning trade to losing trade and profit to loss ratios are conceptually established and quantified, you can proceed to implement your strategic framework by placing your stops in accordance with those ratios and then producing a reasonable expectation for profits.

Yet a third dimension to establishing a profitable trading framework needs your attention before you ever place your first trade. That is your assessment of market direction.

Three-Dimensional Trading

Suppose we take a position that is long the EURO/CHF and we have $10,000 at risk. But the euro unfortunately declines against the Swiss franc, as it has been wont to do all throughout its first two years' introduction to the forex markets. We all know how easy it is to lose $2,000 in a position. Well, with the market declining, our $10,000 indeed becomes $8,000—a 20 percent loss. A mountain has suddenly appeared in front of our friendly trader, and his trader's life just became a lot more complicated.

Now, our friendly trader *must* gain 25 percent of his remaining $8,000 account balance just to recover his 20 percent ($2,000) loss, merely to get back to square one, where he started: $10,000. So large losses create even larger obstacles that then must be overcome if a trader ever hopes to see profits. The judicious use of stops would have preempted such a loss from the unexpected euro's fall and in fact reduced it to a pre-determined level, say, $750. Then from a new $9,250 account balance, our friendly trader would only have had to gain 8 percent to make it back to his original $10,000 starting point—a much more manageable task for him and a much brighter trading future.

Be Opportunistic

If just half of the time you could accurately predict market direction at the time of your entry fills, you would be in an excellent position to garner maximum online currency trading profits. Is that unreasonable? Well, that depends on the trader and those two ratios we talked about. Many traders, like myself, realistically expect to predict market direction less than 50 percent of the time and still see gains because of the 70:30 ratio of profits to losses in our total trades net. How is it that I could err in my predictions more than half the time and then lose three trades out of every five and still profit? Well, that is what minimizing losses is all about. Use all three ratios to structure your stops.

The trader also needs to capture his profits opportunistically, as the circumstances permit, even if that occasionally means smaller gains than his ratios have targeted, because whenever a trader takes a small gain, he is at the same time avoiding those large losses that threaten to put him in the percentage retracement hole we referenced. Opportunistic adjustments to your strategy are relatively easy to do, at least conceptually. Let me illustrate.

Our friendly trader believes the USD will end the day with a gain against the Japanese yen, and he enters the market with a long position that is filled on five contracts at, let's say, 107.50. Our friendly intraday trader is using a 70:30 ratio of profits to losses, and so he places a stop loss sell order at 107.20, which will liquidate his position if the market declines. He also initiates a sell limit gain order at 108.20. As the market makes a small move, let's say in favor of the long trade, he can judge whether or not, with the market then at 107.79, he has confidence that prices will continue higher and indeed touch his 108.20 target, before they fall to 107.20. If he senses that the market will not support more price increases, he will, of course, take his profits, in this case a smaller 29-pip gain, for $1,812.50 on five contracts (table 18.1). Not a bad intraday gain. With his 30-pip stop, all that he risked was $1,875 in five contracts. The market subsequently actually did fall to his stop loss level of 107.20 without ever touching his hoped-for 108.20 price target.

No matter; our friendly trader has adjusted his market expectations to fit the current market price action and in the process stole profits from the jaws of a loss. Notice that for the day, because the market declined at the close, his market expectations for a USD/JPY gain were wrong. (Note, "closing" in forex refers to the closing business hours of 4 P.M. in New York. This is a device to simplify identifying day-to-day changes in price valuations. Of course, the forex market never closes during the week and is a 24-hour market. Traders, however, typically establish an unofficial "trading day" time frame, with opening and closing hours roughly approximating the New York stock exchange.)

Another way, strategically, for our friendly trader to adapt to that market situation is simply to move up his sell stop from 107.20 to 107.70 (table 18.2). If the market indeed continued climbing from 107.79 to 108.20, his original sell limit would kick in to secure the maximum profit his strategy planned for that day. If not, and the market dropped through his new stop level of 107.70, well, then he avoided the loss of 30 pips (107.20) he'd originally built into his strategy and wound up smelling like a rose with a net 20-pip gain from a market that only moved up 29 pips after his trade was filled and subsequently closed lower for the day. That is really maximizing profits and minimizing losses.

The Market Rules

Our friendly trader is someone who has learned well to paint a big picture of what his strategies can accomplish in any given market situation. The lesson that we should take away from this example is important. Have a plan to get out with a smaller-than-planned profit, should it appear doubtful that the market will meet your expectations. Also, as

---

Table 18.1 *Trade Case History No. 1*

USD/JPY market prices open at 107.50.

Trader's market forecast is long USD.

Buy 5 contracts USD/JPY at market filled at 107.50.

Sell stop loss order entered for 107.20.

Sell limit gain order entered for 108.20.

USD/JPY market price moves to 107.79 midday.

Trader elects to liquidate his long position and take profits, due to sense that market move higher may be stalling.

Net profit = 5 contracts at 29 pips each, or $1,812.50.

At-risk Money = $1,875 (5 contracts with 30-pip stop loss at $12.50/pip).

Table 18.2 *Trade Case History No. 2*

Alternative option for trader is to adjust his stops and let market determine P/L.

Market is at 107.79 midday.

Trader has long position of 5 contracts USD/JPY.

Trader adjusts (sell) stop loss to 107.70.

Market falls to 107.30 at the close, stop loss was triggered at 107.70.

Net profit = 5 contracts at 20 pips each or $1,250.

At-risk money = $562.50 (5 contracts with 9-pip potential loss after adjusting stop loss up to 107.70 with market at 107.79. Initial at-risk money was $1,875).

---

part of your strategic plan, when the price environment changes, expect to move your stops in order to preserve your gains as well as limit losses.

In other words, be prepared to adjust your strategies to market action. Let the market rule, do not try to rule the market with your strategic concepts. You will not win that way. Learn to execute any adjustments to your strategies with swift, efficient market orders from your online trading platform.

Another Day, Another Trade

Our friendly trader wants to get back into the market a few days later, as he finds prices on the USD/JPY at 105.00 (table 18.3). This time our trader is bearish the USD against the yen. He initiates a trade from his online platform to sell five contracts at the market on the USD/JPY. He gets his fill at 105.00. Once his confirmation is received for a fill, he enters a buy stop loss at 105.30, which limits his losses to 30 pips. Because he uses a 70:30 ratio for profits to losses in his structural framework, he next enters a buy limit gain order at 104.30. His intraday trade is now structured for a maximum 70-pip gain and a maximum loss of 30 pips, thus a 70:30 profit-to-loss ratio.

In this instance the market is flat, trading sideways all day before falling at the close. It moves in line with our friendly trader's expectation and reaches near but not quite to his buy limit order of 104.30. The market stalls at 104.35. Once again, he decides to exit his trade short of his price target and take his profits. So he enters a market order to buy from his online platform, and he is filled at 104.35 as the trading day closes in New York. His profit on this trade is a nice $4,062.50 for the full five contracts: 65 pips for each of the five contracts at $12.50/pip.

Again, just as in the earlier examples, you can handle this situation an alternative way, strategically, where your stops are not triggered and the market has taken you into the black.

Our friendly trader has a profit in hand when he elects to liquidate his five short contracts on the USD/JPY at 104.35 (table 18.4). Instead, let's say he adjusts his buy limit gain order down from its current 104.30 to 104.00 and observes the price action. He will also move his buy stop loss lower, from 105.30 to 104.65, making it now a trailing stop. Watch what happens.

The market in fact continues lower that evening, as his market prediction proves correct once again. He watches prices break the 104.00 level, triggering his liquidating buy limit order and booking a new total profit at 100 pips/contract for the trade. His profit on this trade then totals $6,250. He gained an additional $2,187.50 by letting the market dictate what it wanted to do with the use of stops.

He uses this intraday trading strategy to reap additional substantial profits without risking any of his account capital. His at-risk money was profits from the trade and amounted to only 30 pips or $1,875 for the five-contract position. (His original risk, of course, was 30 pips, or $1,875, against his account balance for five contracts. But once the market declared itself and his position moved into the black, his new adjusted stop loss position—104.65—put at risk only money already gained from the trade.

Table 18.3   *Trade Case History No. 3*

USD/JPY market prices open at 105.00.

Today's market forecast is short USD/JPY.

   Sell 5 contracts USD/JPY at market—filled at 105.00.

   Buy stop loss order entered for 105.30.

   Buy limit gain order entered for 104.30.

USD/JPY market price moves to 104.35 close of day.

   Trader elects to liquidate his short position and take profits due to near close of day.

Net profit = 5 contracts at 65 pips each or $4,062.50.

At-risk money = $1,875 (5 contracts with 30-pip stop loss at $12.50/pip).

Table 18.4   *Trade Case History No. 4*

Alternative strategy for trader is to adjust his stops and let market determine P/L.

   Trader has short position of 5 contracts USD/JPY filled at 105.00.

Market is at 104.35 near close of day.

   Trader adjusts (buy) stop limit gain to 104.00.

   Trader adjusts (buy) stop loss to 104.65.

Market falls to below 104.00, stop loss was triggered at 104.00.

Net profit = 5 contracts at 100 pips each or $6,250

At-risk money = Initial 30 pips or $1,875; adjusted stop risk is also 30 pips or $1,875.

A Technician's Hierarchy

Technical analysts have a hierarchical category of charting insofar as their three basic formats are concerned. Long-term, medium-term, and short-term charts all have a function to play in that hierarchy. Long-term charts are needed to identify *major* support and resistance levels. The long-term chartist indeed is looking at the big picture of a market's price history.

The medium-term chart is useful for the technician because it can highlight changes in volatility and momentum, as well as affirm any existing trends in prices, while keeping an eye out for trend reversal indicators. The medium-term chart is also of value in confirming *intermediate* support and resistance levels.

The short-term, or intraday, chart is the format of choice for technicians who want to pinpoint volatility and momentum factors in a market on the day they are trading.

The value of identifying support and resistance levels in a price chart lies in the belief among technicians that major support levels are more often than not likely to turn back the market, as the price level approaches them. They are not expected to let the market break through them on the majority of market tests of their support. That is why the intraday trader needs to have the long-term chart as part of his arsenal, as a way to identify a market that is indeed approaching such a major support or resistance price level.

How do you know you have a major support or resistance price level to deal with? Technicians define "major" support or resistance as a historical market turning-point that is distinguished from the current market price profile by two intervening reversals. For now, let's look at another case history of a market that involves a major support price level and see how our friendly trader reacts and how he profits from it.

Our friendly trader has a long-term chart analysis of the USD/JPY that shows a major support level of 111.00 going back some 60 days. At that time, two months earlier, the USD/JPY had fallen to 111.00 but reversed immediately toward the 113.00 level. It subsequently fell back to 112.00, before climbing higher toward 116.00. Then, it once again moved lower to 114.00. It regained upward price momentum, rising to 117.00. It then fell back once more to 113.00, before moving up to 114.00. Finally, as it moved lower, it threw off several head fakes higher, before settling yesterday at 111.50. So the price pattern met the definition for major support noted earlier because of these multiple intervening reversals.

Now, with the market once again declining and testing the 111.00 major support level, our friendly trader takes a long position of five contracts on the USD/JPY, with an order to buy if the market touches 110.50 (table 18.5). He wants the market to marginally break through the 111.00 level before his position is filled.

The market indeed opens New York trading by plummeting to 109.90. His market order was filled at 110.50, but he now finds himself in a losing position by 60 pips or $3,750 for the five contracts.

Following his 70:30 profit-to-loss ratio, he now faces a planning adjustment and directs his online trading platform to enter a sell stop order, minimizing further losses to no more than 60 pips from current price levels, at 109.90. He balances his now modified 140/60 ratio by entering a sell limit order at 140 pips above his fill, which is entered at 111.90.

The major support level of 111.00 for the USD/JPY ultimately holds, and prices rise to 112.60, triggering his sell stop order at 111.90, resulting in a 140-pip mark to the market profit for the trade. The 140-pip gain per contract yields a tidy $8,750 profit for this intraday trade, which saw the USD/JPY hold its support level. Major support levels are considered "intact" even though prices may marginally penetrate the original target number, in this case down through 111.00 to 109.90.

Every trader knows that luck plays a role in profits, and this trade is no exception. One can say that our friendly trader was guided well by his technical analysis strategy, which expects that major supports hold a majority of the times that they are tested. He saw the price break through the support level by 110 basis points, but he was not deterred. Our friendly trader stuck to his plan and persevered, modifying as necessary his 70:30 ratio strategy of stops. Almost immediately, the market obliged with a reversal and ultimate substantial profit.

Adjusting Your Game Plan

We want to show the alternative strategy that our friendly trader could have used in this circumstance (table 18.6), because it shows the importance of reacting to unexpected opportunities for maximizing profits that surface when you are in a winning position and can more easily afford to adjust your strategies, with the express purpose of maximizing profits with minimum risk.

The market, of course, fell through his entry level position of 110.50 for the USD/JPY. When our friendly trader found himself taken down to a 60-pip loss position and owning five contracts on the USD/JPY, he straight ahead placed the tight stop his original plan called for, just 60 pips below the then market price. He proceeded to enter an exit order with a profit target of 140 pips above his fill. So he stayed with his trading structure ratio of 70/30 (140/60). The market indeed turned, holding the support level as it moved higher. At that point, he was in the black by a comfortable margin on the five-contract position. Rather than wait for his stops to take him out of a higher-trending market price pattern, he replaced the original exit gain order with a new one, now positioning himself to exit at 112.50 instead of 111.90. Those additional 60 pips, if filled, would earn him additional profits of $3,750. As we know, the market does indeed continue to rise, filling the exit order at 112.50 and gaining a total profit on the day of $12,500 from this extraordinary 200-pip move.

The lesson here is simply to be prepared and take advantage of a market's momentum trend in your favor. Keep adjusting your exit profit stops and trailing exit-loss stops higher, following the market. Let the market determine your profit level. In other words, follow the time-worn principle that "the market rules."

Fundamental Day Traders

It may surprise many readers to learn that an abundance of fundamental currency traders are using the online format. These fundamental day traders have an interesting take on what moves currency prices in the shortest of short-term time horizons.

Here we want to get a sense of how a fundamental trader who looks at GDP, inflation, interest rates, and so on, makes currency valuations on a short-term time frame. Could a fundamental analyst possibly have a fix on intraday currency moves? And if he does, what can a technician learn from him? Well, the answer to the first question is "he does," and the answer to the second question is "plenty."

A fundamental trader looks at the yen side of the USD/JPY through currency charts, as we have done throughout this book, but he sees something different. He sees a newly independent central bank in the first years of independence from its elected government, opposing its own

Table 18.5 *Trade Case History No. 5*

USD/JPY market prices open at 111.50.

  Trader's market analysis shows major support level of 111.00.

  Trader enters a market if touched buy order for 5 contracts
  at 110.50.

USD/JPY market price falls to 109.90.

Market if touched order is triggered and filled at 110.50.

  Trader immediately enters a new sell limit loss order at 109.90.

  Trader follows with a sell stop gain order at 111.90.

USD/JPY market price rises to 112.60, triggering sell limit gain order
at 111.90.

Sell order to liquidate position is filled at 111.90.

Net profit = 5 contracts at 140 pips each or $8,750.

At-risk money = $3,750 (5 contracts as market forced new stop loss of
109.90, 60 pips below fill price of 110.50).

Table 18.6 *Trade Case History No. 6*

Alternative option for trader to adjust his stops and let market determine P/L.

Market is at 111.60 midday after rising from 109.00 earlier in the day.

  Trader has existing long position of 5 contracts USD/JPY filled
  at 110.50.

  Trader adjusts sell limit loss order from 109.30 to 111.00.

  Trader adjusts sell stop gain order from 111.90 to 112.50.

Market price goes through 112.50 stop gain order near end of day.

Sell stop filled at 112.50.

Net profit = 5 contracts at 200 pips each = $12,500.

At-risk money = $1,875 (adjusted trailing stops maintained a 30-pip
margin × 5 contracts).

finance ministry on a wide array of critically important policy issues at a time when Japan is teetering on the abyss of recession or recovery. The fundamental trader sees ways in which that confrontation will affect currency values. The BoJ, as we know, sterilized the dozens of interventions ordered up by the Ministry of Finance during the 1990s. This decision of the central bank had the effect of immediately and directly neutralizing the impact of the interventions on the economy and monetary base of Japan, in direct contravention to Ministry of Finance's wishes.

Then, to the chagrin of a new Mori administration, in 1999 the BoJ scrapped its ZIRP, zero interest rate policy, and raised interest rates. The administration fought it every step of the way but lost. So the conflict between Japan's MoF and its central bank has a lot of implications for currency valuations from the fundamental trader's perspective, and the fundamental online currency trader studies them all.

The fundamental trader sees the barely marginal economic growth in Japan and the yet-to-be-completed investment in so many structural changes needed in its banking and political structures, which impact currency flow. He sees trade policies and interest rate differentials and makes a judgment about currency valuations. He sees a demographic catastrophe in the long-term pension plans for Japan's growing elderly population.

On the plus side, he has seen some structural reform initiatives take hold, especially in foreign participation in Japan's economy. IT is another area where Japan competes successfully. And Japan enjoys one of the highest savings rates in the world.

From this mix of fundamental data, a fundamental analyst will discern price patterns, the same way a technician might, except that the fundamental trader sees, as the source of those patterns, private sector and government capital expenditures, trade and portfolio flows, and foreign direct investment both into and out of Japan, and from those studies he can make a judgment about big-picture currency valuations. He may even use historical price charts, although he will not consider the MACD, RSI, or other studies that the technician relies on.

Intermarket Spreads

Our friendly fundamental trader calls up a chart from one of his software packages and proceeds to back test his strategies. He then tests them in a simulated platform format that he occasionally uses to shake out new trading strategies. One of the features of his software is the ability to set the two currencies to zero, or parity, as of the start of a new trading day. In his trade-simulation exercises, he follows the price movements of each currency intraday and discovers that a divergence occurs during the day but it then resolves itself before the end of trading each day. This pattern was consistent enough that he elected to develop a strategy to take advantage of it. Following are four case histories (tables 18.7–18.10) that show how such a strategy can be tested and developed. First, a word about the two-currency trading techniques known as intermarket spreads.

Intermarket spreads are positions taken between two different currencies. In the currency markets, fundamental traders especially, but also technicians, have identified relationships between two currency pairs that can move either in tandem or in opposition to one another. That being the case, obviously a signal can be discerned for one currency pair based on the market price action of the other. Also, there may be currencies that from time to time maintain a relative parity. Thus, if one currency moves higher than the other, such disparity may signal an eventual move back into equilibrium to the intermarket spread trader. Traders may take positions in both currencies, or they may elect to trade only one, using the other as signal line, as it were.

Trading in intermarket spreads is a subject unto itself, but we want to give readers a taste of what is involved, and so we have included four case histories, simple enough in nature but that outline this very important feature of the online currency markets.

After the introduction of the euro on January 1, 1999, it soon developed that the EUR/USD and the EUR/JPY moved pretty much in tandem, as the euro skidded in value during its first two years. That might seem rather an obvious conclusion to reach, but not every currency will follow its neighbors against the same base currency like the euro. For instance, the dollar depreciated against the yen in 1999/2000 but appreciated against the euro. The yen, on the other hand, appreciated against both the euro and the dollar. So identifying these unique relationships can be a lucrative pursuit in the currency world. Our friendly trader studied, from a fundamental framework, the EUR/USD and EUR/JPY and concluded that a relationship existed on an intraday basis that would be valid, according to his studies, for an intraday time span.

In our case histories, the EUR/USD gains for a short time in value, while the yen stays flat, and it is this "disparity" between the two at 9 A.M. that, you will see, prompts a trade to exploit this relationship. Go to *http://book.theFinancials.com/interactive/chap18.html* to see the charts that track this price disparity. The EUR/USD gains value while the USD/JPY stays flat as he expects. At midday the EUR/USD has gained 25 pips more than the base pair he is using as his standard, the USD/JPY. At noon, he shorts the EUR/USD, and almost immediately, the value falls, so that by 5 P.M. the EUR/USD is back in parity with the USD/JPY.

For the fundamental trader, this divergence between the EUR/USD and the USD/JPY presented an anomaly that the markets were expected to correct. You will see, when you visit the online resource, that using the same kind of charting resources the technician uses, our fundamental trader pegged the two currency pairs, the EUR/USD and the USD/JPY, as of the start of trading and followed the market's price patterns during the day. The chart on the Web site will show that the two in fact did diverge, peaking at noon, and then found price parity before the end of the trading day.

Table 18.7 *Trade Case History No. 7 (Simulation)*

EUR/USD market prices open at 0.8675.

USD/JPY market prices open at 107.02.

Today's market forecast is disparity between two currency pairs.

Disparity

7 A.M. EUR/USD rises to 0.8700.

7 A.M. USD/JPY remains flat at 107.05.

7:30 A.M. sell 5 contracts EUR/USD filled at 0.8700.

Parity

9 A.M. EUR/USD falls to 0.8675.

9 A.M. USD/JPY remains flat at 107.06.

9 A.M. buy 5 Contracts EUR/USD at the market filled at 0.8675.

Net profit = 5 contracts at 25 pips each or $1,562.50.

At-risk money = $15,000 ($3,000 margins for each of 5 contracts).

Table 18.8   *Trade Case History No. 8 (Simulation)*

EUR/USD market prices open at 0.8675.

USD/JPY market prices open at 107.02.

Today's market forecast is disparity between two currency pairs.

Disparity

   7 A.M. EUR/JPY rises to 0.8700.

   7 A.M. USD/JPY remains flat at 107.05.

   7:30 A.M. sell 5 contracts EUR/USD filled at 0.8700.

   Buy stop loss order entered for 0.8730.

   Sell stop gain order entered for 0.8630.

Parity

   9 A.M. EUR/USD falls to 0.8675.

USD/JPY remains flat at 107.06.

   Trader sees USD/JPY remaining flat and at parity with EUR/USD
   and so enters a liquidation order.

   Buy 5 contracts EUR/USD at the market filled at 0.8675.

Net profit = 5 contracts at 25 pips each or $1,562.50.

At-risk money = $1,875 (5 contracts with 30-pip stop loss at
$12.50/Pip).

Our friendly trader, in reviewing this trade, concludes that his at-risk funds are much too high relative to the expected or likely profit. He addresses that in his next trade simulation (table 18.8).

As we can see, the introduction of stops reduced losses significantly (from theoretically unlimited losses totaling the $15,000 margin requirements, to only $1,875 with stops). One of the benefits of trade simulation is that almost any potential market eventuality can be evaluated. Our friendly trader wants to use this resource to explore all conceivable options. So he prepares for a scenario where either currency may move while the other stays flat. Review the next case history simulation (table 18.9).

Our friendly trader evaluates these results and realizes he forgot to use his stop orders to reduce at-risk funds, so he expands his use of

---

Table 18.9   *Trade Case History No. 9 (Simulation)*

EUR/USD market prices open at 0.8675.

USD/JPY market prices open at 107.02.

Today's market forecast is disparity between the two currency pairs.

Trader places contingent orders to enter the market on both pairs for price rise against USD.

Order entry sell stop EUR/USD entered at 0.8700.

Order entry sell stop USD/JPY entered at 106.77.

Trader places contingent order on both pairs to enter the market for price fall against USD.

Order entry sell stop EUR/USD entered at 0.8650.

Order entry sell stop USD/JPY entered at 107.27.

Disparity

7 A.M. EUR/USD rises to 0.8700.

Sell stop order filled at 0.8700.

All remaining order entries canceled by trader.

The trader now has only one position—short the EUR/USD at 0.8700. If the EUR/USD retraces back to parity with the USD/JPY, the trader will profit 25 pips from his short position with an exit at 0.8675

Parity

9 A.M. EUR/USD falls back to 0.8675.

USD/JPY remains flat at 107.06.

Buy 5 contracts at the market to offset short positioning; EUR/USD—filled at 0.8675.

Net profit = 5 contracts at 25 pips each or $1,562.50.

At-risk money = $15,000 (5 contracts at $3,000 margin/contract).

---

stops in a final trade simulation (table 18.10) before deciding he is ready to use this strategy with at-risk account funds.

Trade simulation and real trading experience are invaluable assets that the successful trader maintains as part of his trading regimen. We next want to look at futures and options case histories.

Table 18.10 *Trade Case History No. 10 (Simulation)*

EUR/USD market prices open at 0.8675.

USD/JPY market prices open at 107.02.

Today's market forecast is disparity in intermarket currency pairs.

Trader places contingent order to enter the market on both pairs for price rise against USD.

Order entry sell stop EUR/USD entered at 0.8700.

Order entry sell stop USD/JPY entered at 106.77.

Trader places contingent order on both pairs to enter the market for price fall against USD.

Order entry sell stop EUR/USD entered at 0.8650.

Order entry sell stop USD/JPY entered at 107.27.

Disparity

7 A.M. EUR/USD rises to 0.8700.

Sell stop order filled at 0.8700.

All remaining order entries canceled by trader.

Trader places contingent orders to reduce risk:

Buy stop loss order entered at 0.8730.

Buy limit gain order entered at 0.8630.

Parity

9 A.M. EUR/USD falls to 0.8675.

USD/JPY remains flat at 107.05, establishing parity with EUR/USD.

Close of trading

Trader concludes market move lower is stalling.

Buy 5 contracts EUR/USD to offset short position; filled at 0.8675.

Net profit = 5 contracts at 25 pips each or $1,562.

At-risk money = $1,875 (5 contracts with 30-pip stop loss at $12.50/pip).

CHAPTER

19

Case Histories of 10 Exchange Futures/Options Trades

Not too long ago, the wife of a former U.S. president related how she, before becoming First Lady, parlayed a $1,000 trading account into a $100,000 profit in cattle futures. One trade, one profit, and no real experience. Stock traders and others, not familiar with exchange futures and options, may rightly feel that if someone can make $100,000 that easily, then someone else can lose it just as easily, and, therefore, this must mean that exchange futures trading is an unreasonably risky business.

Well, yes, trading exchange futures contracts does involve risk, but so, too, does investing in high-tech stocks listed on the Nasdaq exchange. During 2000, the Nasdaq exchange index lost nearly 50 percent of its value at one point. In 1987, the Dow plunged over 20 percent in one day. What about those conservative bond traders? Well, even U.S. Treasury Bonds from time to time generate negative total returns for the year. The point here is that for a responsible, prudent trader, exchange futures markets should be considered no different than stock or bond markets and, indeed, actually are a reasonable-risk enterprise, as long as you follow some common-sense rules of trading.

One of this book's primary goals is to address its readers' worries that futures and options currency markets may be the "wild west" of the financial trading world. They are not. In fact, exchange futures are considered by many to be among the most regulated, fairest markets in the world.

But so many readers are now coming to online currency trading from stock and bond venues, after having heard stories about both fortunes and catastrophes from futures and options trading, that it is important to now balance the perspective for the benefit of those new to online global currency markets.

Exchange Futures As a Risk-Avoidance Venue?

It is well to remember that the futures markets were created and developed initially as risk-avoidance trading venues for small farmers and others who wanted to offset their risk from holding various commodities in the cash markets.

Before futures trading came onto the scene, the cash commodity market was chaotic and captive to seasonal fluctuations that were grossly inefficient and hence cost-laden. A farmer with a corn harvest found himself competing with many other farmers who harvested their crops with him, in the fall of the year, which, of course, drove down prices. Then in the spring, as he was buying seed to replant for next season's harvest, he found that because crops were now scarce, crop prices had been driven higher, but now he had no crops to sell. Concurrently, demand for the seed needed for spring planting had risen, as all the other farmers were seeking, along with him, to buy seed corn all at once. Higher demand sent seed prices higher. So the individual farmer was being squeezed, along with the consumer, who wound up paying higher prices as a result, all due to the inefficiency of the existing cash commodity markets. Such inefficiency, of course, also bred risk.

The idea of creating and then trading contracts based on the future prices of a broad range of commodities successfully accomplished a major reduction in these price inefficiencies for the cash commodity markets and, coincidentally, reduced risk at the same time.

So that is the main lesson our readers need to draw on for an understanding of futures markets—that they in fact reduce risk (rather substantially) for the underlying cash markets. The exchange futures markets themselves, and their futures contracts, which are traded online today, are a marvel of efficiency and risk-avoidance. They offer stock and bond traders an alternative environment that is by far the most protected and safest transfer of ownership venue available in the history of financial markets.

The international exchange futures markets have assumed a major leadership role worldwide, which is to a certain extent unappreciated, misunderstood, and even, for many traders, somewhat feared, at least as far as their own participation is concerned.

Learn from the Best

Traders new to these markets should take a page from the book of successful traders who typically have a realistic big-picture perspective of the markets they invest in and are, by and large, not fearful of their trading environment. Yes, they have a healthy respect for the dangers of open-ended positions, and professional traders are always wary of the changeability in market price sentiment. These *crème de la crème* traders all carry a personal caveat that they keep in front of them at all times. Successful traders remind themselves to be alert to all sorts of risk-inviting inducements that seem to surface in every financial market. Professional traders pretty much universally institutionalize, into their strategic frameworks, risk-avoidance rules that only permit prudent and reasonable-risk scenarios in their trading strategies. Remember, the standard bywords for every investor, whether commodity hedger, forex speculator, or stock portfolio manager, are "minimize losses" and "avoid gratuitous risk."

Really, when viewed from a big-picture perspective, we will find that exchange futures support traders who manage risk well, and they will permit exchange traders an opportunity to profit, with a reasonable and measured risk factor.

Today, family as well as corporate farmers have incorporated exchange futures hedging strategies into their routine crop marketing framework, so as to protect themselves against risk—such as loss from price declines at harvest time. These traders from the farm belt can thank the commodity exchanges for helping them to preserve equity in their family farm.

Similarly, a U.S. exporter doing business in Japan, and having cash revenues due 46 days out, can take a position in the currency futures market that enables him to eliminate the risk of currency exchange rate variations, which could otherwise wipe out his profit margin. In other words, a futures contract will, in fact, eliminate currency exchange risk.

Such businessmen are not looking for risk, and they certainly are not in the habit of gambling on currency rate valuations. They will go a long way to avoid being put in the position of having to "bet" that such currencies like the Japanese yen will buy more U.S. dollars 46 days from now. They are businessmen who routinely seek to eliminate risk from their revenue flow, and the exchange futures markets are there to help them accomplish just that!

Hedging on the Currency Exchange

Let's say a U.S. seller of oranges has a client in Japan who will pay him with a check denominated in yen for a shipment of oranges to Japan coming due in 46 days. The value of the sale is today's equivalent of $100,000, or 10,671,000 yen. If the exchange rate, which today, let's say, is 106.71 yen to the U.S. dollar, happens to be the same in 46 days when delivery is made, then our friendly orange grower will pocket what he can expect to be the same gross dollar sales receipt based on today's valuations, 10,671,000 yen at 106.71 yen/dollar or $100,000.00. On the other hand, if the U.S. dollar strengthens during the 46 days he is waiting for his yen-denominated check, that 10,671,000 yen will yield something less than the $100,000 he needs to make a simple profit. To avoid that risk, he will sell a futures contract on the USD/JPY. Here is how it works.

One mini-futures contract is worth 6,250,000 yen on the CME. He sells a mini-yen December futures contract on September 21, priced at that day's value—0.9513. You will recall that futures contracts valuations are expressed as a price based on the number of U.S. cents/yen. The fill on his order to sell one futures contract comes in at 0.9513, for a December mini-contract on the yen. The spot cash price that day was 106.71. Incidentally, the equivalent of 106.71 yen per USD in cents per yen is 0.009371. Because of the interest rate differentials for futures valuations, the December contract, which was trading at 0.9513 on September 21, is typically much higher than the spot cash equivalent.

In the following 46 days, the futures price of the yen goes from 0.9513 cents per yen on September 21 to 0.9378 on November 6. The spot cash rate fell from 106.71 to 107.51 for the yen. His check comes in for 10,671,000 yen, and the bank converts it at the November 6 exchange rate of 107.51. Our friendly orange exporter finds that he receives not $100,000 but $99,256: 10,671,000 yen/107.51 = $99,256. That creates a net loss of $744 on his client's payment of what he had hoped would be the yen equivalent of $100,000 at an exchange rate of 106.71 yen. So our friendly orange grower suffered from the risks of the cash market.

His futures contract, meanwhile, has decreased from 0.9513 to 0.9378. Use table 19.1 to follow this trade. Since initially he sold the contract, he will now buy it back at the market-friendly rate of 0.9378.

Table 19.1 *Trade Case History No. 1*

On September 21, businessman wants to hedge risk from yen-denominated cash payment due in 46 days.

Amount of payment due = 106,710,000 yen.

Today's exchange rate is 106.71. Dollar value is $100,000.

Businessman sells one CME mini-yen contract at the market/filled at 0.9513.

On November 6, underlying cash market moves (yen) lower to 107.51; futures market falls to 0.9378.

Businessman receives payment for total of 10,671,000 yen.

Today's exchange rate value in USD is 10,671,000/107.51 or $99,256.

Loss of $744 compared to expected value of cash market rate of $100,000.

Futures Contract Summary

Businessman offsets short futures position with a buy of 1 contract, ATM, filled at 0.9378.

Sell futures at 0.9513.

Buy futures at 0.9378.

Net gain 0.0135.

135 ticks at $6.25/tick = $844.

Trade/Payment Summary

Hedge position to eliminate risk from $100,000 value of yen-denominated payment.

Short futures contract dated September 21, with payment due on November 6.

Profit from futures position liquidated on November 6 = $844.

USD value of payment on September 21 = $100,000.

Value of payment in yen on November 6 = $ 99,256.

Loss from cash exchange rate risk on November 6 = $744.

Loss from cash exchange rate risk = $744.

Gain from futures position = $844.

Account at-risk money = $1,810 (margin).

His purchase cost of 0.9378 is subtracted from his selling price of 0.9513, and that difference is 135 ticks. His proceeds, therefore, from the futures position are 135 × $6.25 or $844. Even allowing for trade commission charges, he has protected his company's interest in this uncertain yen-denominated payment through the sale of a single futures contract. Put another way, he used a futures contract to eliminate the cash currency exchange rate risk. Do you see why we can conclude that far from being dangerous, reckless, or even risky, this use of a futures contract was prudent and reasonable? One could even go so far as to say that this is why the futures market can be considered by its nature to be a risk-averse financial environment, if used with knowledge and care.

Another point we should make is that futures trading is cost-efficient. Our friendly orange grower would have had to find other alternatives to avoid risk, if the exchange futures contract had not been available to him. The orange exporter might have sold his client's contract to speculators at a considerable discount. He would have had to look into opening up bank accounts in Japan and think about establishing an office to use his yen-denominated payments to try and purchase materials in Japan, such as office supplies or what have you, in order to try and spend his yen "in-country," thus eliminating currency exchange risk altogether. In short, he would have had to incur substantial additional costs to try to offset the currency risk that a simple futures contract eliminated at essentially no cost or risk to him at all. Go to *http://book.theFinancials.com/interactive/chap19.html* to see the charts on this yen move during the fall of the year 2000.

Note that the orange grower sold a contract because he was interested in protecting his cash position from a market price decline in the yen. If the yen appreciates, he would actually gain from the exchange rate movement, so he needs no risk protection from a yen gain. But let's look anyway at table 19.2, where the value of the yen does increase while the businessman is holding a short position in a yen futures contract, in order to confirm whether this risk-averse strategy holds water even in a rising market environment.

Our friendly orange grower learned that because of the contract specifications in futures markets, dollar-for-dollar hedge covering is approximate. The $89 trade position loss, however, in a rising market is negligible to the businessman, and he considers his hedge against currency valuation loss successful.

Table 19.2 *Trade Case History No. 2*

On September 21, businessman wants to hedge risk from yen-denominated cash payment due in 46 days.

Amount of payment due = 106,710,000 yen.

Today's exchange rate is 106.71. Dollar value is $100,000.

Businessman sells one CME mini-yen futures contract ATM—filled at 0.9513.

On November 6, underlying cash market takes (yen) higher to 105.91. Futures market rises to 0.9648.

Businessman receives payment of 10,671,000 yen.

Today's exchange rate value in USD is 10,671,000/105.91 or $100,755.

Gain in yen value of payment due to exchange rate valuation is $755.

Businessman offsets futures position with a buy of 1 contract, ATM, filled at 0.9648.

Futures Contract Summary

  Buy futures at 0.9648.

  Sell futures at 0.9513.

Net loss 0.0135.

135 ticks at $6.25/tick = $844.

Trade/Payment Summary

Hedge position was taken to eliminate risk to $100,000 value of yen-denominated payment due on November 6.

USD value of yen payment on November 6 = $100,755.

Profit from cash exchange rate = $755.

Loss from futures contract = $844.

Total (net) = $99,911.

Hedge shortage = $89.

Account at-risk money = $1,810 (margin).

Hedgers, Speculators, and Floor Traders

When the futures transaction was filled on September 21, in the CME trading pits, our friendly orange grower's counterparty in the trade may have been another hedge trader like himself—someone who perhaps was buying a futures contract to offset a risk from his own personal cash position. More likely, though, his yen futures contract may have been bought by a speculator. Speculators assume a risk that hedge traders do not wish to take on. A speculator is someone who believes he can profit from a short-term price move in a contract. He is attracted by the leverage that the exchange contract offers.

Then, too, a floor trader may have been the counterparty on this position. Floor traders, we already know, may be looking to offset their contracts in only a matter of moments, through arbitrage, taking a gain from spreads available to them down in the trading pits. None of this is known to the orange exporter. Does that matter?

Well, we should note that the participation of speculators and floor traders makes the futures market more efficient and liquid, and because they assume risk, the exchange market as a whole has less risk for others, like our friendly export hedger. This assures that when you choose to enter your order, someone will take the other side of the trade at a price you find acceptable. So everyone plays a role to make futures markets serve individual traders, according to the different levels of risk tolerance each chooses for himself. It is worth pointing out that the margin this day for a single futures contract set by the CME for the yen was $1,810. In Case History No. 1, our friendly trader had $1,810 of account at-risk and gained a profit of $844, a profit-to-risk ratio of nearly 50 percent, a very nice return over just six weeks.

Margin leverage is another trading benefit that exchange futures offer. It compares to stock margin ratios favorably. One final "marginal" note on margin: On the futures exchange, the margin deposit set aside in a trader's account is not a down payment on a purchase of equity, as many perceive margins to be in the stock markets. No, here your margin is a bond, or good faith deposit, to ensure against trading losses. The CME and other exchanges use a sophisticated, computer-driven model of risk known as SPAN, Security Portfolio Analysis of Risk, based on the mix of futures and options positions you have at any given time. The exchange's SPAN system guarantees currency futures traders a uniformity in margin requirements that is one more component that contributes to the integrity and dependability in prices of exchange futures trading.

Now let's look at table 19.3 as we turn to a trade in the same market that we just examined, but this time from a speculator's perspective. Go to *http://book.theFinancials.com/interactive/chap19.html* and look at the chart of a speculator's technical analysis evaluations in the same declining market, from September 21 to November 6, 2000.

Table 19.3   *Trade Case History No. 3*

September 21, USD/JPY market prices open at 0.9513.

Near term market forecast is bearish the yen.

Speculative trader enters market order—sell 10 futures contracts—JPY, filled at 0.9513.

Speculative trader enters buy stop loss order at 0.9633.

Target price for gain is 0.9233 (note profit to loss ratio of 70:30).

October 6, futures market now at 0.9313.

Technical indicators RSI signals oversold, MACD signals oversold, and parabolic signals hold short position.

Trader elects to stay short the yen.

Trader adjusts his stop loss to previous support level of 0.9450.

October 12, prices retrace higher to 0.9400.

MACD still indicates oversold, but no clear exit-buy signal as yet; RSI signals reversal and buy; parabolic signals reverse trend and buy.

Trader elects to retain short position. Paper profit is 0.9513 – 0.9400 = 113 ticks or $706.25.

October 30, prices touch 0.9250, nearest to profit target of 0.9233. MACD signals oversold, parabolic remains sell, and RSI signals oversold. Because he is close to his target price, trader prepares to offset his short position on the yen. Trader enters buy order to liquidate position; order entry to buy 10 yen contracts filled at 0.9250.

Net profit = 10 contracts at 263 ticks at $6.25/tick or $16,437.50.

At-risk money = 10 margins at $1,810 each or $18,100.

After 46 days, our trader's profits were equal to nearly double his at-risk account funds.

The forces of supply and demand, as we know, are at work in markets to establish price valuations literally by the second. A futures (or options) trader who understands that he can choose his own level of risk, and limit his potential losses from futures trading, is one who will not fear the exchange market, and hence one who can succeed in a fiercely competitive and often fast-paced environment. As noted earlier, one cannot succeed in an environment that one fears.

Options Case Histories

We want to continue with our progression of illustrations of the diminishment of risk in the exchange futures environment with some case histories of options trades. It is appropriate that we progress to options, because options are a vehicle that can limit risk even beyond what we have just discovered in the futures environment.

We know that through the margin leverage available to exchange traders, they can leverage, with a futures contract, value that is equivalent to a cash receivable while using much less at-risk capital. We followed the futures experience of a citrus exporter who had a $100,000 cash receivable due in six weeks. He needed a margin deposit of only $1,810 to leverage a virtually unlimited (well, $100,000, theoretically) decline in the underlying spot cash market through exchange rate volatility. His actual exchange rate loss was $744. But his leverage for the duration of his futures contract actually covered an exchange rate loss for the full $100,000 amount. So leverage, or *gearing*, as it is sometimes called, proves to be a welcome advantage for many traders new to the futures market.

Now comes the exchange currency option. If you thought that the futures contract represented the limits of risk and leverage benefits that the futures exchange has versus the cash markets, well, you were wrong. The options market provides more leverage yet and even less risk.

Our orange exporter could have bought a put on the same December contract for less account money and assumed less risk, while accomplishing an even greater level of protection against exchange rate valuation losses on his cash receivable denominated in yen. Here is how it works.

The futures market was trading the December yen contract (JYZ0) at 0.9513 on September 21, while the forex was valuing the USD/JPY at 106.71. As noted, if the exchange rate of the yen against the U.S.

dollar appreciated, our friendly orange exporter would gain money, so he did not have to worry about protection against a yen appreciation. He did need to protect against a depreciation in the yen versus the U.S. dollar, so this time let's have our friendly orange exporter purchase a put and see how that protection compares with a futures hedge during both a market price increase and decrease in trading case histories Nos. 4 and 5.

Let's suppose the premium for an in-the-money put (96) was 1.00 on September 21. Upon the purchase of the put, which does not require a margin debit entry in the trader's account, the at-risk money for our friendly trader totals $1,250, roughly one-third of the margin requirement of $1,810 needed for a futures position. Also, with a put purchase, $1,250 is all he can lose under any circumstance. So for starters, his at-risk (account debit) money is reduced by 33 percent.

The market, as we know from table 19.4, is going to move lower, and by November 6, the futures price stands at 0.9378, a 135-tick lower value than the September 21 0.9513 value. The put premium, consequently, has gained value. Recall that a put is an option to sell a futures contract, and its value increases as the market declines. The Delta on this put averaged 80 percent, and its premium is now priced at 1.80. Liquidation value for the 1.80 premium is $2,250. That represents a profit upon liquidation of $2,250 – $1,250 or $1,000.

We know that the exchange rate loss was $744. So our friendly orange exporter offset, or hedged, his exchange rate risk and, as it turns out, made a profit. Again, this points out that just as for futures contracts, the structured valuation of options does not permit dollar-for-dollar precision, when hedging. But the leverage with options does result in lower risk per dollar than either cash or futures contract trading, and traders can virtually create a totally hedged protection.

The futures contract requires a margin debit to his account of $1,810. The purchase of the option debited $1,250 to his account, or only two-thirds as much. Yet the gain of $1,000 from the option exceeded the $844 gain from the futures contract hedge, by 15 percent. Readers should take note that the more extensively you participate in the exchange futures and options markets, the more cost effective your trading can become. Using a put gained $1,000. Using a futures contract gained $844. Now we want to evaluate this put option strategy in a rising cash market scenario as shown in table 19.5.

Table 19.4   *Trade Case History No. 4*

On September 21, businessman wants to hedge risk from yen-denominated cash payment due in 46 days.

Amount of payment due = 106,710,000 yen.

Today's exchange rate is 106.71. Dollar value is $100,000.

Businessman buys one 96 put premium value = 1.00.

On November 6, underlying cash market moves (yen) lower to 107.51.

Businessman receives payment for total of 10,671,000 yen.

Today's exchange rate value in USD is 10,671,000/107.51 or $99,256.

Loss of $744 compared to expected value of cash market rate of $100,000.

Businessman offsets put position by selling put ATM, filled at 1.80.

Option Position Summary

　Sell put at 1.80 = $2,250.

　Buy put at 1.00 = $1,250.

Net gain 0.80 = $1,000.

Trade/Payment Summary

Hedge position taken to eliminate risk from $100,000 value of yen-denominated payment dated September 21, due on November 6.

Profit from option position liquidated on November 6 = $1,000.

USD value of contract on September 21 = $100,000.

Value of payment in yen on November 6 = $99,256.

Loss from cash exchange rate risk on November 6 = $744.

Gain from option position = $1,000.

At-risk money = $1,250.

Table 19.5 *Trade Case History No. 5*

On September 21, businessman wants to hedge risk from yen-denominated cash payment due in 46 days.

Amount of payment due = 106,710,000 yen.

Today's exchange rate is 106.71. Dollar value is $100,000.

Businessman buys one put option ATM, premium filled at 1.00.

On November 6, underlying cash market takes (yen) higher to 105.91. Put premium falls to 0.40.

Businessman receives payment for total of 10,671,000 yen.

Today's exchange rate value in USD is 10,671,000/105.91 or $100,755.

Gain of $755 compared to expected value of cash market rate of $100,000.

Businessman offsets put position by selling put ATM, filled at 0.60.

Option Position Summary

Buy put at 1.00 = $1,250.

Sell put at 0.60 = $750.

Net loss 0.40 = $500.

Trade/Payment Summary

Hedge position taken to eliminate risk from $100,000 value of yen-denominated payment dated September 21, due on November 6.

Value of payment in yen on November 6 = $100,755.

USD value of payment on September 21 = $100,000.

Gain from cash exchange rate risk on November 6 = $755.

Loss from option position = $500.

At-risk money = $1,250.

The trade in Case History No. 2 printed a net loss for a futures contract hedge in a rising market. In contrast, this option strategy posts a net gain for the hedge. Once again, we see that options protect extremely well against exchange rate risk in either a rising or declining market.

Why Not Exercise Our Option?

We have, in our case histories to date, liquidated, or as is often said, "offset" an existing option position before expiration. It is estimated that more than 90 percent of trades are offset and liquidated before expiration. But when we purchase an option and pay the premium, we are paying for the right to "exercise" or convert that option into a futures contract. We would then be in the position to liquidate the futures position, obviously at a profit in the futures market.

For instance, when we bought a 96 put and paid $1,250 for the option to sell a futures contract in the futures market at 0.9513, we paid for the right to sell a futures contract at 0.9600. Could we elect to exercise the option and offer a futures contract for sale at 0.9600 with the market trading at 0.9513 as shown in table 19.6? If we did, we would gain 87 ticks. But if we liquidated the futures position, we would lose money.

As we can see, the value of the put premium included time value, so the efficiency of the market prevents that kind of transaction. It is of interest to note that of the $1,250 premium value of the 96 put, $1,087.50 is intrinsic value and the balance, $162.50, is time value. Later, on November 6, we find the futures market trading at 0.9378. Our friendly trader could now exercise his put option, which, remember, is an option to sell one futures contract at 0.9600. If he did, now on November 6, here is what the trade transaction would look like.

Table 19.6 *Exercise of Put Immediately After Purchase*

Purchase of 96 put = $1,250.

Immediate exercise of put.

Sale of futures contract brings 0.9600 − 0.9513 = 87 ticks.

87 ticks at $12.50/tick = $1,087.50.

Cost of put = $1,250.

Proceeds from sale of futures contract = $1,087.50.

Net loss from position = $162.50.

Table 19.7

Purchase of 96 put = $1,250.

Trader elects to exercise or put his option to the market.

Sale of futures contract brings 0.9600 – 0.9378 or 222 ticks.

222 ticks at $12.50/tick = $2,775.

Proceeds from exercising option = $2,775.

Cost of put = $1,250.

Net gain from position = $1,525.

We want to next compare two different trades and illustrate why it is very often in the trader's interest to offset his option, rather than exercise it into a futures contract.

On October 16, a friendly speculator enters an order through his online trading platform, to buy a put at the close of trading that day. His 93 put is filled at 1.11. He believes that the yen futures price will decrease from its present close of 0.9351. Well, let's follow his fortunes as he elects to exercise an option some weeks later with the market at a *slightly lower* level of 0.9326. Go to *http://book.theFinancials.com/interactive/chap19.html*.

On November 3, the futures market indeed does close lower at 0.9326. Our friendly speculator should be printing a gain on this option position, since buying a put is a bearish expectation. As prices decrease, the value of a put will increase, and the put should be able to be sold then at a higher premium, thus establishing a profit for the speculator. Fortune, however, has not smiled on our friendly speculator, as the put's premium has instead declined, even as the market has dropped, an unpredictable though not unusual market occurrence.

He now evaluates what he should do. Should he offset his option or should he exercise his option? Let's see where the least losses lie. The value of his put premium is now only 0.39 on November 10. Even though a market decline should have increased the value of his put, the erosion of the premium's time value trumped the slight underlying futures market drop. So our friendly trader stands to lose by offsetting his put and selling a 93 put at 0.39. His loss then would be 1.11 – 0.39 or 72 ticks. 72 ticks × $12.50 = $900.

On the other hand, he could elect to exercise his put option and sell a futures contract at 0.9300. If he did that, his loss would be 0.9326 − 0.9300 for a 26-tick loss (table 19.8). Add to that the cost of the put, which was 1.11, and his total loss from exercise would be 137 ticks or $1,712.50. Speculation can very often end in unexpected losses, and this speculator, even in a loss scenario, can benefit himself by knowing all the "options" at his disposal. Exercising the option would be substantially more expensive than offsetting the option, and so he elects the better course.

Time value and Delta values play a crucial role in determining option values in a narrow trading range market like this one. Speculation has its share of losses, and this trade is an excellent example of the risks that speculators assume in the exchange futures market.

Although the speculator accurately predicted the direction of the market and properly purchased a put, he found that by the time he was ready to either exercise his put or offset it, time value had eroded its pre-

---

Table 19.8 *Trade Case History No. 6*

October 16, market closes at 0.9351.

Speculator enters with his online trading platform a buy order "at the close" for a 96 put with a premium value of 1.11.

November 10, market falls to 0.9326.

With market lower than at the time of his put purchase, speculator exercises his option to sell a futures contract and "puts" his option to the market upon instructions from his broker. He then sells his futures contract—filled at 0.9300.

Profit/Loss Summary

Market is at 0.9326.

Futures contract at 0.9300.

Loss = 0.0026.

Loss from exercise = 0.0026.

Cost of 93 put = 0.0111.

Net loss = 0.0137.

137 ticks at $12.50/tick = $1,712.50

Table 19.9 *Trade Case History No. 7*

October 16, market closes at 0.9351.

Speculator uses his online platform to enter a buy order "at the close" for a 96 put with a premium value of 1.11.

November 3, market falls to 0.9326.

With market lower than at the time of his put purchase, speculator offsets his put option.

Market is at 0.9326.

Trader liquidates his put option by selling his 93 put for a premium of 0.39.

Profit/Loss Summary

Cost to purchase option = 1.11.

Proceeds from sale of option = 0.39.

Net loss 0.72 ticks at $12.50/tick = $900.

---

mium to the extent that he was facing a loss no matter what he did. He had the presence to evaluate both "options" and table 19.9 tracks how he chose to offset the put and print a $900 loss, rather than exercise into a futures contract and face a nearly $1,712.50 loss. Live and learn!

Spread Risk Reductions

Options traders, as we see, employ a leverage that can minimize their losses when they are wrong in their market expectations, something that happens to all of us. This leverage for minimizing losses is just another way of reducing risk as compared to either the forex trader or futures trader.

If we look at the first two case histories in this chapter, our friendly futures trader gained $844 in a compatible market and then lost $844 in a contrary market, both from a single short contract in a market that moved 135 basis points. For comparison, let's look at tables 19.10 and 19.11, as we follow a very conservative option trader in the same kind of winning and losing market environment who enters a call *ratio* spread position into his online trading platform, and then we will evaluate the results and, in particular, look at the risk reduction available from a spread like this. We can expect to find that using option spreads will provide a level of *risk adjustment* that expands opportunities for online currency traders in various market scenarios. Review the two Case History tables below and then let's talk about it. We will find a bullish option spread gains more than $1,000 in a favorable price environment (table 19.10) and limits losses to $250 in an unfavorable price environment (table 19.11). Go to *http://book.theFinancials.com/interactive/chap19.html* and learn more about ratio spreads.

Table 19.10   *Trade Case History No. 8*

On November 1, position trader believes yen futures market is marginally bullish and wants to take a conservative bull spread option position.

Underlying cash forex market at 107.91. Futures at 0.9400.

Option trader enters a bull call ratio spread online as follows:

Buy 5 December 94 calls
Premium at 2.00 each
Total debit to account = $12,500

Sell 7 December 95 calls
Premium at 1.00 each
Total credit to account = $8,750

Cost of position to trading account = $3,750.

On November 19, market has moved in favor of bullish spread position by 135 ticks.

Underlying USD/JPY cash forex market rises to 106.41. Futures now at 0.9535.

December 94 calls now at 3.08.

December 95 calls now at 1.65.

Position trader elects to liquidate his bull call ratio spread and take gains.

Bought 5 December 94 calls at 2.00 each, now at 3.08.
Gain of $1.08 \times 5 = 5.40$.

Sold 7 December 95 calls at 1.00 each, now at 1.65.
Loss of $0.65 \times 7 = 4.55$.

Net gain from bull call ratio spread position in rising market = 0.85.

Profit is 85 ticks at $12.50/tick = $1,062.50.

At-risk account money = $6,000 (margin)

Table 19.11   *Trade Case History No. 9*

On November 1, position option trader believes yen futures market is marginally bullish and wants to take a conservative bull spread position.

Underlying cash forex market at 107.91 futures at 0.9400.

Position trader enters a bull call ratio spread online as follows:

  Buy 5 December 94 calls
  Premium at 2.00 each = $12,500.

  Sell 7 December 95 calls
  Premium at 1.00 each = $8,750.

Cost of position to account = $3,750.

On November 19, market has moved against bullish position of spread by 135 ticks.

Underlying yen cash forex market falls to 109.41. Yen futures now at 0.9265.

December 94 calls. Premium now at 1.40.

December 95 calls. Premium now at 0.60.

Position trader elects to liquidate his bull call ratio spread and accept loss.

Bought 5 December 94 calls at 2.00 each, now at 1.40.
Loss of 0.60 × 5 = 3.00

Sold 7 December 95 calls at 1.00 each, now at 0.60.
Gain of .40 × 7 = 2.80.

Net loss from bull call ratio spread position in declining market = 0.20.

Loss of 20 ticks at $12.50/tick = $250.

At-risk account Money = $6,000 (margin).

The SPAN margin requirement was $3,620 for a single futures contract (or naked option position). Due to the limited risk that a spread of this kind presents to the trader's account, the SPAN margin requirement is proportionately lower, even though there are multiple options employed in this position. Now let's see how this spread does in a falling market.

Because both options were out-of-the-money, their premiums lose less value per tick as compared to a rising market, which brings them into the money (their Deltas increase then).

Table 19.12

Winning Scenario

Futures trader	Gained $844	At-risk $1,810 (margin)
Option spread trader	Gained $1,062.50	At-risk $6,000 (margin)

Losing Scenario

Futures trader	Lost $844	At-risk $1,810 (margin)
Option spread trader	Lost $250	At-risk $6,000 (margin)

Remember that the market moved the same in both these option spread scenarios as for the futures hedger (Case History Nos. 1 and 2), 135 basis points (see table 19.12). The profit and loss scenarios were as follows: For the futures hedge position and a market that moved 135 ticks, the position gained $844 and lost $844. On the call ratio spread position the market moved 135 ticks and gained $1,062.50 while losing $250. The margin requirements were higher at $6,000 for the option trader, as compared to $3,620 for the futures hedger, because the futures contracts were half-sized e-mini contracts.

The conclusion we can draw from this is rather obvious: Option traders can not only manage their risk better, they can calibrate it to the precise level they are comfortable with in a specific market expectation. The trader only expected a marginal rise in this futures market. That means his assessment and risk level for a declining market had to be a factor in his trading strategy. Hence, he employed a spread position that limited his downside risk while permitting maximum upside gains.

So there is this rather significant trade-off for option spread traders versus futures traders: If you can accept a higher per trade margin ratio, you can use an option spread position to substantially maximize (leverage) your gains while minimizing your losses.

Short Strangles

One of the most popular *and promoted* option spread strategies is the short strangle. Go to *http://book.theFinancials.com/interactive/chap19.html* to learn more about the strangle.

It is a spread position that is quite different than the strategies we are comfortable with, because the risk is unlimited while the profit is limited to the initial credit received when the position initiated. We want to include this in our review, for those who are considering this trade position, and to

---

Table 19.13 *Trade Case History No. 10*

September 19, USD/JPY futures prices open at 0.9300.

Near term forecast is for a narrow trading range.

Trader enters an online market order for a short strangle.

  Sell 5 December 96 calls
  Premium at 0.70 each = 3.50.

  Sell 5 December 90 puts
  Premium at 0.60 each = 3.00.

Total credit to account = 6.50.

On October 21, December yen market increases to 0.9420.

Sold 5 December 96 calls at 0.70 each, now 1.00. Loss = 0.30.

Sold 5 December 90 puts at 0.60 each, now 0.45. Gain = 0.15.

Net loss/position marked to market = 0.15×5 or 75 ticks at \$12.50/tick or \$937.50.

On November 30, December yen market increases to 0.9550.

Sold 5 December 96 calls at 0.70 each, now at 1.50. Loss = 0.80.

Sold 5 December 90 puts at 0.60 each, now at 0.25. Gain = 0.35.

Net loss for position marked to market in account = 0.45×5 or 225 ticks at \$12.50/tick or \$2812.50.

On December 7 expiration, last trading day for options, December yen market increases and closes at 0.9560. Both options expire worthless.

Both options were out-of-the-money; trader keeps all premiums.

Profit/Loss Trading Summary

5 December 96 calls sold/received total 3.50 at \$12.50/tick = \$4,375.

5 December 90 puts sold/received total 3.00 at \$12.50/tick = \$3,750.

Net profit from position = \$8,125.

emphasize that you have to be selective and careful in choosing your spread "option." You have to be alert to the potential of substantial losses. Here is a case history of a short strangle.

Because the options never went into the money (see table 19.13), they would not be exercised by the purchasers. The options seller, who was selling two naked options, faced potentially large losses, as we have seen, and had the market traded above the .9600 level, he faced the possibility that his December 96 calls might be exercised. All option spreads are not created equal.

20

Fateful Decisions

We believe that the most important choices that currency traders ever make result from a relatively small number of big-picture decisions they face. Among the more obvious are the first two that every trader is confronted with. First, "What market am I trading in, forex or exchange futures?" Second, "Which currency am I most comfortable with and confident in?" Our reason for calling attention to the importance of making the right fateful decisions is that the same framework you use to arrive at these two big-picture decisions should be extended to all decisions involving your online currency trading experiences.

We want to help stock traders who are new to currency trading evaluate all of their fateful decisions. For experienced currency traders who are making the transition from voice brokers, we suggest that now is a good time for them to also re-evaluate their basic relationships to the forex or exchange markets and, in the process, consider new opportunities they now may have to explore a rapidly changing electronic currency market. To that end, we want to expand our understanding of the institutions that created and now run the OTC markets, as well as delineate how online traders fit into the big picture of those who really control foreign exchange rates (the institutional dealers), so that traders can more effectively maximize their profits.

Choose Your Market Carefully

The forex markets developed as the Bretton Woods fixed exchange rate infrastructure broke up in the 1970s. A core group consisting of a handful of commercial New York banks began to exploit the opportunities that the new floating international exchange rates offered. These commercial banks, which had already been in the foreign exchange business in a very small way under the Bretton Woods fixed exchange rate regime, soon began finding clients from the corporate and commercial banking sectors knocking at their doors, needing to find buyers and sellers of various currencies to transact their international business deals. Because rates were changing, literally by the minute, a market needed to be developed. So, from this modest beginning, grew what we now know to be the OTC, or interbank forex currency market. It was not long after U.S. banks developed the first over-the-counter market for forex that these interbank "dealers" began to expand *their* interests to include market making in forex for their own profits.

Global Forex Markets

During the intervening years between the collapse of Bretton Woods and the present day, U.S.-based commercial banks have been witness to an inexorable globalization of the world financial community.

One of the important characteristics of our modern currency relationships is the sectorization of the world into three currency zones, or blocks. It is important for traders to be aware that there has been, especially in more recent years, a connection among currencies that divides along the three major world currency zones: the yen, the euro, and the U.S. dollar.

For example, currencies in the Asian zone, like the famous (former) Asian Tigers, owing to their cross-border trade relationships, have exchange values that tend to rise and fall in concert against the Japanese yen.

Then, before the euro was introduced as a single currency into the European zone, we saw euroland currencies trading in virtual lockstep with each other against the German deutschemark. Even after the advent of the single-currency euro, those remaining European currencies that have not yet joined the EMS, not surprisingly, still tend to rise and fall in concert against the new euro.

The U.S. dollar, which is the premier international currency, has also attracted a group of major currencies that move en block with or against the American greenback. There is a collection of trading block countries like Great Britain, New Zealand, Australia, and Canada, whose currencies tend to rise and fall together against the U.S. dollar. Latin American currencies, of course, also tend to follow common exchange values against the U.S. dollar. This currency zone phenomenon, to some, confirms the "global village" nature of modern forex markets.

Something that has greased the skids for the global village development in forex has been the advent of electronic or online trading capabilities. Presently, according to the latest surveys, the total of trades that are electronically matched, through such interbank trading systems as Reuters and EBS, has increased from 6 percent three years ago to over 13 percent of total market volume today. I should note that this 13 percent figure is really a little understated, since major currencies, like the yen, euro, and U.S. dollar, have a much higher percentage of electronic formats, while the minor currencies typically lag behind in electronic matching systems and drag down the percentage totals. Even so, this reported doubling of growth in online currency trading is a tip-off that the electronic format is destined to be the vehicle of choice for trading currencies going forward.

We can predict with some level of confidence that spreads resulting from electronically matched trades will narrow. When spreads narrow, traders' costs of trading go down, sometimes dramatically—a significant benefit of the online currency-trading environment.

U.S. Forex Markets

Financial centers from London all the way to Tokyo have been making inroads into the U.S. market share of the OTC trade. Offshore dealers have, at this point, successfully competed for the largest portion of the interbank market, facilitating its evolution into a truly international market.

Out of the $1.5 trillion daily turnover in the global interdealer system today, U.S. trading houses account for only about 25 percent of that total, or $351 billion/day. U.S. dealers do contribute another $32 billion in currency swaps and options, for a 1998 reporting total of just under $400 billion/day in foreign currency traded by the U.S.-based dealers.

Within the United States, dealing institutions have declined from 148 in 1992 to the 1998 level of 93 dealers. Of those 93, most—82—are commercial banks and 11 are investment houses or other financial institutions that trade forex as a profit-making enterprise. Incidentally, the 10 largest of those control 50 percent of the transactions within U.S. borders.

The most recent surveys also indicate that 58 percent of all the transactions from dealers within the United States are executed by counterparties outside of the country. Add to this the fact that approximately 75 percent of interbank OTC currency transactions occur in non-U.S. banks, and we find a clear affirmation of the global and international character of the forex market.

Within the United States, and as of 1998, 49 percent of OTC trading involved intradealer transactions. That means trading in and among the 93, mostly New York–based, dealers themselves. The remaining balance broke down into 31 percent of the trade being transactions involving other U.S. bank (but nondealer) firms, with the remaining 20 percent coming from U.S. institutional transactors, such as mutual funds, hedge funds, pension funds, and retail traders, in about that order.

This breakdown by category serves to highlight that those forex transactions, which, in one way or another, are business-dependent, are actually in the minority of daily forex transactions. These business-dependent forex transactions include institutional portfolio investments overseas and corporate customers involved in offshore purchases of business or other foreign assets.

So the big-picture conclusion one can draw is that within these three broad categories of forex trading, the participants whom we categorize as "big boys" dominate and will be the controlling factor in determining currency prices and price movements that you, the retail trader, will seek to profit from. And remember, of these, a majority of forex transactions are executed for what might be termed non-business-dependent purposes.

Forex Is Not Regulated

The U.S. forex market is not regulated. When banks or investment houses elect to enter the forex dealing or brokerage fraternity, they do so without any threshold qualification or oversight from any foreign exchange authority. Hours for trading, terms of customer relationships, along with virtually everything else, are unregulated. A set of guidelines is issued by the Foreign Exchange Committee (sponsored by the Federal Reserve), but its rules are only suggestions and are nonbinding on dealers.

Institutional Dealers

We find that the institutional dealers have trading rooms packed with dozens of traders and millions of dollars in equipment. Much of this equipment, owing to the nature of the IT revolution, becomes obsolete only too quickly after its installation. So the investments that the dealers make is enormous, and, as you might imagine, so is their need for profits.

Upon entering the forex-dealing fraternity, many dealer banks can choose to get into the business of making markets in forex. Those market makers are concerned with high volume and small trading-range price targets. They seek to profit from the small spreads in their bid/ask quotes. They quote bid and ask prices and make good on their quotes as these get accepted by traders who participate in their interdealer system. Notice that I call them *interdealers*, because they really perform the functions of a forex dealer, more than those of a bank. From the retail trader's point of view, of course, these market makers happily provide us with liquidity and the competition that keeps the worldwide spreads as narrow as possible.

Some of their personnel function in back-office services, such as in the settlement of executed contracts. A different category of their workers trade with other interbank dealers. Yet another group of workers may trade for their own institutional, proprietary accounts. These proprietary traders will be focused on higher profit margins and longer-term price horizons. In this context, "longer term" may mean hours, instead of the minutes of the market-making fraternity in this office.

Governing all of these activities is the risk-management philosophy of the individual dealer's corporate executives. How much attention needs to be paid to customers and how much to their own proprietary account activity? How much capital in time or personnel needs to be invested in market making? The activity is fast-paced, even occasionally frantic, but always, counterintuitively, controlled.

Action Cycles

There are daily cycles of trading activity and intensity that experienced traders learn to incorporate into their trading practices. Traders should, for their own benefit, keep in mind that it is typical, and somewhat predictable, that the morning (London and New York time) hours of trading each day are the busiest. In fact, savvy traders who see a price move in the late afternoon of the New York trading day, which is so much slower in terms of trading volume, will very often discount that action, preferring instead to wait for the opening of the Asian markets, a few hours later, to assess the significance of such late-afternoon New York market sentiment.

Spots Before Our Eyes

The "spot" price in the forex vernacular, of course, refers to the price "on the spot," or at the moment of trade execution. The forex dealer who buys U.S. dollars at a spot price is actually buying a dollar-denominated deposit in a bank located somewhere in the United States. Another forex dealer, who may be buying Swiss francs, is in reality buying a Swiss franc deposit in a bank somewhere in Switzerland.

When a spot transaction is made, a direct exchange of one currency for another requires transfers through the payment systems of the two countries whose currencies are being traded. Bank Number 1 in Chicago agrees that on October 1, it will sell $1 million for Swiss francs to Bank Number 2 in Zurich. The rate agreed upon in the spot transaction is 1.75 CHF per dollar, for settlement on October 3. On that date, October 3, Bank Number 2 will pay 1.75 million Swiss francs to be credited to Bank Number 1's CHF-denominated account at some bank within Switzerland. Bank Number 1, of course, on October 3 will give $1 million for credit in U.S. dollars to Bank Number 2, which designates its bank in the U.S. for that purpose.

Note that the settlement date is two days subsequent to the trade execution. Because of the international nature of forex interbanking relationships, that is an important consideration. It provides time for these trade agreements, which may take place between parties at opposite ends of the globe, to be consummated. In the geographically proximate nations of the United States and Canada, value dates for settlement need only be one day.

On the issue of settlement dates, there is in the forex markets something known as settlement risk. Simply put, from the date of execution, it has been known to happen that one party may make payment in accordance with the terms of his trade execution. The other party, for a variety of reasons, may be unable to make the payment from his end of the trade. He may default on his agreement to sell 1.75 million Swiss francs, after his counterparty to the trade in the United States has already transferred $1 million to the Swiss trader's bank account.

In October 1994, the New York Foreign Exchange Committee published a widely circulated study, concluding that foreign exchange settlement risk is much greater than generally understood by participants in the forex markets. Then again, in March 1996, the respected Bank for International Settlements, BIS, reinforced the conclusions of the FEC report and called for vigilance by all traders on this issue of settlement risk. In an instance where one party to a trade stands to be defaulted against by the counterparty to his trade, it needs to be known that your forex broker should assume in writing all settlement risk that derives from your trading though him. It is worth repeating, be sure to have in writing from your broker, his affirmation that he, not you, assumes the settlement risk from all your trades.

The proof of the equitable or "leveled" nature of interbank markets is in the confirmation that spreads and prices vary only marginally around the world at any given moment. The price level and spread quoted by a dealer in Tokyo will be very nearly the same as those quoted by a dealer back in New York. This is supported by the fact, which was mentioned earlier, that nearly 60 percent of the transactions made by U.S.-based interbank dealers are with foreign bank counterparties. So the international character of forex trading creates one large pot from which any trader will taste the same stew, irrespective of where in the world he may be dining.

It is estimated that of the 2,000 dealers worldwide, somewhat surprisingly, there are as many as 100 to 200 market makers at any given time. Of those, less than 1 percent, or 10 interbank institutions, are considered major dealers or the biggest of the big interdealer institutions in forex. What these statistics point up is that the OTC forex market is the forerunner and embodiment of a global village, which so many financial market observers have asserted will be the wave of the future, resulting from the information technology revolution.

King Dollar

The U.S. dollar plays a unique and pivotal role in OTC forex trades. Some may not realize how pivotal that role is. For example, the United States accounts for only one-fourth of world output and less than one-fifth of international trade. But when it comes to forex trading, the U.S. dollar is involved in 87 percent of all forex transactions and accumulates a total of 60 percent of the world's currency reserves. This can be accounted for and appreciated if one realizes the multiple roles the U.S. currency plays in world finances. Look at Table 20.1.

Considering Central Banks

The IMF lists 181 national currencies, which our friendly trader can choose to trade in. Many of the cross-currency rates, such as the Turkish lira/Slovakian koruna, simply do not have the liquidity necessary to

Table 20.1 *Role of the U.S. Dollar in World Currency Relationships*

Investment currency	used for	FDI (foreign direct investment)
Reserve currency	used for	Central bank accounts worldwide
Transaction currency	used for	Medium of exchange (e.g. agricultural and oil purchases)
Invoice currency	used for	International contract agreements
Intervention currency	used for	Exchange rate policy by central banks
Vehicle currency	used for	Liquidity: exchange CHF for USD, then USD for Mexican pesos

Use of USD minimizes the need to manage multiple currency pairs.

There is also an efficiency role that the U.S. dollar plays in world currency markets. If a corporation has to deal in 100 currencies, then it could have currency exchange problems in as many as 4,950 different combinations of currencies. But by managing their foreign exchange relationships effectively, those numbers can be reduced to only 99 exchange pairs, by use of the U.S. dollar as a base currency.

make trading that cross-currency pair attractive. Of course, a trader could then, as we have already illustrated, trade the U.S. dollar/Turkish lira, and then the U.S. dollar/Slovakian koruna, to accomplish his trading objectives. So there is always a way for the persistent currency trader to exploit the opportunities that world forex markets offer.

Both the Turkish lira and the Slovakian koruna are floating currencies. But presently, 67 of the 181 international currencies are pegged or fixed, as the Argentine peso is to the U.S. dollar. Pegged rates, needless to say, effectively preempt trading, except in the most unusual of circumstances.

Of the 114 currencies that use a flexible or floating exchange rate valuation system, only a few dozen have the market liquidity to be considered seriously for full-time trading purposes.

The U.S. Central Bank

The U.S. Federal Reserve is the most prominent and, of course, most influential of the world's central banks. Alan Greenspan, its chairman during the recent decade of phenomenal economic growth in the United States, commands unequaled respect when he speaks or makes decisions for his board. If you are trading a currency, like the U.S. dollar, that is subject to central bank intervention, you really must pay attention to the influence that a central bank exerts on its currency's exchange rate.

Remember that the central bank short-circuits the supply-and-demand forces that markets exert on every other price structure. If the Federal Reserve (or any other central bank) raises interest rates, the money supply declines. Normally, in a declining supply environment, prices—or in this case, the exchange rate—can be expected to go up. Also, with higher interest rates, you have to factor in the interest rate differential, which also strengthens the higher interest rate currency vis-à-vis the other currencies. When the Federal Reserve decreases interest rates, supply increases and prices (exchange rates) of the U.S. dollar can be expected to fall. So, one can see that the action of the central banks stands to have a major and immediate impact on currency prices.

Central banks all over the globe intervene from time to time in their currency markets to effect a change to their currency's exchange rate, and they usually succeed, albeit if only in the very short term. Being alert to possible intervention is an important component of every

Table 20.2

Year	Purpose	Amount
1991–1992	Strengthen U.S. dollar	$2.659 billion
1991–1992	Weaken U.S. dollar	$750 million
1993–1995	Strengthen U.S. dollar	$14 billion
1998	Strengthen U.S. dollar	Not officially reported
2000	Buy euro/weaken U.S. dollar	Not officially reported

trader's input data stream. Look at the intervention record of the U.S. Federal Reserve Board in recent years in table 20.2.

So in selecting a currency to trade, you need to take into consideration the interventionist history and role of its central bank. Different national central banks each adopt their own individual, distinctive policies regarding interventions. The Bank of Japan, for instance—not unlike the voters in certain Third World countries or even selected U.S. Midwestern cities—has a history of participating "early and often," in an effort to manage the exchange rate of the yen.

The reason, of course, is that like many Asian nations, Japan's economic growth and its public officials are highly sensitive to export revenue and balance of payments data, which are directly impacted by the exchange rate of their currency.

The mechanism by which central banks intervene is not complex. They hold dollar reserves (and foreign currency reserves) in special funds, like the U.S. Federal Reserve's Exchange Stabilization Fund, for such purposes, and they simply go into the markets and purchase or sell the currency they want to impact. U.S. forex intervention transactions are handled through the offices of the Federal Reserve Bank of New York.

The European Central Bank, under its first president, Wim Duisenberg, was extremely reluctant to intervene in the face of the near 30 percent market devaluation that the euro experienced after its introduction in January 1999. Finally, working with coordination from the United States, Japan, England, and other major world central banks, the ECB intervened for the first time in September 2000. It subsequently followed up this first intervention with several unilateral interventions, in an effort to staunch the plunge of the single currency against the U.S. dollar and Japanese yen.

Virtually all central bank interventions are "sterilized." This term is used to mean, very simply, that whatever addition or withdrawal of the national currency is undertaken by central bank intervention, it is carefully balanced and offset by residual domestic monetary action at the central bank, so as not to impact the existing domestic money supply growth targets in place at the time. Critics maintain that such "sterilization" mitigates or, more accurately perhaps, actually negates the influence of the intervention on exchange rates in the first place.

That argument is undoubtedly true, since you are, after all, putting money one day in the aggregate and taking it back out (in the aggregate) a few days later, in the exact same amount. So obviously, the supply-and-demand dynamics are not being changed when sterilized intervention is used.

Advocates for sterilized interventions argue that central bank action in the forex markets is intended only to bring order to disorderly markets and to communicate to market speculators that their action has the central banks' attention.

Hence, central bank intervention sends a signal to the markets that it believes exchange rates are improperly valued, pressuring traders to re-evaluate their positions and hopefully stabilize the exchange rate to a level and volatility that is in line with economic fundamentals, at least as the central banks see them. Intervention is not supposed to be justified under any other circumstances.

So traders are well advised to keep the central banks' involvement in their currencies in mind at all times. The record shows that central bank action will always have the desired short-term effect. Whether it has a longer-term impact in a direction against the markets is another issue.

Q & A

Question: When I use the online resource search engines for forex and other currency categories, I am overwhelmed by the amount of information and data out there. What is the best way to assimilate and benefit from the near glut of resources available to online currency traders?

Answer: Join the crowd! Online currency traders are indeed beneficiaries in the extreme of an abundance of online resources available. We all have to develop the skills to sort through the chaff and identify only the wheat, to borrow a commodity trader's metaphor. It is vitally important to keep current with what is available online and, as you say, not be overwhelmed by it all. Simply put, organize your search engine results and bookmark helpful Web sites for future use, with clear names. Do not waste time with the redundant or irrelevant information that we are all bombarded with.

Resources

Online Forex Brokers

www.atlantaforex.com
www.cms-forex.com
www.forexcapital.com
www.forextrading.com
www.forex-cmc.com
www.forex-gci.com
www.fxcm.com
www.forexsquare.com
www.iforex.net
www.igforex.com
www.gaincapital.com
www.globalcap.com
www.matchbookfx.com
www.mgforex.com

Online Forex News Sites

www.forexnews.com/news/news.html
www.marketnews.com
www.abilitynews.com
www.cnbc.com

Online Simulated Forex Trading

www.mgforex.com
www.ideal-forex.com
www.imex-fx.com

International Sites of Interest to Forex Traders

www.forexcompass.com
www.fx4business.com
www.ideaglobal.com
www.imex.com
www.opulent-fx.com
www.radaforex.com

URLs of Forex Indexed Sites

www.cas.american.edu
www.fincad.com
www.forexdirectory.net
www.site-by-site.com
www.investorlinks.com
www.marketmaker.co.uk
www.marketuplinks.com
www.x-rates.com
www.global-view.com

Historical Forex Prices

www.is99.com/disktrading.com
www.frbchi.org/econinfo/fin

Online Futures Brokers

www.alaron.com
www.altavest.com
www.ancofutures.com
www.apexfutures.com
www.atticuspartners.com
www.cannontrading.com
www.iepstein.com
www.lind-waldock.com
www.orionfutures.com

Online Simulated Futures Trading

www.auditrack.com
www.mocktrading.com

Futures Related Organizations

www.cftc.com
www.nfafutures.com
www.cme.com
www.phlx.com
www.midam.com
www.fia.com

Options Pricing Sites

www.freeoptionpricing.com
www.mindxpansion.com

Historical Futures/Options Pricing

www.accesstrading.com
www.gpfo.com/futuresguide.com

Commitment of Traders Report

www.commodityquotes.com
www.dacolabs.com
www.marketpit.com
www.visualeconometrics.com

Glossary

All or None A trade entry which requires that the order be treated as a limit order and that the entire quantity of the order be filled at that limit price or better, or none of the order will be executed.

Arbitrage A position where a profit can be made from a temporary price disparity between two markets (or two products within the same market), by taking the long and short side simultaneously.

Assignment The notification to an option seller that the buyer has exercised his right to buy (call) or sell (put) the underlying futures contract. This notification is made by an exchange clearing house.

Associated Person An employee of an FCM, or other accredited professional, whose job is to accept customer orders for trade execution.

At-the-Money (options) An option whose strike price is equivalent to the underlying futures contract market price value.

Bear Spread (options) An option position established by simultaneously buying and selling options in order to profit from a market price decline. One leg will profit from a decline in the underlying currency prices. The other leg of the option spread will profit if the underlying currency value unexpectedly increases.

Bid The price at which a dealer is willing to buy a currency, and at which a trader must sell to enter or exit a currency position.

Black-Scholes Options Pricing Model The theory and formula developed in 1973 by Messers F.Black and M. Scholes that assigns a market value for an option's premium based on the underlying futures price.

Bollinger Bands A technical analysis study which creates moving average and volatility bands above and below the price range so that over 95 percent of the prices are contained within this envelope. A price move outside of the bands can be a trend change indicator.

Bretton Woods, 1944 The agreement to establish fixed exchange rates for the world's major currencies. The U.S. dollar became, de facto, the world's reserve currency and was redeemable for gold from the U.S. Treasury at a guaranteed rate of $35 per ounce. The agreement dissolved in 1971, as the world transitioned to the floating exchange rate system in use today.

Broker A person who matches buyers and sellers in the currency markets, and who does not profit from the price movements in currencies, but rather earns commissions from the trades he matches. The quotes for the orders he executes are established by a dealer, rather than him. Brokers can be Associated Persons, and as such oversee the taking of orders from clients. They can also be on the floor of an exchange, executing orders received from online clients, or FCMs.

Bull Spread An option position established by the simultaneous buying and selling of options in a way that will profit from an increase in the underlying currency market prices. One leg of the option spread will profit if the underlying currency increases. The other leg will gain if the market unexpectedly declines. Thus the two legs together produce an option spread that will on balance, gain from a market increase, while protecting against a market decline by limiting losses in that event.

Call Option A contract that gives authority to the holder of an option to buy the underlying currency at a predetermined price (strike price) at any time until the expiration of the contract. The seller of the option then may be required to take a short position in the underlying currency if the call is subsequently exercised.

CFTC The Commodity Futures Trading Commission was authorized by the Federal Commodity Exchange Act in 1974 and administers the provisions of that act.

Clearing (Member, House) Clearing is the process by which a Clearing House assumes responsibility for guaranteeing futures transactions at its exchange by taking both the buyer's and the seller's side of a transaction. The Clearing House oversees margin administration and the orderly flow of exchange trading execution. A Clearing Member clears all trades of a non Clearing member.

Commitment of Traders Report A report published by the CFTC weekly that accumulates total long or short positions of futures and options traders in U.S. exchange futures markets. Categories are Large Commercial, Large Speculators, and Small Speculators.

Convergence The reduction in the disparity between the (higher) futures contract price and the cash market value of a currency. At expiration, the two prices converge to equivalence.

Dealer A person who functions as a principal in a trade by taking one side, with the intention of quickly offsetting that position through a counterparty, with the goal of profiting from this "dealing."

Delta (options) A fractional value which references the rate of increase (or decrease) in an option premium as the market value of the futures contract increases or decreases. The option premium will rise or fall according to this Delta value.

Dow Theory A theory of market analysis originated by Charles Dow in 1897 which holds that market prices can be categorized into trends that he described as similar to waves. Each wave has its own distinctive characteristic. By identifying those characteristics, you can identify the direction of market prices.

Elliott Wave Named after Ralph Elliott, who believed that financial market price valuations follow the same cyclical patterns found in nature. For example, the Elliott Wave Theory advances the belief that charts can identify discernable price movements according to a pattern of waves: five waves advancing and three waves declining.

Euro The new currency in Europe introduced on Janaury 1, 1999, that combines the values of the member nations' individual currencies into a new, single currency, the euro.

Exercise Price (options) Equivalent to the strike price.

FIA The Futures Industry Association is a professional education and public information group composed of Futures Commission Merchants.

Fibonacci Numbers A sequence of numbers dating back to the 13th century Italian mathematician who posited that formulaic ratios exist in nature that can be applied to almost anything, including currency markets.

Floor Broker An exchange member in the pits who executes trades for other persons.

Floor Trader An exchange member who executes trades in the open outcry pits for his own account. Also referred to as a "local."

Futures Contract A contract to purchase or sell a specified amount of currency on a specified date at the agreed upon price. The futures contract, among other purposes, is used to shift risk that arises from holding assets in the cash markets. This contract defines a standardized framework delineating delivery dates, trading lot sizes, and terms and conditions for contract execution.

Globex 2 The international electronic trading system introduced by the Chicago Mercantile Exchange in 1992 to trade currency futures worldwide after closing hours of the open outcry pit trading on the exchange floor. Participating global exchanges use the system to contribute liquidity to the electronic futures trading markets.

Hedging To take a position in the futures market opposite a position in the cash market for the purpose of minimizing loss from adverse cash market price changes. A hedge may also take the form of a having a position in the futures market to use as a surrogate for a cash transaction that will occur later.

Initial Margin The level of money required by the exchange (or forex dealer) to serve as a surety bond against potential losses resulting in the market.

In-the-Money (options) An option with intrinsic value. For a Call, that means the strike price will be below the underlying contract price. For a Put, the strike price will be above the underlying price of the currency futures contract.

Intrinsic Value (options) The component in an option premium that can be expressed as follows: a value equal to the difference between the strike price and the underlying currency's price level.

Introducing Broker A person other than an Associated Person, who takes and solicits orders for currency contracts at an exchange, but who does not hold money or manage margin.

Limit Order A restrictive order specifying a price at which the trade must be executed by the broker. A limit order protects the fill from being executed at a price worse than the one specified. For instance, a buy limit order will be below the market price of the a currency. When the market reaches the specified fill price, the broker will try to fill the order. If, however, the market then precipitously rises, preventing a fill at the price limit specified or better, then the broker will return the order to the trader as unfilled. So a limit order protects against an adverse market move at the time it is triggered. A sell limit order will specify a price above the underlying currency value.

Liquidation A term used interchangeably with offset. It means to close or offset an existing position in a cash-settled market.

Local See Floor Trader.

MACD A technical analysis study developed in the 1960s that stands for Moving Average Convergence Divergence. This oscillator-based format helped popularize histograms, a bar chart on the bottom of a graph which is used to anticipate price trend changes.

Margin A specified amount of money required by the forex dealer, exchange futures broker or Introducing Broker, to insure against potential losses from outstanding currency market positions. The Initial Margin is established by the various exchanges according to the SPAN formula. A 25 percent reduction establishes a Maintenance Margin level requirement. If a trader's account reaches the Maintenance Margin level, it triggers a margin call. The margin account must then be brought up to the Initial Margin requirement, or the broker/dealer has the right to liquidate all current positions.

Market Maker A dealer in forex who will risk his own capital by offering both buy and sell quotes in a currency market. Such market makers have the effect of adding liquidity to the overall market environment.

Market Order An order which instructs a broker to execute the trade at the best available price immediately and without restrictions.

Mark-To-Market A valuation system that takes place daily. The closing prices of a futures contract or option premium is revalued at the hour of the exchange's daily closing. It is used to determine daily margin and cash settlement requirements for the exchange futures markets. In a marked-to-market system, the current daily value of all positions is established, regardless of whether the positions are settled that day or remain outstanding as of the close of business.

Momentum A technical analysis study tool that measures the relative change in price within a specific time interval.

Naked Option An option position where the trader sells an option but does not hold the underlying futures contract as a backstop against possible exercise of the option he has sold. Naked options have unlimited potential losses.

National Futures Association A self-regulating organization to which all trading professionals employed in the futures business must belong. It is organized under CFTC authority by federal law. It conducts arbitration and mediation services for traders and others who may have a complaint involving exchange futures trading or relationships.

Not Held Order This is an order that brokers and dealers may accept from a client, but that they do not obligate themselves to abide by in the same way they would for the execution of a market order. A Not Held order means the broker who accepts it is not held responsible if the order cannot, or is not, executed at the specified price, or time, or for any other reason. An OCO, or order cancels order trade entry could be an example of a "not held" order by a broker.

Offer The price at which a dealer would be willing to sell a currency; also the price at which traders must buy a currency.

Order Cancels Order This instruction to the broker has two parts. If one order is executed, then the remaining order is to be canceled. Also referred to as "One Cancels Other."

Option A contract which gives the holder a right, but not an obligation, to purchase the underlying futures contract, at a price and time specified in the option. Thus a 90 March Call option will give the buyer the "option" to buy a futures contract at a price level of 0.9000 before the option expires in March.

Out-of-the-Money (options) An option whose premium value has no intrinsic worth, but does have time value. For a call, that would mean the strike price is higher than the underlying currency futures price. For a put, the strike price is lower than the underlying currency futures price level. The premium value for an out-of-the-money option is referred to as having only "time value."

Pip The smallest incremental value by which an exchange rate move is measured in forex markets.

Point and Figure Charts A method of charting that uses price levels to generate patterns and where price trends are discerned by direction alone and not in relationship to time.

Premium (options) The price that must be paid to acquire rights to hold an option against an underlying futures contract. For the buyer of an option, the premium is the price paid. For the seller or writer of an option, the premium is the price received.

Purchasing Power Parity This theory of fundamental analysis suggests that the exchange rates between two currencies will adjust so that goods in both countries will cost the same.

Put Option A contract that gives an authority to the buyer of this option a right to sell the underlying currency future at a predetermined price (strike price) at any time up to the expiration of the contract. The seller of the option may then be required to take a long position in the underlying currency if the put is exercised.

Random Walk A current theory which holds that price movements cannot be predicted from past history or trends, and that future market values will be determined by totally random factors that cannot be defined through either technical or fundamental analysis.

Resistance A price level in technical analysis which anticipates that selling pressure may reverse an upward price movement. A resistance level is where selling in the past has in fact resisted an uptrending price pattern.

Retracement A price move reversal within a major price trend.

RSI A technical analysis study known as the Relative Strength Index. The RSI scale is 0 to 100, and uses an oscillator form of moving averages to signal overbought and oversold market price conditions.

Scalper A person who is generally found on the trading floor and who gets into and out of positions rapidly. A scalper seeks to garner very small profits as frequently as possible during the trading day. For instance, a scalper will initiate purchases only fractions below the last transaction price and then seek to sell at only a fraction above the last traded price. Scalpers do, from the standpoint of the other market participants, produce liquidity for the broader market.

Settlement Price (futures) The Clearing House clears all trades and settles all positions. A settlement process involves those trades that have been liquidated or offset, so that the buyer and seller can have their accounts credited or debited as the case may be on a daily basis. If some positions have not been traded, they will be assigned a settlement price as that option's designated closing price for the day, in order to permit the mark-to-market requirement.

SPAN The Standard Portfolio of Risk Analysis. This model factors in various elements of the market environment to establish a standardized valuation for margin requirements at an exchange.

Spot Price The execution price for a currency which then will be delivered or settled two days hence, or in the case of USD/CAD, one day.

Stochastics A technical analysis study originated by George Lane. A Stochastics chart measures the position of a currency price in relation to its own recent trading range. Like all oscillators it uses a range, in this case, 0 percent to 100 percent, for overbought and oversold signals. There are multiple variations including fast and slow Stochastics studies.

Stop Order An order entry which is designed to be executed when the market price reaches a predetermined level. For an existing position, the stop will specify a price level which when reached by the market, will trigger a market order for immediate fill at the best available price to exit the position. When used to enter a position, a stop will become a market order for execution when the market reaches a predetermined price level the trader wishes to have as an entry point in a currency.

Straddle (options) An option position designed to take advantage of a market price move either up or down. It consists of two options, one a call and the other a put, having the same expiration contract date and the same strike prices.

Strangle (options) An option position designed to profit from a range-bound market price environment. It consists of two options, one a call and the other a put, both having the same contract expiration dates, but different strike prices. A strangle can be either a long or a short spread.

Strike Price (options) Also referred to as the exercise price. The strike price is the price in the option contract at which the holder of the option may buy or sell an underlying futures contract by exercising his option. Hence, a Dec 90 call has a 90 strike price. This call option contract grants the holder a right to buy the underlying futures contract at the price level of 0.9000 anytime during the life of the option contract.

Support A technical analysis term meaning a price level where buying may be expected to reverse a downward trending market. Support is the level where buying in the past has in fact halted a downtrending market price direction.

Technical analysis An evaluation of market prices that anticipates future price movements based on previous patterns of market price history. This can include momentum, volume open interest, and many other types of studies.

Tick The smallest increment of price change in an exchange traded futures contract or option.

Time Value (options) Refers to that value of an option premium that is separate from and, for the case of an in-the-money option, in addition to, intrinsic value. Time value includes volatility, time until expiration, and other factors that are extrinsic in the sense that they are distinct from the intrinsic value in the option premium.

Volatility The degree of price movement within a range of time.

Index

A

Abbreviation standards, 24
Accumulation/Distribution (AD) charts, 183–185
Action cycles, 328
Adjusting strategies, 292–293
Alerts, e-mail, 159–160
Arbitrage, 269, 308
Arbitration, 262
    benefits of process, 282
    damages, claims for, 277, 279
    discovery proceedings, 278–279
    flexibility of procedure, 279–280
    hearing procedures, 280–282
    panel members, 280
    procedure, 277–278
    state court appeals, 282
    state law and, 279
    subpoenas in proceedings, 281
    witnesses at hearing, 280
Argentine peso, 42
Asia, 14–16. *See also* specific countries
    currency crisis, 5, 15–16
Asia Fund, 14–15
Asian Tigers, 13, 324
    International Monetary Fund (IMF) loans, 15
Asking price, 26
ATM (at-the-money) options, 140
    Delta and, 143
Australia
    base currency, 24
    Chicago Mercantile Exchange currency trading, 24
    Globex2, dollar on, 263
    margin requirements, 64
    as trading block country, 325
Austrian schilling, 5

B

Bank for International Settlements (BIS), 329
Bank of England (BoE), 22
Bank of Japan (BoJ), 22
    call rate, 97–98
    market price breakout, 91–92
    Ministry of Finance interventions and, 295
    role of, 332
    ZIRP (zero interest rate policy), 52, 250, 295
Banks. *See also* specific banks
    euro, intervention for, 239–240
    as major forex players, 43
Bear call spreads. *See* Options
Belgian franc, 5
Belgium Futures & Options Exchange (Belfox), 59
Bids and offers, 26
    inside the spread, 46
Black-Scholes pricing model, 146
Bollinger Bands, 44, 132–134
    uses of, 162
Bond markets
    interest rates and, 92
    United States bonds, 93, 100

Brazil
  Chicago Mercantile Exchange currency
    trading, 24
  Globex2, real on, 263
  margin requirements, 64
Brazilian Mercantile and Futures Exchange
  (BMF), 57, 59
Breakout, 178
Bretton Woods conference, 6–8, 324. See also
  Exchange rates
Brokers. See also Arbitration; Errors; Online
  trading
  accountability of, 68
  choosing a broker, 45–46
  competition among, 80
  damages claims against, 277, 279
  futures margins, 65
  Globex2, interfacing with, 264
  language of brokers, learning, 265–266
Budapest Commodity Exchange (BCE), 59
Budget surpluses, 93
Buffet, Warren, 242
Bull call spreads. See Options
Bullish trends, 190
Buy/sell signals
  in Point and Figure charts, 176–180
  Stochastics and, 218–220
  Stop and Reversal (SAR) charts and, 183
  Ultimate Oscillator and, 212
Buy stop orders
  defined, 51
  for short-term traders, 167

C

Cable, 24
Calls. See Puts and calls
Canada
  Chicago Mercantile Exchange currency
    trading, 24
  Globex2, dollar on, 263
  margin requirements, 64
  as trading block country, 325
Candlestick charts, 42
Cash forex, 62, 63
Cell phones, 160
Central banks, 43
  euro, intervention for, 239–240
  in forex market, 330–331
  sterilization, 333

Charts. See also MACD charts; Point and Figure
  charts; Stochastics
  Accumulation/Distribution (AD) charts,
    183–185
  daily charts, 161–162
  details in, 158
  elements of, 120
  Pivot Point system, 185–186
  selection of, 160–162
  Stop and Reversal (SAR) charts, 180–183
  time zone Fibonacci charts, 194
  trends and, 120
Chicago Board of Trade (CBOT), 57, 58–59
  TOPS (Trade Order Processing System), 79
Chicago Mercantile Exchange (CME), 7–8, 23.
  See also Globex2
  currencies traded, 24
  futures and options trading, 57
  hours of operation, 63
  TOPS (Trade Order Processing System),
    78–79
  transparent margin format, 63–64
  world's largest futures exchange, 57–59
China, 19
Choosing markets, 41–42, 3243
Clearinghouse guarantees, 67–68
Closing account statements, 273
Closing out, 260, 261
Closing positions, 28, 29
Commissions
  limit orders and, 49
  waiver of, 50
Commitment of Traders weekly report, 267–270
  effective use of, 270
Commodity Channel Index (CCI), 127–131
  late signals on trends, 129–130
Commodity Futures Trading Commission
  (CFTC), 33, 262
  forex dealers in, 275
  futures exchange markets regulation, 66–67
  reportable trades data, 267–270
Common market thesis, 248
Communication in online trading, 272
Congested price action, 178
Cost savings, euro and, 10–11
Credit spreads, 229
Cross currencies, 24
Currency swaps
  benefits of, 35–36
  motivation for, 34–35
  plain vanilla swaps, 33–35

Currency trends, software showing, 105
Currency zones/blocks, 324–325
Czech Republic, euro in, 11

D

Daily charts, 161–162
DaimlerChrysler Corporation, 10
Damages claims against brokers, 277, 279
Data source providers, 42
Day Order option, 48
Dealers, 42
Debit spread, 226–227
Delta
    Gamma and, 147–148
    options, Delta value of, 142–143, 316
    software data, 145
Demo accounts, 81–84
    liquidating options, 84–86
    spread format, 83
    stop orders in, 83–84
Denmark in European Monetary Union (EMU), 9
Derivatives, options as, 126
Details
    attention to, 156–157
    in charts, 158
De-Trender, Price, 210–211
Divergence indicators. *See also* MACD charts;
    Stochastics
    Accumulation/Distribution (AD) charts, 184
    in Relative Strength Index (RSI), 116
    Ultimate Oscillator as, 211–212
Dollar. *See* specific currencies
Dow, Charles, 190, 194, 195
Dow Jones Industrial Average
    options, 222
    risk in trading, 301
    Trade Deficit theory and, 249–250
Dow Jones Transportation Average, 190
Downtrend lines, 120
Dow Theory, 190
Drawdowns, 156
Druckenmiller, Stanley, 53
Duisenberg, Wim, 332
Dutch guilder, 5

E

Eastern Europe, euro in, 11
EBS, 325

Elliott, Ralph, 195, 196
Elliott Wave Theory, 190, 195–201
    corrective waves, 197
    Fibonacci influence on, 197–201
    Grand Supercycle in, 196
    impulsive waves, 197
    peak price levels in, 199–200
E-mail price alerts, 159–160
E-Mini euro on Globex2, 263, 264
E-Mini yen on Globex2, 263, 264
End-of-day closing account statements, 273
England. *See* Great Britain
Entry orders, 164–167
    OCOs (one cancels other), 167–168
Entry points, 160
Errors. *See also* Arbitration
    communication errors, 262
    dealing with, 272–274
    with exit orders, 273
    National Futures Association, claims with,
        276–278
Estonia, euro in, 11
Euro, 4, 8–11, 324
    as base currency, 24
    benchmark exchange rate, 10–11
    fundamental traders and, 44–45
    on Globex2, 263
    introduction of, 4–5, 6
    margin requirements, 64
    real business, effect on, 10–11
    September 2000 intervention, 239–240
Eurodollars, 32–33
    accounts, 95
European Central Bank (ECB), 22, 239–240,
    332–333
European Currency Union (ECU), 45
European monetary system (EMS), 8
European Monetary Union (EMU), 9
European Union, 8, 19. *See also* Euro
Euro-zone returns, 248
    Interest Rate Parity theory, 251
Exchange futures. *See* Futures exchange markets
Exchange Rate Mechanism (ERM), 9
Exchange rates, 7. *See also* Euro
    currency swaps and, 34
    for Eurodollars, 32
    floating exchange rates, 21
    market-driven rates, 19
    official rates, 5
Existing position hedged futures strategy, 144
Exit orders, errors with, 273

Exit points, 106, 160
  Stop and Reversal (SAR) charts, 180–183
Exponential moving averages (EMAs), 107
  defined, 124–125
  in MACD study, 108
  short-term traders and, 158

F

Fair market value approach, 243
Fannie Mae bonds, 93
Federal Reserve. *See* United States Federal
  Reserve
Fibonacci, Leonardo, 190, 197
Fibonacci numbers, 190–194, 195
  Elliott Wave Theory and, 197–201
  price values, ratio relationship as, 196
  ratio chart, 195
Financials.com Web site, 283–284
  intermarket spreads, 297
  ratio spreads, 318
  speculator's technical analysis evaluations,
    309
  on strangles, 320
  yen, moves by, 306
Fines from National Futures Association, 276
Finex Exchange, 57, 58
Finnish markka, 5
Flat markets, 289
Floating exchange rates, 21
Floor traders, 308–310
Foreign exchange (forex). *See* Forex
Forex, 4. *See also* Options
  abbreviation standards, 24
  basic transactions, 23–25
  cash forex, 62, 63
  central banks, role of, 330–331
  closing in, 287
  comparative survey of dealers, 25
  Elliott Wave Theory and, 200–201
  euro currency and, 10–11
  exchange futures compared, 56–57
  expanding opportunities, 104–105
  global character of, 29
  global markets, 324–325
  growth of, 20–21
  institutional dealers, 327
  major players in, 43
  market bids/asks, 66
  regulated forex, 274–278
  regulation of United States market, 326–327

simultaneous currency positions, 258
spot price in, 27–30, 328–329
structure of market, 22–23
technical analysis for, 187–201
United States markets, 325–326
up *vs.* down language, 29
Forwards, 33, 36–38
  formulas for, 38
France, 4, 5
  Chicago Mercantile Exchange currency
    trading, 24
  Globex2, franc on, 263
  gold reserves and, 7–8
  margin requirements, 64
Freddie Mac bonds, 93
Free demos, 50
Fundamental analysis, 44–45, 90
  central bank intervention and, 239–240
  fair value approach, 243
  interest rate differentials, 92–93
  Interest Rate Parity theory, 251
  intrinsic value requirement, 244
  online trading and, 293–295
  and Phillips Curve, 245–246
  Purchasing Power Parity theory, 247–249
  Rukeyser, Louis and, 242
  technical analysis and, 239–252
  Trade Deficit theory, 249–250
Futures commission merchants (FCMs), 66, 68–69
Futures exchange markets, 23. *See also* Globex2;
  Options
  clearinghouse guarantees, 67–68
  cost-efficiency of, 306
  demo accounts, 81–84
  derivatives, futures as, 136
  existing position hedged futures strategy, 144
  forex compared, 56–57
  futures commission merchants (FCMs), 68–69
  gaps affecting, 72
  global futures exchanges, 59–60
  international exchange futures markets, 302
  long-term strategies, 126–131
  margins, 63–66
    costs, 73–75
    deposits, 308–309
  market bids/asks, 66
  maximizing profits, blueprint for, 71–86
  oscillators in, 204–205
  Price De-Trender, 210–211
  Price Oscillator, 208–210
  profits and losses, 75–78
  quarterly settlement prices, 60–62

quoting futures prices, 60–63
regulation of, 66–67
risk-avoidance trading venues, 302
risk in, 301–302
short-term strategies, 131–132
simultaneous currency positions, 258
software strategies, 123–124
stock exchanges compared, 73–75
strangles, 234–236
strategies for trading in, 119–134
structural pricing distinctions, 63
technical analysis in, 203–220
trends in, 120–122
Ultimate Oscillator, 211–212
United States markets, 57–58
Volume Oscillator, 205–208

G

Gamma, 145–146, 147–149
    Delta and, 147–148
    meaning of readings, 148
Gaps in futures market trading, 72
Gentz, Manfred, 10
Germany, 4, 5, 324
    Chicago Mercantile Exchange currency
        trading, 24
    Globex2, mark on, 263
Global foreign markets, 3
Globalization, 4
    nations embracing, 20–21
Globex2, 23, 57–58, 262–266
    stop limit orders on, 264
Gold reserves, 7–8
Gold standard
    postwar standard, 7
    tests on, 7–8
Good Till Canceled instruction, 48
Great Britain
    base currency, 24
    Chicago Mercantile Exchange currency
        trading, 24
    European Monetary Union (EMU), 9
    Exchange Rate Mechanism (ERM) and, 9
    Globex2, pound on, 263
    London market, 22
    margin requirements, 64
    as trading block country, 325
Greece, 9, 11
Greenspan, Alan, 103–104, 156, 331
    on Russian economy, 12–13
Guaranteed fills, 50

H

Hayami, Masaru, 43
Hedges, 304–307
    options as, 143–145
    traders, 308–310
Holland, margin requirements, 64
Hong Kong Futures Exchange, 57, 59
Hungary
    Budapest Commodity Exchange (BCE), 59
    euro in, 11

I

Immediate-term trends, 121
IMM (International Monetary Market), 8
Indonesia
    International Monetary Fund (IMF)
        loans, 15
    short-term debt, 16
Inflation
    euro-zone interest rates, 248
    Purchasing Power Parity theory and, 249
    United States dollar and, 7–8
Initial account minimums, 50
Inside-the-spread fills, 46, 50
Institutional dealers, 327
Institutional market data, 266–267
Interbank markets, 329
Interest Rate Parity theory, 251
Interest rates
    Current Account deficit and, 95–96
    differentials, 92–93
    Eurodollars and, 32–33
    euro-zone interest rates, 248
    forwards and, 36–37
    influences of, 94
    Interest Rate Parity theory, 251
    in Japan, 99–100
    in Russia, 12
    spot rollovers and, 31
    Trade Deficit theory and, 249–250
    in United States, 2000, 93
Intermarket spreads, 295–300
Intermediate-term traders, daily charts used by,
    161–162
International Monetary Fund (IMF), 6
    Asian currency crisis, 15–16
    loans from, 7
    Russia, loan to, 12

Internet. *See also* Online trading
    currency-related site categories, 89
    daily opportunities on, 52
    problems with, 272
Internet Service Providers (ISPs), 50
Intraday trading options, 150–154
Intrinsic value of option, 140
Investors' Business Daily, 242
Irish punt, 5
ISDA (International Swaps and Derivatives
    Association), 33
ISO (International Standards Organization), 24
Italian lira, 4, 5
IT (information technology), 4, 16
    benefits of, 16–17
ITM (in-the-money) options, 139, 141
    Delta and, 143

J

Japan. *See also* Bank of Japan (BoJ)
    appreciation of yen, 21, 43–44
    Chicago Mercantile Exchange currency
        trading, 24
    debt, 98
    Financial.com Web site on yen, 306
    40 percent gain by yen, 91–92
    fundamental traders and, 293–295
    gains in, 97
    Globex2, yen on, 263
    interest rate in, 99–100
    long-term trends of yen, 121–122
    margin requirements, 64
    recession in, 96–97
    repatriation of profits in, 95
    role of yen, 13–14
    Tokyo International Financial Futures
        Exchange (TIFFE), 60
    ZIRP (zero interest rate policy), 52, 250

L

Lane, George, 212, 214, 216, 218–219
Large Commercial positions, 268–269
Large Speculators' positions, 268, 269–270
Latin America, 12, 325
Level I information area, 47
Level II information area, 47, 49
Limit orders, 164–167
    defined, 51
    for short-term traders, 165, 167
Liquidation values errors, 274–275
Liquidity
    Asian currency crisis and, 15
    in demo accounts, 84–86
    forex OTC environment, 222
    institutional money managers and, 269
    of markets, 42
    options, 144
    spreads and, 26
Liquid markets, 42
Loans from International Monetary Fund (IMF),
    7
Long positions
    Stop and Reversal (SAR) charts signaling,
        182–183
    strangles, 235
Long-term indicators, 126, 291
Long-term strategies, 126–131
Long-term trends, 121
Losses. *See* Profits and losses
Lots, specification of, 25
LTCM, 43–44, 91
    losses of, 156
Luxembourg franc, 5

M

Maastrict Treaty, 8
MACD charts, 108
    divergence signals, 112–113
    histogram in, 110–111
    Price Oscillator and, 208–209
    prices, tracking, 108–113
    reading, 109–111
    uses of, 162–164
Major support/resistance levels, 291–292
Malaysia, 15
    short-term debt, 16
Margin calls, 78
    exiting trade on, 262
Margin leverage, 308–309
Margins. *See also* Futures exchange markets
    description of, 65–66
    errors with, 272
    euro currency contracts, 11
    forex OTC dealers setting, 55–56
    intraday options trading and, 151
    profits and losses and (*See* Profits and losses)
    SPAN margin system, 59
    standard ratios, 66

Mark. *See* Germany
Market direction, predicting, 286
Market-driven currency exchange rates, 19
Market makers, 329
Market orders, 164–167
  defined, 51
  for short-term trader, 165
Market rules, 91–92, 287–288
  adjusting strategies to, 292–293
Markets, evaluating, 41–42
Market trading systems, 42
Maximizing profits, 285
Mediation of claims, 262
Medium-term charts, 291
Mexico
  Chicago Mercantile Exchange currency
    trading, 24
  exchange futures price of peso, 72
  Globex2, peso on, 263
  margin requirements, 64
Mid-American Futures Exchange, 57, 58–59
Mini-futures contracts, 304
Minimum trades, 25
Misjudging market, 260–261
MIT (market-if-touched) orders, 164–167
  defined, 51
  for short-term trader, 165–166
Momentum, 107. *See also* MACD charts
Moscow International Commodity Exchange
  (Micex), 60
Moving Average Convergence Divergence chart
  study. *See* MACD charts
Moving averages, 44, 107. *See also* Exponential
  moving averages (EMAs); Oscillators
  Commodity Channel Index (CCI) and,
    127–131
  defined, 124–125
  noise in, 158
  in Relative Strength Index (RSI), 115–116
Multinational corporations, 43

N

NAFTA (North American Free Trade
  Agreement), 19
NAIRU (non-accelerating inflation rate of
  unemployment) standard, 245–246, 251
Naked options, 141, 224–225
Nasdaq
  Nikkei compared, 98–99
  options, 222

risk in trading, 301
Trade Deficit theory and, 249–250
National Futures Association (NFA), 67, 262. *See
  also* Arbitration
  claims, traders filing, 276–278
  Conduct Committee, disciplinary action by, 278
  dispute resolution formats, 277–278
  forex dealers in, 275
  futures brokers and, 68
  rules for members, 276
New Concepts in Technical Trading Systems
  (Wilder), 183
New developments, 156
New Economy debate, 244–246
New York Board of Trade (NYBOT), 57, 58
New York Foreign Exchange Committee, 329
New Zealand
  base currency, 24
  Chicago Mercantile Exchange currency
    trading, 24
  Globex2, dollar on, 263
  margin requirements, 64
  as trading block country, 325
Niche for trading, establishing, 258, 261
Nikkei stock market, 28, 52
  Nasdaq compared, 98–99
Nippon Telegraph & Telephone, 14
Noise, 158
  lowering noise level, 158–159

O

OCOs (one cancels other), 167–168
Offers. *See* Bids and offers
Offsetting option positions, 314–317
Offshore dealers, 325
Omega, 149
O'Neil, William, 242
Online trading. *See also* Globex2
  bull call spreads in, 266
  clarifying orders, 264–265
  communication in, 272
  confirming orders, 264–265
  forex and, 325
  by fundamental day traders, 293–295
  instant bid/ask recognition, 104
  major support/resistance levels, 291–292
  placing orders, 264–265
  platforms, 17
  printing out orders, 273
  transition to, 323

Opening of markets, 22–23
Opening positions, 28, 29
Options, 135–154. *See also* Puts and calls
    American-style options, 137
    balancing risk and reward, 222–224
    bear call spreads, 150–153, 229–232
        stopping option losses, 233–234
    bull call spreads, 150–153, 226–227
        in online trading, 266
    case histories, 310–313
    credit spreads, 229
    Delta values of, 142–143, 316
    as derivatives, 136
    European-style options, 137
    existing position hedged futures strategy, 144
    expired options, 224
    Gamma formula, 145–146, 147–149
    as hedge, 143–145
    intraday trading, 150–154
    ITM (in-the-money) options, 139, 141
    list of option spreads, 228–229
    list of strategies, 152
    maximizing profits with spreads, 232–233
    naked options, 141, 224–225
    offsetting option positions, 314–317
    OTC options, 221–222
    OTM (out-of-the-money) options, 141
    prices, 137–139
    reasonable uses of, 136–137
    risks, limiting, 310
    selling options, 224–225
    short option losses, limiting, 225–229
    software data, use of, 145–146
    spreads, 150–154, 228–229
        maximizing profits with, 232–233
        minimizing losses with, 150–153, 229–232
        strangles, 234–236
    stops with bear spreads, 233–234
    strangles, 234–236
    structured valuation of, 311
    technical analysis for, 221–237
    time value/intrinsic value, 139–140
    using options, 141–142
    Vega number, 148, 149, 150
    as wasting assets, 140
Order entries, 50–51
Oscillators, 107, 124–125. *See also* MACD
        charts; Relative Strength Index (RSI);
        Stochastics
    Accumulation/Distribution (AD) charts,
        183–185
    defined, 125

    details in, 158
    in futures exchange markets, 204–205
    Price De-Trender, 210–211
    Price Oscillator, 208–210
    Ultimate Oscillator, 211–212
    Volume Oscillator, 205–208
OTC markets, 55
OTM (out-of-the-money) options, 141
Overbought/oversold oscillators
    Accumulation/Distribution (AD) charts,
        183–185
    Stochastics and, 216–217
Over-the-counter (OTC) trading
    markets for, 55
    options, 221–222
    in United States, 326

P

Parabolic Time and Price System, 181–183
Penalties from National Futures Association, 276
P/E ratios, 245
Permissible losses, identifying, 260
Phases of price movement, 190
Philadelphia Stock Exchange (Philx), 23, 50, 57
Philippines, 15
    short-term debt, 16
Phillips Curve, 245–246, 251
Pho, 149
Pip, value of, 26–27
Pit trading, 262, 264
Pivot Point system, 185–186
Plain vanilla swaps, 33–35
Point and Figure charts, 171–172
    buy/sell signals in, 176–180
    creating charts, 175
    day-to-day price changes on, 175–176
    description of, 173–175
    price movements shown with, 163
    sideways movement in, 177–178
    trends, focus on, 174–175
Poland, euro in, 11
Portfolio flows, 248
Portuguese escudo, 5
Position traders, 44
Price alerts, online, 159–160
Price De-Trender, 210–211
Price Oscillator, 208–210
Profitability, elements of, 42
Profits and losses
    adjusting strategies, 292–293

bull call spread and, 150–153, 226–227
entry orders and, 166
futures exchange markets, 75–78
generating profits, 155–156
opportunistic capturing of profits, 286
options, tracking for, 153
permissible losses, identifying, 260
ratios, 284–285
strangles and, 235–236
Proprietary software trading systems, 125–126
Purchasing Power Parity theory, 247–249
Puts and calls, 137–138
Delta and, 143
immediately after purchasing, exercising, 314–315
ITM (in-the-money) options, 139, 141
OTM (out-of-the-money) options, 141
premium value, 139–140
pricing values, 138–139

R

Ratio spread positions, 317–320
Regulated forex, 274–278
Relative Strength Index (RSI), 108, 113–114, 204
buy signal, 156–157
confirmation sources for, 115
details in, 158
divergence factors in, 116
implications of, 115–117
moving averages in, 115–116
reading the, 114–115
signal references, 116
uses of, 162–164
Reportable trades data from CFTC, 267–270
Reserve currency, 7
Resistance levels, 44, 120, 122–123
long-term charts for, 291
major levels, 291
Pivot Point system calculating, 186
technical analysis and, 240
Retracements in Elliott Wave Theory, 200
Reuters, 325
Risk
intermarket spreads and, 298–299
options limiting, 310
settlement risk, 329
speculators assuming, 308
spreads and, 318
Risk capital, 258–261
Robertson, Julian, 155–156

Romanian Futures Exchange (SMFCE), 59
Rukeyser, Louis, 241–242
Russia
Chicago Mercantile Exchange currency trading, 24
devaluation of ruble, 11–13
Globex2, ruble on, 263
margin requirements, 64

S

Sakikibara, Eisuke, 14–15
Schumpeter, Joseph, 159
Search engines for forex, 333–334
SEC (Securities and Exchange Commission), 33
futures exchange markets regulation, 66
Sell limit orders, 49, 287
Sell orders, 47
defined, 51
Settlement risk, 329
Short positions, 101, 225–229
Stop and Reversal (SAR) charts signaling, 182
strangles, 235
Short strangles, 320–322
Short-term indicators, 126, 291
Short-term moving averages, 209
Short-term strategies
Bollinger Bands, using, 132–134
in futures exchange markets, 131–132
Short-term traders
entry orders for, 165–166
OCOs (one cancels other), 167–168
Short term trends, 121
Simultaneous currency positions, 258
Skills development, 256
Slovakian koruna, 330–331
Slovenia, euro in, 11
Software programs, 17, 105–106. See also Online trading
archived price data, 101
Bollinger Bands, 132–134
in futures exchange markets, 123–124
MACD format in, 110–111
for options traders, 145–146
Point and Figure charts, 180
proprietary software trading systems, 125–126
technical analysis studies, 125–126
Soros, George, 11, 53, 155–156
South Africa
Chicago Mercantile Exchange currency trading, 24

South Africa *(continued)*
    Globex2, rand on, 263
    margin requirements, 64
South African Futures Exchange (SAFEX), 60
South Korea
    IMF loans to, 15
    Korean Futures Exchange, 60
Spanish peseta, 5
SPAN (Security Portfolio Analysis of Risk), 59,
    63–64, 308–309
    for single futures contract, 319
Speculators, 308–310
Spot transactions, 27–30, 328–329. *See also*
    Forwards
    rollovers, 30–31
Spreads. *See also* Options
    bear call spreads, 85, 150–153, 229–232
    bids and offers, 26
    bull call spreads, 150–153, 226–227
    dealing the, 26–27
    demo spread format, 83
    five-pip spread, 45
    interbank markets and, 329
    intermarket spreads, 295–300
    ratio spread positions, 317–320
    risk reductions, 317–320
    strangles, 234–236
    technology reducing, 50
    value of pip, 26–27
Sterilized interventions, 333
Sterling, 24
Stochastics, 42, 212, 214–219
    description of, 215–218
    formulas for calculating, 216, 217
    interpreting, 218–219
    Raw K study, 217
Stock markets, 240–241. *See also* Nikkei stock
    market
    futures exchanges compared, 73–75
    margin costs, 73–74
    portfolio flows, 248
Stop and Reversal (SAR) charts, 180–183
Stop limit orders, 164–165
    defined, 51
    illustration of, 165
    for short-term traders, 166
Stop orders, 29
    with bear spreads, 234
    defined, 51
    in demo accounts, 83–84
    developing skills, 256

    on Globex2, 264
    intermarket spreads and, 298–299
    Stop and Reversal (SAR) charts on, 182
Strangles, 234–236
    description of, 235
    short strangles, 320–322
Subpoenas in arbitration proceedings, 281
Successful traders, 303
Support levels, 44, 120, 122–123
    long-term charts for, 291
    major levels, 291–292
    Pivot Point system calculating, 186
Swaps. *See* Currency swaps
Sweden in European Monetary Union (EMU), 9
Swing traders, 44
Swiss francs, 42
    Chicago Mercantile Exchange currency
      trading, 24
    futures prices, 61
    on Globex2, 263
    margin requirements, 64
    spot transactions, 328–329

T

Technical analysis, 90, 106. *See also* Charts;
    Stochastics
    Commodity Channel Index (CCI), 127–131
    and fair value approach, 243
    for forex markets, 187–201
    fundamental analysis and, 239–252
    in futures exchange markets, 203–220
    hierarchical category of charting, 291–292
    momentum and, 107
    for options, 221–237
    oscillators, 107
    patterns, study of, 124
    Pivot Point system, 185–186
    Relative Strength Index (RSI), 113–114
    Rukeyser, Louis and, 241–242
    support and resistance, 122–123
Technicians, learning from, 44
Thailand
    International Monetary Fund (IMF) loans, 15
    short-term debt, 16
Theoretical pricing software, 145–147
Theta, 149
30-Year T-bonds, 93
Three-dimensional trading, 285–286
TIF (Time in Force) box, 47–48

Tiger Fund, 43, 91
    losses from, 155–156
Time value of options, 140, 316
Time zone Fibonacci charts, 194
Tokyo International Financial Futures Exchange
    (TIFFE), 60
TOPS (Trade Order Processing System), 78–80
    cost of trades, 79–80
Trade Deficit theory, 249–250
Trade entry points, 106
Trader-to-trader transactions, 50
Trade simulation, 296, 298–299
Trading day, 287
Trading pits, 68–69
Trading platforms, 42
    types of, 46–50
Transparent margin format, 63–64
Treaty of Rome, 8
Treble damages in arbitration, 277–279
Trends
    in futures exchange markets, 120–122
    phases of price movement, 190
    Point and Figure charts and, 174–175
    Price Oscillator and, 209
    reversals, 106
    Stochastics and, 217–218
    Stop and Reversal (SAR) charts signaling,
        182–183
    support and resistance evaluation, 123
    Ultimate Oscillator, 211–212
Turkish lira, 330–331

U

Ultimate Oscillator, 211–212
    rules for using, 213
United States bonds, 93, 100
United States Congress and futures exchange
    markets regulation, 66–67
United States Current Account, 94–95
    interest rates and, 95–96
United States dollars, 6–8, 325
    Eurodollars, 32
    in forex trading, 24
    inflation and, 7–8

noncitizen holders of, 95
    role of, 330
    at spot price, 328
United States Federal Reserve, 22, 331–332
    Bank of Japan and, 52
    Exchange Stabilization Fund, 332
    funds rate, 97–98
United States Treasury, 12
    reserve currency, 7
Uptrend lines, 120

V

Vega, 148, 149, 150
Voice squawk box feeds, 50
Volatility
    Bollinger Bands showing, 132
    Gamma formula and, 145–146
    short-term trading and, 131–132
    Vega number measuring, 150
Volume
    as stock market indicator, 242
    thinning volume, 261–262
    volatility and, 132
    Volume Oscillator, 205–208
Volume Oscillator, 205–208

W

Wall Street Week, 241–242
Williams, Larry, 211–212
Williams Ultimate Oscillator, 211–212
Winning trades, rule of thumb for, 284
World Bank, 6

Y

Yen. *See* Japan

Z

ZIRP (zero interest rate policy), 52, 250, 295